# *THE NEW FOLGER LIBRARY SHAKESPEARE*

Designed to make Shakespeare's great plays available to all readers, the New Folger Library edition of Shakespeare's plays provides accurate texts in modern spelling and punctuation, as well as scene-by-scene action summaries, full explanatory notes, many pictures clarifying Shakespeare's language, and notes recording all significant departures from the early printed versions. Each play is prefaced by a brief introduction, by a guide to reading Shakespeare's language, and by accounts of his life and theater. Each play is followed by an annotated list of further readings and by a "Modern Perspective" written by an expert on that particular play.

Barbara A. Mowat is Director of Research at the Folger Shakespeare Library, Executive Editor of *Shakespeare Quarterly,* Chair of the Folger Institute, and author of *The Dramaturgy of Shakespeare's Romances* and of essays on Shakespeare's plays and their editing.

Paul Werstine is Professor of English at the Graduate School and at King's University College at the University of Western Ontario. He is general editor of the New Variorum Shakespeare and author of many papers and articles on the printing and editing of Shakespeare's plays.

# Folger Shakespeare Library

The Folger Shakespeare Library in Washington, D.C., is a privately funded research library dedicated to Shakespeare and the civilization of early modern Europe. It was founded in 1932 by Henry Clay and Emily Jordan Folger, and incorporated as part of Amherst College in Amherst, Massachusetts, one of the nation's oldest liberal arts colleges, from which Henry Folger had graduated in 1879. In addition to its role as the world's preeminent Shakespeare collection and its emergence as a leading center for Renaissance studies, the Folger Shakespeare Library offers a wide array of cultural and educational programs and services for the general public.

EDITORS

BARBARA A. MOWAT
*Director of Research*
*Folger Shakespeare Library*

PAUL WERSTINE
*Professor of English*
*King's University College at the University of Western Ontario, Canada*

apoplectic - objective
- overcome w/ anger,
extremely indignant

FOLGER SHAKESPEARE LIBRARY

# Coriolanus

By

WILLIAM SHAKESPEARE

EDITED BY BARBARA A. MOWAT
AND PAUL WERSTINE

SIMON & SCHUSTER PAPERBACKS
NEW YORK LONDON TORONTO SYDNEY

Simon & Schuster Paperbacks
A Division of Simon & Schuster, Inc.
1230 Avenue of the Americas
New York, NY 10020



This Simon & Schuster paperback edition September 2009

SIMON & SCHUSTER PAPERBACKS and colophon are registered trademarks of Simon & Schuster, Inc.

For information regarding special discounts for bulk purchases, please contact Simon & Schuster Special Sales at 1-800-456-6798 or business@simonandschuster.com.

The Simon & Schuster Speakers Bureau can bring authors to your live event. For more information or to book an event, contact the Simon & Schuster Speakers Bureau at 1-866-248-3049 or visit our website at www.simonspeakers.com.

Manufactured in the United States of America

10 9 8 7 6 5 4 3

ISBN 978-0-671-72258-6

# From the Director of the Library

Shakespeare has never been more alive as author and playwright than he is today, with productions being staged all over the world, new film versions appearing on screen every year, and millions of students in classrooms at all levels absorbed in the human drama and verbal richness of his works.

The New Folger Library Shakespeare editions welcome the interested reader with newly edited texts, commentary in a friendly facing-page format, and illustrations, drawn from the Folger archives, that wonderfully illuminate references and images in the plays. A synopsis of every scene makes the action clear.

In these editions, students, teachers, actors, and thousands of other readers will find the best of modern textual scholarship, along with up-to-date critical essays, written especially for these volumes, that offer original and often surprising interpretations of Shakespeare's characters, action, and language.

I thank editors Barbara Mowat and Paul Werstine for undertaking this ambitious project, which is nothing less than an entirely new look at the texts from the earliest printed versions. Lovers of Shakespeare everywhere must be grateful for the breadth of their learning, the liveliness of their imaginations, and the scholarly rigor that they bring to the challenge of reediting the plays.

Gail Kern Paster, Director
The Folger Shakespeare Library

For Stephen Llano,
this—and all the others.

# Contents

# Editors' Preface

In recent years, ways of dealing with Shakespeare's texts and with the interpretation of his plays have been undergoing significant change. This edition, while retaining many of the features that have always made the Folger Shakespeare so attractive to the general reader, at the same time reflects these current ways of thinking about Shakespeare. For example, modern readers, actors, and teachers have become interested in the differences between, on the one hand, the early forms in which Shakespeare's plays were first published and, on the other hand, the forms in which editors through the centuries have presented them. In response to this interest, we have based our edition on what we consider the best early printed version of a particular play (explaining our rationale in a section called "An Introduction to This Text") and have marked our changes in the text—unobtrusively, we hope, but in such a way that the curious reader can be aware that a change has been made and can consult the "Textual Notes" to discover what appeared in the early printed version.

Current ways of looking at the plays are reflected in our brief introductions, in many of the commentary notes, in the annotated lists of "Further Reading," and especially in each play's "Modern Perspective," an essay written by an outstanding scholar who brings to the reader his or her fresh assessment of the play in the light of today's interests and concerns.

As in the Folger Library General Readers' Shakespeare, which this edition replaces, we include explanatory notes designed to help make Shakespeare's language clearer to a modern reader, and we place the notes on the page facing the text that they explain. We also follow the earlier edition in including illustrations—of objects, of clothing, of mythological figures—from books and manuscripts in the Folger Library collection. We provide fresh accounts of the life of Shakespeare, of the publishing of his plays, and of the theaters in which his plays were performed, as well as an introduction to the text itself. We also include a section called "Reading Shakespeare's Language," in which we try to help readers learn to "break the code" of Elizabethan poetic language.

For each section of each volume, we are indebted to a host of generous experts and fellow scholars. The "Reading Shakespeare's Language" section, for example, could not have been written had not Arthur King, of Brigham Young University, and Randall Robinson, author of *Unlocking Shakespeare's Language,* led the way in untangling Shakespearean language puzzles and shared their insights and methodologies generously with us. "Shakespeare's Life" profited by the careful reading given it by the late S. Schoenbaum; "Shakespeare's Theater" was read and strengthened by Andrew Gurr, John Astington, and William Ingram; and "The Publication of Shakespeare's Plays" is indebted to the comments of Peter W. M. Blayney. We, as editors, take sole responsibility for any errors in our editions.

We are grateful to the authors of the "Modern Perspectives"; to Leeds Barroll and David Bevington for their generous encouragement; to the Huntington and Newberry Libraries for fellowship support; to King's University College for the grants it has provided to Paul Werstine; to the Social Sciences and Humanities Research Council of Canada, which has provided him with Research Time Stipends; to R. J. Shroyer of the University of Western Ontario for essential computer support; to the Folger Institute's Center for

Shakespeare Studies for its sponsorship of a workshop on "Shakespeare's Texts for Students and Teachers" (funded by the National Endowment for the Humanities and led by Richard Knowles of the University of Wisconsin), a workshop from which we learned an enormous amount about what is wanted by college and high school teachers of Shakespeare today; to Alice Falk for her expert copyediting; and especially to Stephen Llano, our production editor at Simon & Schuster, whose expertise and attention to detail are essential to this project. Our special thanks to David George for sharing with us his draft textual notes for the New Variorum edition of *Coriolanus*. Of the editions we consulted, we found Lee Bliss's 2000 New Cambridge edition especially useful. Other editions to which we refer in our commentary are Philip Brockbank's 1976 New Arden and R. B. Parker's 1994 Oxford Shakespeare.

Our biggest debt is to the Folger Shakespeare Library—to Gail Kern Paster, Director of the Library, whose interest and support are unfailing (and whose scholarly expertise is an invaluable resource) and to Werner Gundersheimer, the Library's Director from 1984 to 2002, who made possible our edition; to Deborah Curren-Aquino, who provides extensive editorial and production support; to Jean Miller, the Library's former Art Curator, who combs the Library holdings for illustrations, and to Julie Ainsworth, Head of the Photography Department, who carefully photographs them; to Peggy O'Brien, former Director of Education at the Folger and now Director of Communications for the District of Columbia Public Schools, who gave us expert advice about the needs being expressed by Shakespeare teachers and students (and to Martha Christian and other "master teachers" who used our texts in manuscript in their classrooms); to Mary

Bloodworth and Michael Poston for their expert computer support; to the staff of the Research Division, especially Christina Certo (whose help is crucial), Mimi Godfrey, Jennifer Rahm, Kathleen Lynch, Carol Brobeck, Owen Williams, Sarah Werner, and Adrienne Schevchuk; and, finally, to the generously supportive staff of the Library's Reading Room.

Barbara A. Mowat and Paul Werstine

# Shakespeare's *Coriolanus*

*Coriolanus* is set in the earliest days of the Roman Republic. When the play opens, Rome's kings, the Tarquins, have only recently been expelled, and its citizens are negotiating, sometimes violently, about how Rome is to be ruled. The common people or plebeians are up in armed revolt against the patricians, in whom all power rests and whom they accuse of starving them. The people—represented by Shakespeare as perceptive and articulate, if sometimes irresolute, easily swayed, and cowardly in battle—win the right to be represented in government by tribunes, who will themselves foment more unrest. Nor is this civil dissension the sole threat to Rome, which also has foreign enemies close to its gates. Historically, centuries will pass before the Roman empire of Shakespeare's *Titus Andronicus, Julius Caesar,* and *Antony and Cleopatra* will range across continents. In *Coriolanus,* Rome's territories can be crossed on foot in a matter of days, and thus assaults on the city itself can be swiftly mounted by its Italian neighbors. The patrician Menenius is convinced that the Roman state, which he identifies with his own noble class, will prevail over all opposition, both within and without—"you may as well / Strike at the heaven . . . as . . . / Against the Roman state, whose course will on / The way it takes, cracking ten thousand curbs"—and history will prove him right; at the moment of the play, however, Rome is vulnerable.

The play explores in its treatment of the Roman family one of the reasons why the state will achieve such spectacular success. Family bonds inspire reverence from the characters. Cominius, the Roman general, speaks of his "dear wife's" reputation and of his children as the "treasure of [his] loins." Coriolanus's esteem for his mother, Volumnia, so dominates him that he almost obsessively puts his life at risk in bids to win her approval. Yet even the value of family is subordinate to loyalty to the Roman state. As Cominius asserts, "I do love / My country's good with a respect more tender, / More holy and profound, than" life or family. When a Roman's obligation to the city becomes aligned with duty toward family, the combined pressure is simply irresistible.

Coriolanus himself has been so thoroughly imbued by Volumnia with devotion to his patrician family and to Rome that he finds intolerable his fellow patricians' decision to cede some of their power to the plebeians by granting them representation in government. In the eyes of Coriolanus, the creation of the tribunes' office—especially as its power is exercised by the two tribunes Sicinius and Brutus—elevates unworthy plebeians to a status equal with his own family and class, to the great disadvantage of his ideal of Rome. His principled decision to sacrifice his own political career, if necessary, in his attempt to have the tribunate abolished drives him into irresolvable conflict with the plebeians. When he loses this struggle and is banished from Rome, his disgust with both his fellow patricians and the lowly populace ignites in him an apparently insatiable vengefulness against the state that he has been raised to idealize; it also opens up a tragic divide within himself, pitting him against his own mother and family. Threatened in the action of the play is Rome's very existence: it seems that Rome will never fulfill the destiny that Menenius has foreseen for it, but will be consumed in the fire of Coriolanus's revenge.

When you have finished the play, we invite you to read the essay printed after it, "*Coriolanus:* A Modern Perspective," by Professor Heather James of the University of Southern California.

# Reading Shakespeare's Language: *Coriolanus*

For many people today, reading Shakespeare's language can be a problem—but it is a problem that can be solved. Those who have studied Latin (or even French or German or Spanish), and those who are used to reading poetry, will have little difficulty understanding the language of poetic drama. Others, though, need to develop the skills of untangling unusual sentence structures and of recognizing and understanding poetic compressions, omissions, and wordplay. And even those skilled in reading unusual sentence structures may have occasional trouble with Shakespeare's words. Four hundred years of "static" intervene between his speaking and our hearing. Most of his vocabulary is still in use, but a few of his words are no longer used, and many of his words now have meanings quite different from those they had in the seventeenth century. In the theater, most of these difficulties are solved for us by actors who study the language and articulate it for us so that the essential meaning is heard—or, when combined with stage action, is at least *felt*. When we are reading on our own, we must do what each actor does: go over the lines (often with a dictionary close at hand) until the puzzles are solved and the lines yield up their poetry and the characters speak in words and phrases that are, suddenly, rewarding and wonderfully memorable.

## Shakespeare's Words

As you begin to read the opening scenes of a Shakespeare play, you may notice occasional unfamiliar words. Some are unfamiliar simply because we no longer use them. In the early scenes of *Coriolanus,* for example, one finds the words *unactive* (i.e., lazy), *bemock* (i.e., flout), *mammocked* (i.e., tore to pieces), and *vaward* (i.e., vanguard). Words of this kind are explained in notes to the text and will become familiar the more Shakespeare plays you read.

In *Coriolanus,* as in all of Shakespeare's writing, more problematic are the words that are still in use but that now have different meanings. In the opening scenes of *Coriolanus,* for example, the word *nerves* is used where we would say "sinews," *cranks* where we would say "channels," and *disease* where we would say "trouble." Such words will be explained in the notes to the text, but they, too, will become familiar as you continue to read Shakespeare's language.

Some words are strange not because of the "static" introduced by changes in language over the past centuries but because these are words that Shakespeare is using to build a dramatic world that has its own space, time, and history. In the opening scene of *Coriolanus,* for example, the dramatist quickly establishes the setting in the very early days of Rome by delineating its civil strife between what he has his patricians call the "helms o' th' state" (i.e., themselves) and the "dissentious rogues" as they fight over "the weal o' th' common." He also arms the "mutinous rascals" with "pikes" and "staves." Such language quickly constructs Coriolanus's Rome; the words and the world they create will become increasingly familiar as you get further into the play.

## Shakespeare's Sentences

In an English sentence, meaning is quite dependent on the place given each word. "The dog bit the boy" and "The boy bit the dog" mean very different things, even though the individual words are the same. Because English places such importance on the positions of words in sentences, on the way words are arranged, unusual arrangements can puzzle a reader. Shakespeare frequently shifts his sentences away from "normal" English arrangements—often to create the rhythm he seeks, sometimes to use a line's poetic rhythm to emphasize a particular word, sometimes to give a character his or her own speech patterns or to allow the character to speak in a special way. When we attend a good performance of the play, the actors will have worked out the sentence structures and will articulate the sentences so that the meaning is clear. When reading the play, we need to do as the actor does: that is, when puzzled by a character's speech, check to see if words are being presented in an unusual sequence.

Often Shakespeare rearranges subjects and verbs (i.e., instead of "He goes" we find "Goes he"). In *Coriolanus,* when the eponymous hero says "Yonder comes news" (1.4.1), he uses such a construction. So does Cominius when he says "dare I never" (1.6.82). The "normal" order would be "news comes yonder" and "I never dare." Shakespeare also frequently places the object before the subject and verb (i.e., instead of "I hit him," we might find "Him I hit"). The First Volscian Senator provides an example of this inversion when he says "Our gates, / . . . we have but pinned with rushes" (1.4.23–25), and Coriolanus another example when he says of some Roman looters "Cushions, leaden spoons, / Irons of a doit . . . these base slaves . . .

pack up" (1.5.5–8). The "normal" order would be "we have but pinned our gates with rushes" and "these base slaves pack up cushions, leaden spoons, irons of a doit."

Inversions are not the only unusual sentence structures in Shakespeare's language. Often in his sentences words that would normally appear together are separated from each other. Again, this is frequently done to create a particular rhythm or to stress a particular word, or else to draw attention to a needed piece of information. Take, for example, Cominius's

> the dull tribunes,
> That with the fusty plebeians hate thine honors,
> Shall say against their hearts "We thank the gods
> Our Rome hath such a soldier."
>
> (1.9.6–10)

Here the subject ("the dull tribunes") is separated from its verb ("shall say") by the adjective clause "That [i.e., who] with the fusty plebeians hate thine honors." As the purpose of the sentence is to assert that Coriolanus's martial feats are so impressive that even the tribunes, his detractors, will have to admire them, the adjective clause characterizing the tribunes as hating his fame has an importance that gives it precedence over the verb. Or take Volumnia's self-justification for allowing Coriolanus to go to war when still a boy:

> I, considering how honor would become such a person—that it was no better than picturelike to hang by th' wall, if renown made it not stir—was pleased to let him seek danger where he was like to find fame.
>
> (1.3.10–14)

Here the subject and verb ("I . . . was pleased") are separated by a participial phrase ("considering . . .") that involves first one clause ("how honor . . ."), then another ("that it was . . .") and another ("if renown . . ."). This accumulation of language separating subject and verb focuses attention on what was intrinsically appropriate for the boy Coriolanus ("such a person"), as if Volumnia's desires exercised no influence on her judgment to risk her young son's life and health in battle. Even when the verb finally arrives, it is passive ("was pleased"); thus Volumnia's language continues to deny her any role in the action of the son she so obviously shapes to her wishes. In order to create sentences that seem more like the English of everyday speech, one can rearrange the words, putting together the word clusters ("The dull tribunes shall say . . ." and "I was pleased to let . . ."). The result will usually be an increase in clarity but a loss of rhythm or a shift in emphasis.

Often in *Coriolanus,* rather than separating basic sentence elements, Shakespeare simply holds them back, delaying them until other material to which he wants to give greater emphasis has been presented. He puts this kind of construction in the mouth of Menenius, who says "Why, masters, my good friends, mine honest neighbors, / Will you undo yourselves?" (1.1.63–65). The basic sentence elements ("will you undo") are here delayed for a moment until Menenius addresses the armed plebeians in three different complimentary ways ("masters, my good friends, mine honest neighbors") in his effort to mollify them. Cominius employs the same kind of sentence structure—in this case also creating an elaborate example of inversion—when he lavishes the spoils of war on Coriolanus in recompense for the younger man's extraordinary contribution to the Roman victory, delaying the basic sentence elements of subject and verb ("we render") in order to place first, and thus to stress, the magnitude of the booty in which Coriolanus will have such a large share:

> Of all the horses—
> Whereof we have ta'en good and good store—of all
> The treasure in this field achieved and city,
> We render you the tenth[.]
>
> (1.9.36–39)

Finally, in Shakespeare's plays, sentences are sometimes complicated not because of unusual structures or interruptions but because the dramatist omits words and parts of words that English sentences normally require. (In conversation, we, too, often omit words. We say, "Heard from him yet?" and our hearer supplies the missing "Have you.") Sometimes in *Coriolanus* ellipsis contributes to the formality with which Rome's highest officials speak, as when a senator yields precedence to Coriolanus in order to honor him: "Right worthy you priority" (1.1.279). With the omitted words conjecturally supplied, the senator might be understood to mean "Right worthy *are* you *of* priority" (i.e., "You are truly deserving to go first"). At other times, ellipsis conveys brutal vulgarity. After Coriolanus, alone among the Romans, is shut into the hostile Volscian city of Corioles, the Roman soldiers who failed to accompany him into the city predict his ignominious death. "To th' pot, I warrant him" (1.4.62); conjectural expansion yields "*he will be sent* to the *cooking* pot, I warrant him," suggesting that Coriolanus will be hacked to pieces like food to be boiled in a pot on a fire.

## Shakespeare's Wordplay

Shakespeare plays with language so often and so variously that entire books are written on the topic. Here we will mention only two kinds of wordplay, metaphors and puns. A metaphor is a play on words in which one object or idea is expressed as if it were something else, something with which the metaphor suggests it shares common features. For instance, when the First Citizen describes the effects of a famine on the common people of Rome, he says "we become rakes" (1.1.22–23), comparing himself and his companions in their emaciated condition to ordinary farm implements and invoking the proverb "As lean as a rake." In discussing a fable that likens the state to a body, the Second Citizen employs a series of metaphors that equate each part with one function: "The counselor heart, the arm our soldier, / Our steed the leg, the tongue our trumpeter" (1.1.119–20). These metaphors seem neutral in tone when set against Coriolanus's scathing characterization of the plebeians' behavior in warfare: "He that trusts to you, / Where he should find you lions, finds you hares; / Where foxes, geese" (1.1.181–83). Here Coriolanus uses metaphor to link the common people of Rome with undesirable features of animals—hares are quick to flee danger, and geese readily become the prey of foxes.

A pun is a play on words that sound the same but have different meanings (or on a single word that has more than one meaning). Menenius uses the first kind of pun when he refers to the tribunes as "wealsmen" (2.1.55). Literally, the word means "men devoted to the public good," but it sounds like "wellsmen," and Menenius may thus be subtly ridiculing the tribunes for their habit—obvious in the play's dialogue—of overusing the word *well*. The same character is given the second kind of pun earlier in the play when he instructs the famine-stricken citizens to cease their armed revolt against the Senate and instead turn to prayer: "For the dearth, / The gods, not the patricians, make it, and / Your knees to them, not arms, must help" (1.1.74–76). Here Menenius puns on the word *arms*, which means both "weapons" and, as is underscored by its placement after the word *knees*, "the upper limbs of the body."

## Implied Stage Action

Finally, in reading Shakespeare's plays we should always remember that what we are reading is a performance script. The dialogue is written to be spoken by actors who, at the same time, are moving, gesturing, picking up objects, weeping, shaking their fists. Some stage action is described in what are called "stage directions"; some is signaled within the dialogue itself. We must learn to be alert to such signals as we stage the play in our imaginations.

Often the dialogue offers an immediately clear indication of the action that is to accompany it. For example, when Menenius says "Take my cap, Jupiter" (2.1.108), he can be assumed to toss his cap in the direction of Jupiter—that is, up into the air. Therefore we feel fairly confident about adding the stage direction "*He throws his cap in the air,*" putting it in square half-brackets to signal that it is our interpolation, rather than words appearing in the earliest printed text. Again when Volumnia addresses the kneeling Coriolanus with the words "Nay, my good soldier, up" (2.1.179), it seems likely that Coriolanus would immediately obey—first, because he is presented throughout the play as such a dutiful son, and, second, because almost immediately after this exchange he is greeting his wife and others in a way that demands he be standing. Therefore we add the stage direction *"He stands"* to this line, again putting it in half-brackets.

Occasionally, in *Coriolanus,* signals to the reader are not so clear. At the end of 1.8, the First Folio presents the fight between Martius (who is not yet Coriolanus) and Aufidius in the following sequence of stage directions and dialogue:

*Heere they fight, and certaine Volces come in the ayde of Auffi. Martius fights til they be driuen in breathles.*

[*Aufidius.*] Officious and not valiant, you haue
sham'd me
In your condemned Seconds.

(1.8.19 SD–22)

At least two puzzles arise from this passage. First, if read literally, it sets up a dramatic impossibility: Aufidius's chastisement of the Volscians for coming to his aid cannot be heard by them if Martius has already driven them offstage (*"in"*) before Aufidius issues his rebuke. Second, it is not clear how the scene is to end: the Folio provides no exit for the two main combatants, Aufidius and Martius. Do they exit the stage continuing to fight, with the outcome of their contest left to be reported in later dialogue? Or does their battle end when Aufidius is shamed by the unfair intervention of the Volscians repulsed by Martius, and do he and Martius then exit separately? We have edited the passage as follows to address these questions:

*Here they fight, and certain Volsces come in the aid of Aufidius.*

⌜*To the Volsces.*⌝ Officious and not valiant, you have shamed me
In your condemnèd seconds.

*Martius fights till they be driven in breathless.*
⌜*Aufidius and Martius exit separately.*⌝

Such editorial change allows the Volscians the opportunity to hear their general's repudiation of their unwanted intrusion and also resolves the question of how the fight between Aufidius and Coriolanus ends. In the present text, it concludes with Coriolanus's defeat of the Volscians who come to Aufidius's aid. However, we would not argue that our (provisional) solution is the only one possible. Hence our use of square half-brackets around the stage direction we have devised; hence too our preservation of the Folio's version in our Textual Notes, to allow the reader to grapple independently with the problems presented by the Folio.

Practice in reading the language of stage action repays one many times over when one reaches scenes heavily dependent on stage business. Think, for example, of scene 1.4, in which the Romans capture Corioles. The battle begins when the Volscian army enters the stage, presumably through a single door, as if issuing out of the gates of their city. They drive the Romans offstage, presumably through another door, as if "back to their trenches." While the Volscians are still onstage, Martius reenters from the door through which the Romans have retreated. He rallies the Romans, in turn, to drive the Volscians offstage, back through the door from which they first issued. Alone he follows them through. The stage is now occupied only by the Romans who have abandoned him and who discuss his fate—until he reenters from the door that has come to represent the gates of Corioles. Bleeding from his ongoing fight with the Volscians, he keeps the door (gates) open to admit the Romans and enable them to take the city.

It is immensely rewarding to work carefully with Shakespeare's language—with the words, the sentences, the wordplay, and the implied stage action—as readers for the past four centuries have discovered. It may be more pleasurable to attend a good performance of a play—though not everyone has thought so. But the joy of being able to stage a Shakespeare play in one's imagination, to return to passages that continue to yield further meanings (or further questions) the more one reads them—these are pleasures that, for many, rival (or at least augment) those of the performed text, and certainly make it worth considerable effort to "break the code" of Jacobean poetic drama and let free the remarkable language that makes up a Shakespeare text.

# CATECHISMVS

*paruus pueris primùm Latinè qui ediſcatur, proponendus in Scholis.*

LONDINI

Apud Iohannem Dayum Typographum. An. 1573.

Cum Priuilegio Regiæ Maieſtatis.

Title page of a 1573 Latin and Greek catechism for children.

# Shakespeare's Life

Surviving documents that give us glimpses into the life of William Shakespeare show us a playwright, poet, and actor who grew up in the market town of Stratford-upon-Avon, spent his professional life in London, and returned to Stratford a wealthy landowner. He was born in April 1564, died in April 1616, and is buried inside the chancel of Holy Trinity Church in Stratford.

We wish we could know more about the life of the world's greatest dramatist. His plays and poems are testaments to his wide reading—especially to his knowledge of Virgil, Ovid, Plutarch, Holinshed's *Chronicles,* and the Bible—and to his mastery of the English language, but we can only speculate about his education. We know that the King's New School in Stratford-upon-Avon was considered excellent. The school was one of the English "grammar schools" established to educate young men, primarily in Latin grammar and literature. As in other schools of the time, students began their studies at the age of four or five in the attached "petty school," and there learned to read and write in English, studying primarily the catechism from the Book of Common Prayer. After two years in the petty school, students entered the lower form (grade) of the grammar school, where they began the serious study of Latin grammar and Latin texts that would occupy most of the remainder of their school days. (Several Latin texts that Shakespeare used repeatedly in writing his plays and poems were texts that schoolboys memorized and recited.) Latin comedies were introduced early in the lower form; in the upper form, which the boys entered at age ten or eleven, students wrote their own Latin orations and declamations, studied Latin historians and rhetoricians, and began the study of Greek using the Greek New Testament.

Since the records of the Stratford "grammar school" do not survive, we cannot prove that William Shakespeare attended the school; however, every indication (his father's position as an alderman and bailiff of Stratford, the playwright's own knowledge of the Latin classics, scenes in the plays that recall grammar-school experiences—for example, *The Merry Wives of Windsor,* 4.1) suggests that he did. We also lack generally accepted documentation about Shakespeare's life after his schooling ended and his professional life in London began. His marriage in 1582 (at age eighteen) to Anne Hathaway and the subsequent births of his daughter Susanna (1583) and the twins Judith and Hamnet (1585) are recorded, but how he supported himself and where he lived are not known. Nor do we know when and why he left Stratford for the London theatrical world, nor how he rose to be the important figure in that world that he had become by the early 1590s.

We do know that by 1592 he had achieved some prominence in London as both an actor and a playwright. In that year was published a book by the playwright Robert Greene attacking an actor who had the audacity to write blank-verse drama and who was "in his own conceit [i.e., opinion] the only Shake-scene in a country." Since Greene's attack includes a parody of a line from one of Shakespeare's early plays, there is little doubt that it is Shakespeare to whom he refers, a "Shake-scene" who had aroused Greene's fury by successfully competing with university-educated dramatists like Greene himself. It was in 1593 that Shakespeare became a published poet. In that year he published his long narrative poem *Venus and Adonis;*

in 1594, he followed it with *Lucrece.* Both poems were dedicated to the young earl of Southampton (Henry Wriothesley), who may have become Shakespeare's patron.

It seems no coincidence that Shakespeare wrote these narrative poems at a time when the theaters were closed because of the plague, a contagious epidemic disease that devastated the population of London. When the theaters reopened in 1594, Shakespeare apparently resumed his double career of actor and playwright and began his long (and seemingly profitable) service as an acting-company shareholder. Records for December of 1594 show him to be a leading member of the Lord Chamberlain's Men. It was this company of actors, later named the King's Men, for whom he would be a principal actor, dramatist, and shareholder for the rest of his career.

So far as we can tell, that career spanned about twenty years. In the 1590s, he wrote his plays on English history as well as several comedies and at least two tragedies (*Titus Andronicus* and *Romeo and Juliet*). These histories, comedies, and tragedies are the plays credited to him in 1598 in a work, *Palladis Tamia,* that in one chapter compares English writers with "Greek, Latin, and Italian Poets." There the author, Francis Meres, claims that Shakespeare is comparable to the Latin dramatists Seneca for tragedy and Plautus for comedy, and calls him "the most excellent in both kinds for the stage." He also names him "Mellifluous and honey-tongued Shakespeare": "I say," writes Meres, "that the Muses would speak with Shakespeare's fine filed phrase, if they would speak English." Since Meres also mentions Shakespeare's "sugared sonnets among his private friends," it is assumed that many of Shakespeare's sonnets (not published until 1609) were also written in the 1590s.

A stylized representation of the Globe theater.
From Claes Jansz Visscher, *Londinum florentissima Britanniae urbs* . . . [c. 1625].

In 1599, Shakespeare's company built a theater for themselves across the river from London, naming it the Globe. The plays that are considered by many to be Shakespeare's major tragedies (*Hamlet, Othello, King Lear,* and *Macbeth*) were written while the company was resident in this theater, as were such comedies as *Twelfth Night* and *Measure for Measure.* Many of Shakespeare's plays were performed at court (both for Queen Elizabeth I and, after her death in 1603, for King James I), some were presented at the Inns of Court (the residences of London's legal societies), and some were doubtless performed in other towns, at the universities, and at great houses when the King's Men went on tour; otherwise, his plays from 1599 to 1608 were, so far as we know, performed only at the Globe. Between 1608 and 1612, Shakespeare wrote several plays—among them *The Winter's Tale* and *The Tempest*—presumably for the company's new indoor Blackfriars theater, though the plays seem to have been performed also at the Globe and at court. Surviving documents describe a performance of *The Winter's Tale* in 1611 at the Globe, for example, and performances of *The Tempest* in 1611 and 1613 at the royal palace of Whitehall.

Shakespeare wrote very little after 1612, the year in which he probably wrote *King Henry VIII.* (It was at a performance of *Henry VIII* in 1613 that the Globe caught fire and burned to the ground.) Sometime between 1610 and 1613 he seems to have returned to live in Stratford-upon-Avon, where he owned a large house and considerable property, and where his wife and his two daughters and their husbands lived. (His son Hamnet had died in 1596.) During his professional years in London, Shakespeare had presumably derived income from the acting company's profits as well as from his own career as an actor, from the sale of his play manuscripts to the acting company, and,

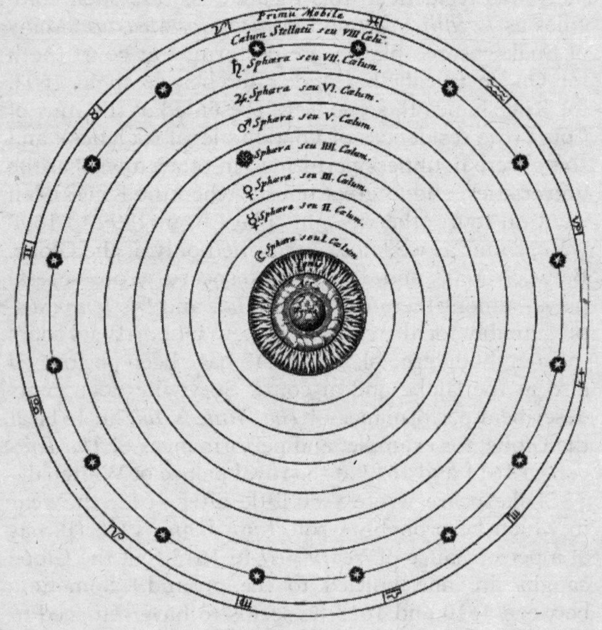


The Ptolemaic system.
From Marcus Manilius, *The sphere of* . . . (1675).

after 1599, from his shares as an owner of the Globe. It was presumably that income, carefully invested in land and other property, which made him the wealthy man that surviving documents show him to have become. It is also assumed that William Shakespeare's growing wealth and reputation played some part in inclining the crown, in 1596, to grant John Shakespeare, William's father, the coat of arms that he had so long sought. William Shakespeare died in Stratford-upon-Avon on April 23, 1616 (according to the epitaph carved under his bust in Holy Trinity Church) and was buried on April 25. Seven years after his death, his collected plays were published as *Mr. William Shakespeares Comedies, Histories, & Tragedies* (the work now known as the First Folio).

The years in which Shakespeare wrote were among the most exciting in English history. Intellectually, the discovery, translation, and printing of Greek and Roman classics were making available a set of works and worldviews that interacted complexly with Christian texts and beliefs. The result was a questioning, a vital intellectual ferment, that provided energy for the period's amazing dramatic and literary output and that fed directly into Shakespeare's plays. The Ghost in *Hamlet,* for example, is wonderfully complicated in part because he is a figure from Roman tragedy—the spirit of the dead returning to seek revenge—who at the same time inhabits a Christian hell (or purgatory); Hamlet's description of humankind reflects at one moment the Neoplatonic wonderment at mankind ("What a piece of work is a man!") and, at the next, the Christian disparagement of human sinners ("And yet, to me, what is this quintessence of dust?").

As intellectual horizons expanded, so also did geographical and cosmological horizons. New worlds—both North and South America—were explored, and in them were found human beings who lived and worshiped in ways radically different from those of Renaissance Europeans and Englishmen. The universe during these years also seemed to shift and expand. Copernicus had earlier theorized that the earth was not the center of the cosmos but revolved as a planet around the sun. Galileo's telescope, created in 1609, allowed scientists to see that Copernicus had been correct: the universe was not organized with the earth at the center, nor was it so nicely circumscribed as people had, until that time, thought. In terms of expanding horizons, the impact of these discoveries on people's beliefs—religious, scientific, and philosophical—cannot be overstated.

London, too, rapidly expanded and changed during the years (from the early 1590s to around 1610) that Shakespeare lived there. London—the center of England's government, its economy, its royal court, its overseas trade—was, during these years, becoming an exciting metropolis, drawing to it thousands of new citizens every year. Troubled by overcrowding, by poverty, by recurring epidemics of the plague, London was also a mecca for the wealthy and the aristocratic, and for those who sought advancement at court, or power in government or finance or trade. One hears in Shakespeare's plays the voices of London—the struggles for power, the fear of venereal disease, the language of buying and selling. One hears as well the voices of Stratford-upon-Avon—references to the nearby Forest of Arden, to sheepherding, to small-town gossip, to village fairs and markets. Part of the richness of Shakespeare's work is the influence felt there of the various worlds in which he lived: the world of metropolitan London, the world of small-town and rural England, the world of the theater, and the worlds of craftsmen and shepherds.

That Shakespeare inhabited such worlds we know from surviving London and Stratford documents, as well as from the evidence of the plays and poems themselves. From such records we can sketch the dramatist's life. We know from his works that he was a voracious reader. We know from legal and business documents that he was a multifaceted theater man who became a wealthy landowner. We know a bit about his family life and a fair amount about his legal and financial dealings. Most scholars today depend upon such evidence as they draw their picture of the world's greatest playwright. Such, however, has not always been the case. Until the late eighteenth century, the William Shakespeare who lived in most biographies was the creation of legend and tradition. This was the Shakespeare who was supposedly caught poaching deer at Charlecote, the estate of Sir Thomas Lucy close by Stratford-upon-Avon; this was the Shakespeare who fled from Sir Thomas's vengeance and made his way in London by taking care of horses outside a playhouse; this was the Shakespeare who reportedly could barely read but whose natural gifts were extraordinary, whose father was a butcher who allowed his gifted son sometimes to help in the butcher shop, where William supposedly killed calves "in a high style," making a speech for the occasion. It was this legendary William Shakespeare whose Falstaff (in *1* and *2 Henry IV*) so pleased Queen Elizabeth that she demanded a play about Falstaff in love, and demanded that it be written in fourteen days (hence the existence of *The Merry Wives of Windsor*). It was this legendary Shakespeare who reached the top of his acting career in the roles of the Ghost in *Hamlet* and old Adam in *As You Like It*—and who died of a fever contracted by drinking too hard at "a merry meeting" with the poets Michael Drayton and Ben Jonson. This legendary Shakespeare is a rambunctious, undisciplined man, as attractively "wild" as his plays were seen by earlier generations to be. Unfortunately, there is no trace of evidence to support these wonderful stories.

Perhaps in response to the disreputable Shakespeare of legend—or perhaps in response to the fragmentary and, for some, all-too-ordinary Shakespeare documented by surviving records—some people since the mid–nineteenth century have argued that William Shakespeare could not have written the plays that bear his name. These persons have put forward some dozen names as more likely authors, among them Queen Elizabeth, Sir Francis Bacon, Edward de Vere (earl of Oxford), and Christopher Marlowe. Such attempts to find what for these people is a more believable author of the plays is a tribute to the regard in which the plays are held. Unfortunately for their claims, the documents that exist that provide evidence for the facts of Shakespeare's life tie him inextricably to the body of plays and poems that bear his name. Unlikely as it seems to those who want the works to have been written by an aristocrat, a university graduate, or an "important" person, the plays and poems seem clearly to have been produced by a man from Stratford-upon-Avon with a very good "grammar school" education and a life of experience in London and in the world of the London theater. How this particular man produced the works that dominate the cultures of much of the world almost four hundred years after his death is one of life's mysteries—and one that will continue to tease our imaginations as we continue to delight in his plays and poems.

# Shakespeare's Theater

The actors of Shakespeare's time performed plays in a great variety of locations. They played at court (that is, in the great halls of such royal residences as Whitehall, Hampton Court, and Greenwich); they played in halls at the universities of Oxford and Cambridge, and at the Inns of Court (the residences in London of the legal societies); and they also played in the private houses of great lords and civic officials. Sometimes acting companies went on tour from London into the provinces, often (but not only) when outbreaks of bubonic plague in the capital forced the closing of theaters to reduce the possibility of contagion in crowded audiences. In the provinces the actors usually staged their plays in churches (until around 1600) or in guildhalls. Though surviving records show only a handful of occasions when actors played at inns while on tour, London inns were important playing places up until the 1590s.

The building of theaters in London had begun only shortly before Shakespeare wrote his first plays in the 1590s. These theaters were of two kinds: outdoor or public playhouses that could accommodate large numbers of playgoers, and indoor or private theaters for much smaller audiences. What is usually regarded as the first London outdoor public playhouse was called simply the Theatre. James Burbage—the father of Richard Burbage, who was perhaps the most famous actor in Shakespeare's company—built it in 1576 in an area north of the city of London called Shoreditch. Among the more famous of the other public playhouses that capitalized on the new fashion were the Curtain and the Fortune (both also built north of the city), and the Rose, the Swan, the Globe, and the

Hope (all located on the Bankside, a region just across the Thames south of the city of London). All these playhouses had to be built outside the jurisdiction of the city of London because many civic officials were hostile to the performance of drama and repeatedly petitioned the royal council to abolish it.

The theaters erected on the Bankside (a region under the authority of the Church of England, whose head was the monarch) shared the neighborhood with houses of prostitution and with the Paris Garden, where the blood sports of bearbaiting and bullbaiting were carried on. There may have been no clear distinction between playhouses and buildings for such sports, because the Hope was used for plays and baiting, and Philip Henslowe, owner of the Rose and, later, partner in the ownership of the Fortune, was also a partner in a monopoly on baiting. All these forms of entertainment were easily accessible to Londoners by boat across the Thames or over London Bridge.

Evidently Shakespeare's company prospered on the Bankside. They moved there in 1599. Threatened by difficulties in renewing the lease on the land where their first playhouse (the Theatre) had been built, Shakespeare's company took advantage of the Christmas holiday in 1598 to dismantle the Theatre and transport its timbers across the Thames to the Bankside, where, in 1599, these timbers were used in the building of the Globe. The weather in late December 1598 is recorded as having been especially harsh. It was so cold that the Thames was "nigh [nearly] frozen," and there was heavy snow. Perhaps the weather aided Shakespeare's company in eluding their landlord, the snow hiding their activity and the freezing of the Thames allowing them to slide the timbers across to the Bankside without paying tolls for repeated trips over London Bridge. Attractive as this narrative is, it remains just as likely that the heavy snow hampered transport of the timbers in wagons through the London streets to the river. It also must be remembered that the Thames was, according to report, only "nigh frozen" and therefore as impassable as it ever was. Whatever the precise circumstances of this fascinating event in English theater history, Shakespeare's company was able to begin playing at their new Globe theater on the Bankside in 1599. After the first Globe burned down in 1613 during the staging of Shakespeare's *Henry VIII* (its thatch roof was set alight by cannon fire called for by the play), Shakespeare's company immediately rebuilt on the same location. The second Globe seems to have been a grander structure than its predecessor. It remained in use until the beginning of the English Civil War in 1642, when Parliament officially closed the theaters. Soon thereafter it was pulled down.

The public theaters of Shakespeare's time were very different buildings from our theaters today. First of all, they were open-air playhouses. As recent excavations of the Rose and the Globe confirm, some were polygonal or roughly circular in shape; the Fortune, however, was square. The most recent estimates of their size put the diameter of these buildings at 72 feet (the Rose) to 100 feet (the Globe), but they were said to hold vast audiences of two or three thousand, who must have been squeezed together quite tightly. Some of these spectators paid extra to sit or stand in the two or three levels of roofed galleries that extended, on the upper levels, all the way around the theater and surrounded an open space. In this space were the stage and, perhaps, the tiring house (what we would call dressing rooms), as well as the so-called yard. In the yard stood the spectators who chose to pay less, the ones whom Hamlet contemptuously called "groundlings."

For a roof they had only the sky, and so they were exposed to all kinds of weather. They stood on a floor that was sometimes made of mortar and sometimes of ash mixed with the shells of hazelnuts, which, it has recently been discovered, were standard flooring material in the period.

Unlike the yard, the stage itself was covered by a roof. Its ceiling, called "the heavens," is thought to have been elaborately painted to depict the sun, moon, stars, and planets. Just how big the stage was remains hard to determine. We have a single sketch of part of the interior of the Swan. A Dutchman named Johannes de Witt visited this theater around 1596 and sent a sketch of it back to his friend, Arend van Buchel. Because van Buchel found de Witt's letter and sketch of interest, he copied both into a book. It is van Buchel's copy, adapted, it seems, to the shape and size of the page in his book, that survives. In this sketch, the stage appears to be a large rectangular platform that thrusts far out into the yard, perhaps even as far as the center of the circle formed by the surrounding galleries. This drawing, combined with the specifications for the size of the stage in the building contract for the Fortune, has led scholars to conjecture that the stage on which Shakespeare's plays were performed must have measured approximately 43 feet in width and 27 feet in depth, a vast acting area. But the digging up of a large part of the Rose by archaeologists has provided evidence of a quite different stage design. The Rose stage was a platform tapered at the corners and much shallower than what seems to be depicted in the van Buchel sketch. Indeed, its measurements seem to be about 37.5 feet across at its widest point and only 15.5 feet deep. Because the surviving indications of stage size and design differ from each other so much, it is possible that the stages in other playhouses, like the

Theatre, the Curtain, and the Globe (the outdoor playhouses where Shakespeare's plays were performed), were different from those at both the Swan and the Rose.

After about 1608 Shakespeare's plays were staged not only at the Globe but also at an indoor or private playhouse in Blackfriars. This theater had been constructed in 1596 by James Burbage in an upper hall of a former Dominican priory or monastic house. Although Henry VIII had dissolved all English monasteries in the 1530s (shortly after he had founded the Church of England), the area remained under church, rather than hostile civic, control. The hall that Burbage had purchased and renovated was a large one in which Parliament had once met. In the private theater that he constructed, the stage, lit by candles, was built across the narrow end of the hall, with boxes flanking it. The rest of the hall offered seating room only. Because there was no provision for standing room, the largest audience it could hold was less than a thousand, or about a quarter of what the Globe could accommodate. Admission to Blackfriars was correspondingly more expensive. Instead of a penny to stand in the yard at the Globe, it cost a minimum of sixpence to get into Blackfriars. The best seats at the Globe (in the Lords' Room in the gallery above and behind the stage) cost sixpence; but the boxes flanking the stage at Blackfriars were half a crown, or five times sixpence. Some spectators who were particularly interested in displaying themselves paid even more to sit on stools on the Blackfriars stage.

Whether in the outdoor or indoor playhouses, the stages of Shakespeare's time were different from ours. They were not separated from the audience by the dropping of a curtain between acts and scenes. Therefore the playwrights of the time had to find other ways of signaling to the audience that one scene (to be imagined as occurring in one location at a given time) had ended and the next (to be imagined at perhaps a different location at a later time) had begun. The customary way used by Shakespeare and many of his contemporaries was to have everyone onstage exit at the end of one scene and have one or more different characters enter to begin the next. In a few cases, where characters remain onstage from one scene to another, the dialogue or stage action makes the change of location clear, and the characters are generally to be imagined as having moved from one place to another. For example, in *Romeo and Juliet,* Romeo and his friends remain onstage in Act 1 from scene 4 to scene 5, but they are represented as having moved between scenes from the street that leads to Capulet's house into the house itself. The new location is signaled in part by the appearance onstage of Capulet's servingmen carrying napkins, something they would not take into the streets. Playwrights had to be quite resourceful in the use of hand properties, like the napkin, or in the use of dialogue to specify where the action was taking place in their plays because, in contrast to most of today's theaters, the playhouses of Shakespeare's time did not use stage sets to make the location precise. As another consequence of this difference, however, the playwrights of Shakespeare's time did not have to specify exactly where the action of their plays was set when they did not choose to do so, and much of the action of their plays is tied to no specific place.

Usually Shakespeare's stage is referred to as a "bare stage," to distinguish it from the stages of the past two or three centuries with their elaborate sets. But the stage in Shakespeare's time was not completely bare: Philip Henslowe, owner of the Rose, lists in his inventory of stage properties a rock, three tombs, and two mossy banks. Stage directions in plays of the time also call for such things as thrones (or "states"), banquets (presumably tables with plaster replicas of food on them), and beds and tombs to be pushed onto the stage. Thus the stage often held more than the actors.

The actors did not limit their performing to the stage alone. Occasionally they went beneath the stage, as the Ghost appears to do in the first act of *Hamlet*. From there they could emerge onto the stage through a trapdoor. They could retire behind the hangings across the back of the stage, as, for example, the actor playing Polonius does when he hides behind the arras. Sometimes the hangings could be drawn back during a performance to "discover" one or more actors behind them. When performance required that an actor appear "above," as when Juliet is imagined to stand at the window of her chamber in the famous and misnamed "balcony scene," then the actor probably climbed the stairs to the gallery over the back of the stage and temporarily shared it with some of the spectators. The stage was also provided with ropes and winches so that actors could descend from, and re-ascend to, the "heavens."

Perhaps the greatest difference between dramatic performances in Shakespeare's time and ours was that in Shakespeare's England the roles of women were played by boys. (Some of these boys grew up to take male roles in their maturity.) There were no women in the acting companies, only in the audience. It had not always been so in the history of the English stage. There are records of women on English stages in the thirteenth and fourteenth centuries, two hundred years before Shakespeare's plays were performed. After the accession of James I in 1603, the queen of England and her ladies took part in entertainments at court called masques, and with the reopening of the theaters in

1660 at the restoration of Charles II, women again took their place on the public stage.

The chief competitors for the companies of adult actors, such as the one to which Shakespeare belonged and for which he wrote, were companies of exclusively boy actors. The competition was most intense in the early 1600s. There were then two principal children's companies: the Children of Paul's (the choirboys from St. Paul's Cathedral, whose private playhouse was near the cathedral); and the Children of the Chapel Royal (the choirboys from the monarch's private chapel, who performed at the Blackfriars theater built by Burbage in 1596, which Shakespeare's company had been stopped from using by local residents who objected to crowds). In *Hamlet* Shakespeare writes of "an aerie [nest] of children, little eyases [hawks], that cry out on the top of question and are most tyrannically clapped for 't. These are now the fashion and . . . berattle the common stages [attack the public theaters]." In the long run, the adult actors prevailed. The Children of Paul's dissolved around 1606. By about 1608 the Children of the Chapel Royal had been forced to stop playing at the Blackfriars theater, which was then taken over by the King's company of players, Shakespeare's own troupe.

Acting companies and theaters of Shakespeare's time seem to have been organized in various ways. With the building of the Globe, Shakespeare's company apparently managed itself, with the principal actors, Shakespeare among them, having the status of "sharers" and the right to a share in the takings, as well as the responsibility for a part of the expenses. Five of the sharers, including Shakespeare, owned the Globe. As actor, as sharer in an acting company and in ownership of theaters, and as playwright, Shakespeare was about as involved in the theatrical industry as one could imagine. Although Shakespeare and his fellows prospered, their status under the law was conditional upon the protection of powerful patrons. "Common players"—those who did not have patrons or masters—were classed in the language of the law with "vagabonds and sturdy beggars." So the actors had to secure for themselves the official rank of servants of patrons. Among the patrons under whose protection Shakespeare's company worked were the lord chamberlain and, after the accession of King James in 1603, the king himself.

In the early 1990s we seemed on the verge of learning a great deal more about the theaters in which Shakespeare and his contemporaries performed—or, at least, opening up new questions about them. At that time about 70 percent of the Rose had been excavated, as had about 10 percent of the second Globe, the one built in 1614. It was then hoped that more would become available for study. However, excavation was halted at that point, and while it is not known if or when it will resume at these sites, archaeological discoveries in Shoreditch in 2008 in the vicinity of the Theatre may yield new information about the playhouses of Shakespeare's London.

# The Tragedy of Coriolanus.

## *Actus Primus. Scœna Prima.*

*Enter a Company of Mutinous Citizens, with Staues, Clubs, and other weapons.*

1. *Citizen.*

BEfore we proceed any further, heare me ſpeake.

*All.* Speake, ſpeake.

1. *Cit.* You are all reſolu'd rather to dy then to famiſh?

*All.* Reſolu'd, reſolu'd.

1. *Cit.* First you know, *Caius Martius* is chiefe enemy to the people.

*All.* We know't, we know't.

1. *Cit.* Let vs kill him, and wee'l haue Corne at our own price. Is't a Verdict?

*All.* No more talking on't; Let it be done, away, away

2. *Cit.* One word, good Citizens.

1. *Cit.* We are accounted poore Citizens, the Patricians good: what Authority ſurfets one, would releeue vs. If they would yeelde vs but the ſuperfluitie while it were wholſome, wee might gueſſe they releeued vs humanely: But they thinke we are too deere, the leanneſſe that afflicts vs, the obiect of our miſery, is as an inuentory to particularize their abundance, our ſufferance is a gaine to them. Let vs reuenge this with our Pikes, ere we become Rakes. For the Gods know, I ſpeake this in hunger for Bread, not in thirſt for Reuenge.

2. *Cit.* Would you proceede eſpecially againſt *Caius Martius.*

*All.* Againſt him firſt: He's a very dog to the Commonalty.

2. *Cit.* Conſider you what Seruices he ha's done for his Country?

1. *Cit.* Very well, and could bee content to giue him good report for't, but that hee payes himſelfe with beeing proud.

*All.* Nay, but ſpeak not malicioully.

1. *Cit.* I ſay vnto you, what he hath done Famouſlie, he did it to that end: though ſoft conſcienc'd men can be content to ſay it was for his Countrey, he did it to pleaſe his Mother, and to be partly proud, which he is, euen to the altitude of his vertue.

2. *Cit.* What he cannot helpe in his Nature, you account a Vice in him: You muſt in no way ſay he is couetous.

1. *Cit.* If I muſt not, I neede not be barren of Accuſations he hath faults (with ſurplus) to tyre in repetition.

*Showts within.*

What ſhowts are theſe? The other ſide a'th City is riſen: why ſtay we prating heere? To th'Capitoll.

*All.* Come, come.

1 *Cit.* Soft, who comes heere?

*Enter Menenius Agrippa.*

2 *Cit.* Worthy *Menenius Agrippa,* one that hath alwayes lou'd the people.

1 *Cit.* He's one honeſt enough, wold al the reſt wer ſo.

*Men.* What work's my Countrimen in hand?
Where go you with Bats and Clubs? The matter
Speake I pray you.

2 *Cit.* Our buſines is not vnknowne to th'Senat, they haue had inkling this fortnight what we intend to do, w now wee'l ſhew em in deeds: they ſay poore Suters haue ſtrong breaths, they ſhal know we haue ſtrong arms too.

*Menen.* Why Maſters, my good Friends, mine honeſt Neighbours, will you vndo your ſelues?

2 *Cit.* We cannot Sir, we are vndone already.

*Men.* I tell you Friends, moſt charitable care
Haue the Patricians of you for your wants.
Your ſuffering in this dearth, you may as well
Strike at the Heauen with your ſtaues, as lift them
Againſt the Roman State, whoſe courſe will on
The way it takes: cracking ten thouſand Curbes
Of more ſtrong linke aſſunder, then can euer
Appeare in your impediment. For the Dearth,
The Gods, not the Patricians make it, and
Your knees to them (not armes) muſt helpe. Alacke,
You are tranſported by Calamity
Thether, where more attends you, and you ſlander
The Helmes o'th State; who care for you like Fathers,
When you curſe them, as Enemies.

2 *Cit.* Care for vs? True indeed, they nere car'd for vs yet. Suffer vs to famiſh, and their Store-houſes cramm'd with Graine: Make Edicts for Vſurie, to ſupport Vſurers; repeale daily any wholſome Act eſtabliſhed againſt the rich, and prouide more piercing Statutes daily, to chaine vp and reſtraine the poore. If the Warres eate vs not vppe, they will; and there's all the loue they beare vs.

*Menen.* Either you muſt
Confeſſe your ſelues wondrous Malicious,
Or be accus'd of Folly. I ſhall tell you
A pretty Tale, it may be you haue heard it,
But ſince it ſerues my purpoſe, I will venture
To ſcale't a little more.

2 *Citizen.* Well,
Ile heare it Sir: yet you muſt not thinke
To fobbe off our diſgrace with a tale:
But and't pleaſe you deliuer.

*Men.* There was a time, when all the bodies members
Rebell'd againſt the Belly; thus accus'd it:
That onely like a Gulfe it did remaine

 Th

From the 1623 First Folio.
(Copy 5 in the Folger Library Collection.)

# The Publication of Shakespeare's Plays

Eighteen of Shakespeare's plays found their way into print during the playwright's lifetime, but there is nothing to suggest that he took any interest in their publication. These eighteen appeared separately in editions in quarto or, in the case of *Henry VI, Part 3,* octavo format. The quarto pages are not much larger than the ones you are now reading, and the octavo pages are even smaller; these little books were sold unbound for a few pence. The earliest of the quartos that still survive were printed in 1594, the year that both *Titus Andronicus* and a version of the play now called *Henry VI, Part 2* became available. While almost every one of these early quartos displays on its title page the name of the acting company that performed the play, only about half provide the name of the playwright, Shakespeare. The first quarto edition to bear the name Shakespeare on its title page is *Love's Labor's Lost* of 1598. A few of the quartos were popular with the book-buying public of Shakespeare's lifetime; for example, quarto *Richard II* went through five editions between 1597 and 1615. But most of the quartos were far from best sellers; *Love's Labor's Lost* (1598), for instance, was not reprinted in quarto until 1631. After Shakespeare's death, two more of his plays appeared in quarto format: *Othello* in 1622 and *The Two Noble Kinsmen,* coauthored with John Fletcher, in 1634.

In 1623, seven years after Shakespeare's death, *Mr. William Shakespeares Comedies, Histories, & Tragedies* was published. This printing offered readers in a single book thirty-six of the thirty-eight plays now thought to have been written by Shakespeare, including eighteen that had never been printed before. And it offered them in a style that was then reserved for serious literature and scholarship. The plays were arranged in double columns on pages nearly a foot high. This large page size is called "folio," as opposed to the smaller "quarto," and the 1623 volume is usually called the Shakespeare First Folio. It is reputed to have sold for the lordly price of a pound. (One copy at the Folger Shakespeare Library is marked fifteen shillings—that is, three-quarters of a pound.)

In a preface to the First Folio entitled "To the great Variety of Readers," two of Shakespeare's former fellow actors in the King's Men, John Heminge and Henry Condell, wrote that they themselves had collected their dead companion's plays. They suggested that they had seen his own papers: "we have scarce received from him a blot in his papers." The title page of the Folio declared that the plays within it had been printed "according to the True Original Copies." Comparing the Folio to the quartos, Heminge and Condell disparaged the quartos, advising their readers that "before you were abused with divers stolen and surreptitious copies, maimed, and deformed by the frauds and stealths of injurious impostors." Many Shakespeareans of the eighteenth and nineteenth centuries believed Heminge and Condell and regarded the Folio plays as superior to anything in the quartos.

Once we begin to examine the Folio plays in detail, it becomes less easy to take at face value the word of Heminge and Condell about the superiority of the Folio texts. For example, of the first nine plays in the Folio (one-quarter of the entire collection), four were essentially reprinted from earlier quarto printings that Heminge and Condell had disparaged, and four have now been identified as printed from copies written in the hand of a professional scribe of the 1620s named

Ralph Crane; the ninth, *The Comedy of Errors,* was apparently also printed from a manuscript, but one whose origin cannot be readily identified. Evidently, then, eight of the first nine plays in the First Folio were not printed, in spite of what the Folio title page announces, "according to the True Original Copies," or Shakespeare's own papers, and the source of the ninth is unknown. Because today's editors have been forced to treat Heminge and Condell's pronouncements with skepticism, they must choose whether to base their own editions upon quartos or the Folio on grounds other than Heminge and Condell's story of where the quarto and Folio versions originated.

Editors have often fashioned their own narratives to explain what lies behind the quartos and Folio. They have said that Heminge and Condell meant to criticize only a few of the early quartos, the ones that offer much shorter and sometimes quite different, often garbled, versions of plays. Among the examples of these are the 1600 quarto of *Henry V* (the Folio offers a much fuller version) or the 1603 *Hamlet* quarto. (In 1604 a different, much longer form of the play got into print as a quarto.) Early-twentieth-century editors speculated that these questionable texts were produced when someone in the audience took notes from the plays' dialogue during performances and then employed "hack poets" to fill out the notes. The poor results were then sold to a publisher and presented in print as Shakespeare's plays. More recently this story has given way to another in which the shorter versions are said to be re-creations from memory of Shakespeare's plays by actors who wanted to stage them in the provinces but lacked manuscript copies. Most of the quartos offer much better texts than these so-called bad quartos. Indeed, in most of the quartos we find texts that are at least equal to or better than what is printed in the Folio. Many Shakespeare enthusiasts persuaded themselves that most of the quartos were set into type directly from Shakespeare's own papers, although there is nothing on which to base this conclusion except the desire for it to be true. Thus speculation continues about how the Shakespeare plays got to be printed. All that we have are the printed texts.

The book collector who was most successful in bringing together copies of the quartos and the First Folio was Henry Clay Folger, founder of the Folger Shakespeare Library in Washington, D.C. While it is estimated that there survive around the world only about 300 copies of the First Folio, Mr. Folger was able to acquire more than seventy-five copies, as well as a large number of fragments, for the library that bears his name. He also amassed a substantial number of quartos. For example, only fourteen copies of the First Quarto of *Love's Labor's Lost* are known to exist, and three are at the Folger Shakespeare Library. As a consequence of Mr. Folger's labors, scholars visiting the Folger Library have been able to learn a great deal about sixteenth- and seventeenth-century printing and, in particular, about the printing of Shakespeare's plays. And Mr. Folger did not stop at the First Folio, but collected many copies of later editions of Shakespeare, beginning with the Second Folio (1632), the Third (1663–64), and the Fourth (1685). Each of these later folios was based on its immediate predecessor and was edited anonymously. The first editor of Shakespeare whose name we know was Nicholas Rowe, whose first edition came out in 1709. Mr. Folger, and the library named for him, collected this edition and many, many more by Rowe's successors, and the collecting continues.

# An Introduction to This Text

*Coriolanus* was first printed in the 1623 collection of Shakespeare's plays now known as the First Folio. The present edition is based directly upon that printing.* For the convenience of the reader, we have modernized the punctuation and the spelling of the Folio text. Sometimes we go so far as to modernize certain old forms of words; for example, usually when *a* means *he,* we change it to *he;* we change *mo* to *more,* and *ye* to *you.* It is not our practice in editing any of the plays to modernize words that sound distinctly different from modern forms. For example, when the early printed texts read *sith* or *apricocks* or *porpentine,* we have not modernized to *since, apricots, porcupine*. When the forms *an, and,* or *and if* appear instead of the modern form *if,* we have reduced *and* to *an* but have not changed any of these forms to their modern equivalent, *if*. We also modernize and, where necessary, correct passages in foreign languages, unless an error in the early printed text can be reasonably explained as a joke.

Whenever we change the wording of the First Folio or add anything to its stage directions, we mark the change by enclosing it in superior half-brackets (⌜ ⌝). We want our readers to be immediately aware when we have intervened. (Only when we correct an obvious typographical error in the First Folio does the change not get marked.) Whenever we change either the First Folio's wording or its punctuation so that meaning changes, we list the change in the textual notes at the

---

*We have also consulted the computerized text of the First Folio provided by the Text Archive of the Oxford University Computing Centre, to which we are grateful.

back of the book, even if all we have done is fix an obvious error.

We regularize spellings of a number of the proper names in the dialogue and stage directions, as is the usual practice in editions of the play. For example, the First Folio occasionally uses the forms "Latius" and "Marcus" but our edition uses only the more usual Folio spellings "Lartius" and "Martius."

This edition differs from many earlier ones in its efforts to aid the reader in imagining the play as a performance. Thus stage directions and speech prefixes are written and arranged with reference to the stage. For example, at the end of 1.4, which presents the Roman army entering the gates of the Volscian city Corioles to capture it, the First Folio offers a stage direction written entirely in terms of the play's fictive action: "They fight, and all enter the City." We supplement the Folio's direction with the words "exiting the stage" in order to aid our readers in imagining not just the fictive action but also the way that action would be realized in a production. Through such directions, we hope to help our readers stage the play in their own imaginations in a way that more closely approximates an experience in the theater.

Whenever it is reasonably certain, in our view, that a speech is accompanied by a particular action, we provide a stage direction describing the action, setting the added direction in brackets to signal that it is not found in the Folio. (Occasional exceptions to this rule occur when the action is so obvious that to add a stage direction would insult the reader.) Stage directions for the entrance of a character in mid-scene are, with rare exceptions, placed so that they immediately precede the character's participation in the scene, even though these entrances may appear somewhat earlier in the early printed texts. Whenever we move a stage direction, we record this change in the textual notes. Latin stage directions (e.g., *Exeunt*) are translated into English (e.g., *They exit*).

We expand the often severely abbreviated forms of names used as speech headings in early printed texts into the full names of the characters. We also regularize the speakers' names in speech headings, using only a single designation for each character, even though the early printed texts sometimes use a variety of designations. For example, in the First Folio the Roman military leader Titus Lartius is given a variety of speech prefixes—"*Titus Lartius.*," "*Lartius.*," "*Latius.*," "*Tit.*," "*Lart.*," and "*Lar.*" However, in this edition, he has a single speech prefix, "LARTIUS." An exception to this principle arises with the play's leading character, who because of his prowess is given a new name partway through the play. Before he is honored for his bravery in the battle of Corioles, he is usually addressed in dialogue as "Martius," the name we therefore use as his speech prefix. However, after he is awarded the honor of the name "Coriolanus" in 1.9, he is usually addressed by that name, and it becomes his speech prefix for the rest of this edition. Variations in the speech headings of the early printed texts are recorded in the textual notes.

In the present edition, as well, we mark with a dash any change of address within a speech, unless a stage direction intervenes. When the -ed ending of a word is to be pronounced, we mark it with an accent. Like editors for the past two centuries, we print metrically linked lines in the following way:

MESSENGER
Where's Caius Martius?
MARTIUS Here. What's the matter?
(1.1.246–47)

However, when there are a number of short verse-lines that can be linked in more than one way, we do not, with rare exceptions, indent any of them.

## The Explanatory Notes

The notes that appear on the pages facing the text are designed to provide readers with the help that they may need to enjoy the play. Whenever the meaning of a word in the text is not readily accessible in a good contemporary dictionary, we offer the meaning in a note. Sometimes we provide a note even when the relevant meaning is to be found in the dictionary but when the word has acquired since Shakespeare's time other potentially confusing meanings. In our notes, we try to offer modern synonyms for Shakespeare's words. We also try to indicate to the reader the connection between the word in the play and the modern synonym. For example, Shakespeare sometimes uses the word *head* to mean *source,* but, for modern readers, there may be no connection evident between these two words. We provide the connection by explaining Shakespeare's usage as follows: "**head:** fountainhead, source." On some occasions, a whole phrase or clause needs explanation. Then, if space allows, we rephrase in our own words the difficult passage, and add at the end synonyms for individual words in the passage. When scholars have been unable to determine the meaning of a word or phrase, we acknowledge the uncertainty. Biblical quotations are from the Geneva Bible (1560), with spelling modernized.

# CORIOLANUS

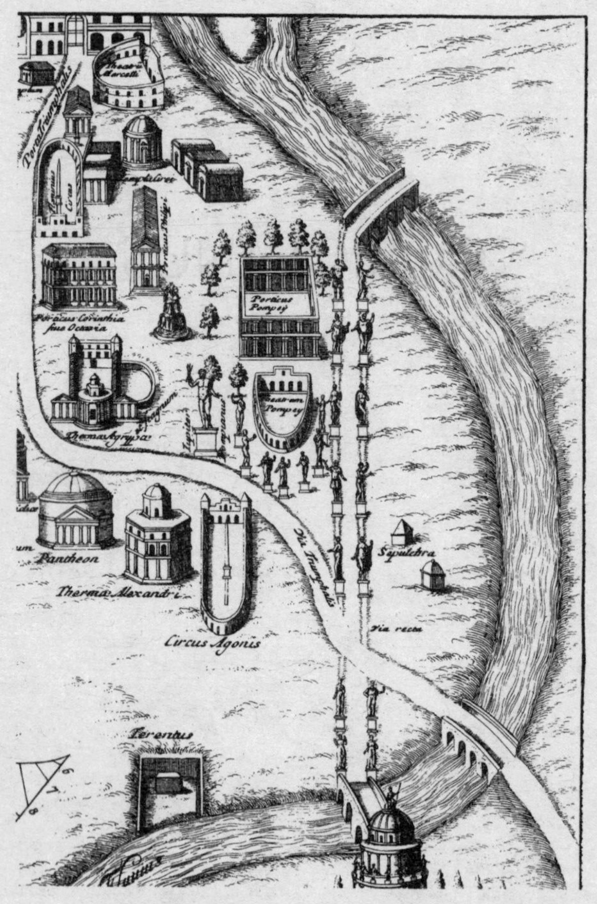


Tiber River and "great Rome" as it appeared some centuries after the time of Coriolanus. (3.1.403)
From Alessandro Donati, . . . *Roma* . . . (1694).

# Characters in the Play

Caius MARTIUS, later Caius Martius CORIOLANUS
VOLUMNIA, his mother
VIRGILIA, his wife
YOUNG MARTIUS, their son
VALERIA, friend to Volumnia and Virgilia
A GENTLEWOMAN, Volumnia's attendant

MENENIUS Agrippa, patrician
COMINIUS, patrician and general
Titus LARTIUS, patrician and military officer
SICINIUS Velutus, tribune
Junius BRUTUS, tribune
Roman SENATORS, PATRICIANS, NOBLES
Roman LIEUTENANT
Roman OFFICERS
Roman AEDILES
Roman HERALD
Roman SOLDIERS
Roman CITIZENS or PLEBEIANS
Roman MESSENGERS
A ROMAN defector, Nicanor

Tullus AUFIDIUS, general of the Volscians
Volscian CONSPIRATORS of his faction
Three of his SERVINGMEN

Volscian SENATORS, LORDS
Volscian LIEUTENANT
Volscian SOLDIERS
Two of the Volscian WATCH
Volscian PEOPLE

A VOLSCIAN spy, Adrian
CITIZEN of Antium

Roman Lords, Gentry, Captains, Lictors, Trumpeters, Drummers, Musicians, Attendants, and Usher.

# CORIOLANUS

## ACT 1

**1.1** Rome's famished plebeians threaten revolt, and the patrician Menenius attempts to placate them. Martius announces that the plebeians, whom he hates, have been granted tribunes to represent them in government. Then news arrives of a Volscian army, led by Aufidius, threatening Rome.

---

0 SD. **mutinous:** rebellious; **staves:** staffs, cudgels

1. **proceed:** With this word there begins a sequence of legal terms that continues to line 45 with **hear, resolved, verdict, accusations.**

10. **corn:** wheat, grain

12. **on 't:** i.e., about it

14. **poor:** (1) impoverished; (2) bad

14–15. **patricians:** members of the noble families, with exclusive rights to the Senate (See picture, page 8.)

15. **good:** (1) **good** for credit; (2) worthy; **authority:** i.e., the **patricians; surfeits:** feasts gluttonously

17. **while . . . wholesome:** i.e., before it went bad; **guess:** think, suppose

19. **dear:** costly; **object:** spectacle

20. **inventory:** itemized account; **particularize:** possible wordplay on (1) itemize; (2) restrict to a particular class

21. **sufferance:** suffering; **gain:** benefit, profit

22. **pikes:** pickaxes or pitchforks (with wordplay on soldiers' spears); **ere:** before

# ACT 1

## Scene 1

*Enter a company of mutinous Citizens with staves, clubs, and other weapons.*

FIRST CITIZEN Before we proceed any further, hear me speak.

ALL Speak, speak!

FIRST CITIZEN You are all resolved rather to die than to famish?

ALL Resolved, resolved!

FIRST CITIZEN First, you know Caius Martius is chief enemy to the people.

ALL We know 't, we know 't!

FIRST CITIZEN Let us kill him, and we'll have corn at our own price. Is 't a verdict?

ALL No more talking on 't; let it be done. Away, away!

SECOND CITIZEN One word, good citizens.

FIRST CITIZEN We are accounted poor citizens, the patricians good. What authority surfeits on would relieve us. If they would yield us but the superfluity while it were wholesome, we might guess they relieved us humanely. But they think we are too dear. The leanness that afflicts us, the object of our misery, is as an inventory to particularize their abundance; our sufferance is a gain to them. Let us revenge this with our pikes ere we become

23. **rakes:** Proverbial: "As lean as a rake."

27. **dog:** i.e., cruel enemy

27–28. **commonalty:** common people

36. **famously:** excellently, splendidly; **to that end:** i.e., to be **proud** (line 33)

36–37. **soft-conscienced:** i.e., tenderhearted

38–39. **to be partly proud:** i.e., **partly** in order **to be proud**

40. **virtue:** valor

46. **repetition:** recitation

46 SD. **within:** offstage

47. **is risen:** has revolted, has taken up arms

47–48. **prating:** talking

48. **Capitol:** temple of Jupiter on the Capitoline hill, presented here as the meeting place of the Senate (See picture, page 120, and note to 2.2.0 SD.)

50. **Soft:** i.e., wait a minute

53. **Would:** i.e., I wish

A Roman patrician. (1.1.14–15)
From Cesare Vecellio, *Degli habiti antichi et moderni* . . . (1590).

rakes; for the gods know I speak this in hunger for bread, not in thirst for revenge.

SECOND CITIZEN Would you proceed especially against Caius Martius?

ALL Against him first. He's a very dog to the commonalty.

SECOND CITIZEN Consider you what services he has done for his country?

FIRST CITIZEN Very well, and could be content to give him good report for 't, but that he pays himself with being proud.

⌜SECOND CITIZEN⌝ Nay, but speak not maliciously.

FIRST CITIZEN I say unto you, what he hath done famously he did it to that end. Though soft-conscienced men can be content to say it was for his country, he did it to please his mother and to be partly proud, which he is, even to the altitude of his virtue.

SECOND CITIZEN What he cannot help in his nature you account a vice in him. You must in no way say he is covetous.

FIRST CITIZEN If I must not, I need not be barren of accusations. He hath faults, with surplus, to tire in repetition. (*Shouts within.*) What shouts are these? The other side o' th' city is risen. Why stay we prating here? To th' Capitol!

ALL Come, come!

*Enter Menenius Agrippa.*

FIRST CITIZEN Soft, who comes here?

SECOND CITIZEN Worthy Menenius Agrippa, one that hath always loved the people.

FIRST CITIZEN He's one honest enough. Would all the rest were so!

57. **bats:** sticks, staffs; **matter:** reason, cause

58 SP. SECOND CITIZEN: Many editions assign this speech, and the following speeches of the Second Citizen, to the First Citizen. See longer note, page 283.

59. **inkling:** rumor, report

61. **suitors:** petitioners

63. **masters:** gentlemen, sirs

65. **undo:** destroy, ruin

68. **For:** i.e., as **for**

71. **course:** onward movement, path (The word *course* also means "a gallop on horseback" and "horserace," meanings picked up in **curbs** and **impediment.**) **on:** i.e., go **on**

72. **curbs:** A *curb* is a chain used for controlling a horse, passing under its lower jaw and fastened to the bit. **Curbs,** more generally, are checks or restraints.

74. **your impediment:** barriers or hindrances you set up

76. **arms:** weapons (with wordplay on **arms** as opposed to **knees**)

78. **attends:** awaits

79. **helms o' th' state:** i.e., rulers (nautical language)

82. **Suffer:** allow

83. **make edicts for:** proclaim laws about

84–85. **wholesome:** beneficial

MENENIUS
What work 's, my countrymen, in hand? Where go you
With bats and clubs? The matter? Speak, I pray you.

SECOND CITIZEN Our business is not unknown to th' Senate. They have had inkling this fortnight what we intend to do, which now we'll show 'em in deeds. They say poor suitors have strong breaths; they shall know we have strong arms too.

MENENIUS
Why, masters, my good friends, mine honest neighbors,
Will you undo yourselves?

SECOND CITIZEN
We cannot, sir; we are undone already.

MENENIUS
I tell you, friends, most charitable care
Have the patricians of you. For your wants,
Your suffering in this dearth, you may as well
Strike at the heaven with your staves as lift them
Against the Roman state, whose course will on
The way it takes, cracking ten thousand curbs
Of more strong link asunder than can ever
Appear in your impediment. For the dearth,
The gods, not the patricians, make it, and
Your knees to them, not arms, must help. Alack,
You are transported by calamity
Thither where more attends you, and you slander
The helms o' th' state, who care for you like fathers,
When you curse them as enemies.

SECOND CITIZEN Care for us? True, indeed! They ne'er cared for us yet. Suffer us to famish, and their storehouses crammed with grain; make edicts for usury to support usurers; repeal daily any wholesome act established against the rich, and provide more piercing statutes daily to chain up and re-

89. **wondrous:** i.e., wondrously, remarkably

92. **pretty:** pleasing; artful

94. **stale 't:** i.e., make it stale (through repeating it)

96. **fob off:** set aside, deceitfully put off; **disgrace:** misfortune; **an 't:** i.e., if it

97. **deliver:** tell, relate

98. **members:** parts, i.e., organs, limbs

100. **gulf:** whirlpool (devouring everything)

101. **unactive:** inactive, lazy

102. **Still:** always; **cupboarding:** shutting up, hoarding; **viand:** food; **bearing:** enduring

103. **where:** whereas; **instruments:** parts of the body, organs

104. **devise:** plan, contrive

105. **participate:** i.e., participating

105–6. **minister / Unto:** attend to, serve

106. **affection:** disposition

107. **Of:** i.e., to

110. **ne'er . . . lungs:** i.e., was not a belly laugh

111. **look you:** pay attention to this

114. **his receipt:** what he took in; **even so most fitly:** with precisely the same appropriateness (sarcastic)

115. **for that:** because

118. **kingly crownèd head:** wordplay on *crown* as **head** and on **kingly** as dignified, majestic, and as belonging to a king; and on **head** as the seat of **kingly** reason

119. **counselor heart:** i.e., **heart** which serves as adviser (See Shakespeare's *Much Ado About Nothing* 3.2.13: "what his **heart** thinks.")

strain the poor. If the wars eat us not up, they will; and there's all the love they bear us.

MENENIUS
Either you must confess yourselves wondrous
malicious
Or be accused of folly. I shall tell you
A pretty tale. It may be you have heard it,
But since it serves my purpose, I will venture
To ⌜stale⌝'t a little more.

SECOND CITIZEN Well, I'll hear it, sir; yet you must not think to fob off our disgrace with a tale. But, an 't please you, deliver.

MENENIUS
There was a time when all the body's members
Rebelled against the belly, thus accused it:
That only like a gulf it did remain
I' th' midst o' th' body, idle and unactive,
Still cupboarding the viand, never bearing
Like labor with the rest, where th' other instruments
Did see and hear, devise, instruct, walk, feel,
And, mutually participate, did minister
Unto the appetite and affection common
Of the whole body. The belly answered—

SECOND CITIZEN Well, sir, what answer made the belly?

MENENIUS
Sir, I shall tell you. With a kind of smile,
Which ne'er came from the lungs, but even thus—
For, look you, I may make the belly smile
As well as speak—it ⌜tauntingly⌝ replied
To th' discontented members, the mutinous parts
That envied his receipt; even so most fitly
As you malign our senators for that
They are not such as you.

SECOND CITIZEN Your belly's answer—what?
The kingly crownèd head, the vigilant eye,
The counselor heart, the arm our soldier,

121. **muniments:** defenses, fortifications; furnishings

122. **fabric:** structure (i.e., body)

124. **'Fore me:** a mild oath (equivalent to "by my word")

125. **cormorant:** greedy (Cormorants are large, voracious seabirds.) See picture, page 24.

126. **sink:** sewer

128. **former agents:** i.e., **head, eye,** etc. (lines 118–20)

131. **small:** i.e., **small** quantity

132. **you'st:** i.e., you must

133. **long:** i.e., taking a **long** time

134. **Note me:** pay attention to, observe (**Me** is an ethical dative.)

135. **Your . . . belly:** i.e., this **most** serious **belly** of which we speak

137. **incorporate:** united; embodied (with wordplay on the Latin word for *body: corpus*)

138. **the general:** i.e., all the

139. **fit:** fitting, appropriate

140. **shop:** organ of production

144. **cranks:** channels, courses; **offices:** parts of a house devoted to specific household services

145. **nerves:** sinews

146. **natural competency:** i.e., sufficient supply for their nature

148. **mark:** pay attention to

Our steed the leg, the tongue our trumpeter,
With other muniments and petty helps
In this our fabric, if that they—

MENENIUS
What then?
'Fore me, this fellow speaks. What then? What then?

SECOND CITIZEN
Should by the cormorant belly be restrained,
Who is the sink o' th' body—

MENENIUS
Well, what then?

SECOND CITIZEN
The former agents, if they did complain,
What could the belly answer?

MENENIUS
I will tell you,
If you'll bestow a small—of what you have little—
Patience awhile, you'st hear the belly's answer.

SECOND CITIZEN
You're long about it.

MENENIUS
Note me this, good friend;
Your most grave belly was deliberate,
Not rash like his accusers, and thus answered:
"True is it, my incorporate friends," quoth he,
"That I receive the general food at first
Which you do live upon; and fit it is,
Because I am the storehouse and the shop
Of the whole body. But, if you do remember,
I send it through the rivers of your blood
Even to the court, the heart, to th' seat o' th' brain;
And, through the cranks and offices of man,
The strongest nerves and small inferior veins
From me receive that natural competency
Whereby they live. And though that all at once,
You, my good friends"—this says the belly, mark
me—

SECOND CITIZEN
Ay, sir, well, well.

153. **make my audit up:** compile **my** balance sheet for an auditor

154. **flour:** the finer part of meal (The word retained its original sense of *the flower,* meaning "the choicest part" of something.)

155. **bran:** husks of grain

157. **senators:** See picture, page 94.

159. **digest:** ponder over; apprehend (with wordplay on "assimilate food")

160. **Touching:** regarding; **weal o' th' common:** welfare of the common people (with wordplay on *commonweal* or general good, prosperity of the people)

166. **For that:** because

168. **rascal:** (1) member of the rabble or mob; (2) inferior dog; **worst in blood:** (1) of the lowest breed; (2) most desperate; (3) poorest spirited

169. **vantage:** advantage, profit

170. **stiff:** hard

171. **at the point:** on the very verge

172. **have bale:** suffer harm

174. **dissentious:** quarrelsome; **rogues:** idle vagrants, rascals

176. **scabs:** wordplay on (1) crusts covering healing wounds; (2) scoundrels

MENENIUS "Though all at once cannot
See what I do deliver out to each,
Yet I can make my audit up, that all
From me do back receive the flour of all,
And leave me but the bran." What say you to 't?

SECOND CITIZEN
It was an answer. How apply you this?

MENENIUS
The senators of Rome are this good belly,
And you the mutinous members. For examine
Their counsels and their cares, digest things rightly
Touching the weal o' th' common, you shall find
No public benefit which you receive
But it proceeds or comes from them to you
And no way from yourselves. What do you think,
You, the great toe of this assembly?

SECOND CITIZEN I the great toe? Why the great toe?

MENENIUS
For that, being one o' th' lowest, basest, poorest,
Of this most wise rebellion, thou goest foremost.
Thou rascal, that art worst in blood to run,
Lead'st first to win some vantage.
But make you ready your stiff bats and clubs.
Rome and her rats are at the point of battle;
The one side must have bale.

*Enter Caius Martius.*

Hail, noble Martius.

MARTIUS
Thanks.—What's the matter, you dissentious rogues,
That, rubbing the poor itch of your opinion,
Make yourselves scabs?

SECOND CITIZEN We have ever your good word.

MARTIUS
He that will give good words to thee will flatter
Beneath abhorring. What would you have, you curs,

180. **nor peace:** i.e., neither **peace**

181. **proud:** arrogant

183. **surer:** more to be relied on

185. **virtue:** excellence, distinction

186. **make him worthy:** i.e., honor the man; **whose . . . him:** i.e., who is justly punished for committing an **offense**

187. **Who:** i.e., he **who**

188. **affections:** inclinations, penchants; **are:** i.e., **are** like

190. **evil:** disease

191. **favors:** goodwill

195. **now your hate:** recently the object of **your** hatred

196. **your garland:** i.e., the one you most prized

197. **several:** various

199. **which:** i.e., who; **else:** otherwise

200. **What's their seeking:** i.e., what do they want

201. **corn:** grain

205. **like:** i.e., likely

206. **side:** support, countenance

207. **give out:** announce, proclaim

209. **feebling:** enfeebling, weakening

210. **cobbled:** patched

212. **Would the nobility:** i.e., if only **the nobility would; ruth:** pity

213. **quarry:** pile of dead bodies

That like nor peace nor war? The one affrights you;
The other makes you proud. He that trusts to you,
Where he should find you lions, finds you hares;
Where foxes, geese. You are no surer, no,
Than is the coal of fire upon the ice
Or hailstone in the sun. Your virtue is
To make him worthy whose offense subdues him,
And curse that justice did it. Who deserves greatness
Deserves your hate; and your affections are
A sick man's appetite, who desires most that
Which would increase his evil. He that depends
Upon your favors swims with fins of lead,
And hews down oaks with rushes. Hang you! Trust
  you?
With every minute you do change a mind
And call him noble that was now your hate,
Him vile that was your garland. What's the matter,
That in these several places of the city
You cry against the noble senate, who,
Under the gods, keep you in awe, which else
Would feed on one another?—What's their seeking?

MENENIUS
For corn at their own rates, whereof they say
The city is well stored.

MARTIUS Hang 'em! They say?
They'll sit by th' fire and presume to know
What's done i' th' Capitol, who's like to rise,
Who thrives, and who declines; side factions and
  give out
Conjectural marriages, making parties strong
And feebling such as stand not in their liking
Below their cobbled shoes. They say there's grain
  enough?
Would the nobility lay aside their ruth
And let me use my sword, I'd make a quarry

214. **quartered slaves:** rascals cut to pieces, or cut in four (The penalty imposed on commoners for treason in Shakespeare's England was hanging, drawing [disemboweling], and quartering.)

215. **pick:** pitch, hurl (northern dialect)

217. **discretion:** discernment

218. **passing:** surpassingly, extremely

219. **troop:** i.e., of rebellious citizens

220. **dissolved:** dispersed

222. **an-hungry:** hungry

225. **meat:** food

231. **break the heart of:** crush; **generosity:** nobility

234. **horns o' th' moon:** i.e., ends of the crescent **moon**

235. **emulation:** i.e., hatred of their superiors

237. **vulgar:** plebeian

239. **'Sdeath:** i.e., God's or Christ's death (a strong oath)

241. **Ere:** i.e., before they should have; **It:** i.e., **the rabble** (line 240)

242. **Win upon:** get the better of; **power:** government, authority (i.e., the patricians)

245. **fragments:** a term of contempt (literally, scraps of uneaten food)

With thousands of these quartered slaves as high
As I could pick my lance.

MENENIUS
Nay, these are almost thoroughly persuaded;
For though abundantly they lack discretion,
Yet are they passing cowardly. But I beseech you,
What says the other troop?

MARTIUS They are dissolved. Hang 'em!
They said they were an-hungry, sighed forth proverbs
That hunger broke stone walls, that dogs must eat,
That meat was made for mouths, that the gods sent not
Corn for the rich men only. With these shreds
They vented their complainings, which being answered
And a petition granted them—a strange one,
To break the heart of generosity
And make bold power look pale—they threw their caps
As they would hang them on the horns o' th' moon,
Shouting their emulation.

MENENIUS What is granted them?

MARTIUS
Five tribunes to defend their vulgar wisdoms,
Of their own choice. One's Junius Brutus,
Sicinius Velutus, and I know not. 'Sdeath!
The rabble should have first ⌜unroofed⌝ the city
Ere so prevailed with me. It will in time
Win upon power and throw forth greater themes
For insurrection's arguing.

MENENIUS This is strange.

MARTIUS Go get you home, you fragments.

*Enter a Messenger hastily.*

249. **on 't:** i.e., of it; **vent:** get rid of

250. **musty superfluity:** bad-tempered superfluous people (literally, moldy excess food)

252. **that:** i.e., **that** which; **lately:** recently

255. **put you to 't:** challenge you, drive you to extremities

260. **Were . . . ears:** if **half the world were** fighting with the other **half**

261. **party:** side

262. **Only . . . with:** i.e., **my only** war against

265. **Attend upon:** go with; i.e., serve under

270. **stiff:** i.e., too old to fight; **Stand'st out:** i.e., are you not taking part

A Roman soldier.
From Cesare Vecellio,
*Degli habiti antichi et moderni* . . . (1590).

MESSENGER
Where's Caius Martius?

MARTIUS
Here. What's the matter?

MESSENGER
The news is, sir, the Volsces are in arms.

MARTIUS
I am glad on 't. Then we shall ha' means to vent
Our musty superfluity.

*Enter Sicinius Velutus, Junius Brutus,* ⌜*(two Tribunes)*;⌝ *Cominius, Titus Lartius, with other Senators.*

See our best elders.

FIRST SENATOR
Martius, 'tis true that you have lately told us:
The Volsces are in arms.

MARTIUS
They have a leader,
Tullus Aufidius, that will put you to 't.
I sin in envying his nobility,
And, were I anything but what I am,
I would wish me only he.

COMINIUS
You have fought together?

MARTIUS
Were half to half the world by th' ears and he
Upon my party, I'd revolt, to make
Only my wars with him. He is a lion
That I am proud to hunt.

FIRST SENATOR
Then, worthy Martius,
Attend upon Cominius to these wars.

COMINIUS
It is your former promise.

MARTIUS
Sir, it is,
And I am constant.—Titus ⌜Lartius,⌝ thou
Shalt see me once more strike at Tullus' face.
What, art thou stiff? Stand'st out?

273. **business:** affair (i.e., the war)

274. **true bred:** i.e., behaving in a way that reflects well on one's ancestry and training

276. **attend:** wait for

279. **Right worthy you priority:** i.e., you truly deserve to precede us

285. **Worshipful:** honorable, distinguished; **mutineers:** rebels

286. **puts well forth:** i.e., displays itself **well;** or, perhaps, promises **well** (like a plant sending out buds or leaves) See longer note, page 284.

290. **Marked:** observed

292. **moved:** angered; **spare to gird:** i.e., refrain from sneering at

293. **Bemock:** mock at, flout; **modest moon:** The **moon** is **modest** because its goddess is the chaste Diana.

294. **The present:** i.e., may **the present**

295. **Too . . . valiant:** perhaps, excessively **proud** of being **valiant**

A cormorant. (1.1.125)
From Ulisse Aldrovandi, . . . *Ornithologiae* . . . (1599–1603).

LARTIUS No, Caius Martius,
I'll lean upon one crutch and fight with t' other
Ere stay behind this business.

MENENIUS O, true bred!

⌜FIRST⌝ SENATOR
Your company to th' Capitol, where I know
Our greatest friends attend us.

LARTIUS, ⌜*to Cominius*⌝ Lead you on.—
⌜*To Martius.*⌝ Follow Cominius. We must follow you;
Right worthy you priority.

COMINIUS Noble Martius.

⌜FIRST⌝ SENATOR, ⌜*to the Citizens*⌝
Hence to your homes, begone.

MARTIUS Nay, let them follow.
The Volsces have much corn; take these rats thither
To gnaw their garners.

*Citizens steal away.*

Worshipful mutineers,
Your valor puts well forth.—Pray follow.

*They exit. Sicinius and Brutus remain.*

SICINIUS
Was ever man so proud as is this Martius?

BRUTUS He has no equal.

SICINIUS
When we were chosen tribunes for the people—

BRUTUS
Marked you his lip and eyes?

SICINIUS Nay, but his taunts.

BRUTUS
Being moved, he will not spare to gird the gods—

SICINIUS
Bemock the modest moon.

BRUTUS
The present wars devour him! He is grown
Too proud to be so valiant.

297. **Tickled with:** prompted by; **good:** advantageous; **success:** outcome

299. **insolence:** pride

302. **whom:** i.e., which (referring to **fame**)

304. **place:** rank, position; **miscarries:** is unsuccessful

306. **To th' utmost of a man:** i.e., as well as any **man** could; **giddy:** inconstant, foolish; **censure:** hostile criticism

307. **of Martius:** concerning **Martius**

308. **borne:** undertaken

310. **Opinion:** (1) reputation; (2) popular judgment; **sticks on:** is fastened upon

311. **his demerits:** i.e., Cominius's merits

313. **are to:** i.e., **are** credited **to**

314. **his:** i.e., Cominius's

316. **In . . . not:** i.e., Martius deserves nothing

318. **dispatch:** sending off; **made:** effected

319. **singularity:** self-aggrandizement

320. **present:** current; **action:** engagement with the enemy

**1.2** Aufidius and Volscian senators discuss the Roman preparations for war.

---

2. **are entered in:** have been given information about

SICINIUS Such a nature,
Tickled with good success, disdains the shadow
Which he treads on at noon. But I do wonder
His insolence can brook to be commanded
Under Cominius.

BRUTUS Fame, at the which he aims,
In whom already he's well graced, cannot
Better be held nor more attained than by
A place below the first; for what miscarries
Shall be the General's fault, though he perform
To th' utmost of a man, and giddy censure
Will then cry out of Martius "O, if he
Had borne the business!"

SICINIUS Besides, if things go well,
Opinion that so sticks on Martius shall
Of his demerits rob Cominius.

BRUTUS Come.
Half all Cominius' honors are to Martius,
Though Martius earned them not, and all his faults
To Martius shall be honors, though indeed
In aught he merit not.

SICINIUS Let's hence and hear
How the dispatch is made, and in what fashion,
More than his singularity, he goes
Upon this present action.

BRUTUS Let's along.

*They exit.*

## ⌜Scene 2⌝

*Enter Tullus Aufidius with Senators of Corioles.*

FIRST SENATOR
So, your opinion is, Aufidius,
That they of Rome are entered in our counsels
And know how we proceed.

5. **Whatever:** i.e., what things

7. **Had circumvention:** i.e., got the better of us by craft; **gone:** i.e., ago

8. **thence:** from there (i.e., from Rome)

10. **pressed:** impressed, forced into service; **power:** army

15. **of Rome:** i.e., by or in **Rome; of you:** by you

17. **preparation:** force prepared for war

18. **Whither:** to whatever place; **bent:** directed, aimed

21. **made doubt but:** doubted that

22. **answer us:** encounter us; i.e., fight with us

24. **pretenses:** purposes

25. **needs must show:** i.e., **must** of necessity reveal

25–26. **in the hatching:** i.e., while still being contrived or devised

27. **appeared to:** became known in; **discovery:** revelation, disclosure

28. **shortened:** curtailed; **aim:** course

29. **take in:** capture; **ere almost:** i.e., even before

32. **hie you:** hurry; **bands:** troops

33. **Let us alone:** i.e., leave it to us, rely on us

34. **set down before 's:** lay siege to us; **for the remove:** i.e., in order to raise the siege

37. **doubt not that:** i.e., do **not doubt that** they are **prepared for us** (line 36)

AUFIDIUS Is it not yours?
Whatever have been thought on in this state
That could be brought to bodily act ere Rome
Had circumvention? 'Tis not four days gone
Since I heard thence. These are the words—I think
I have the letter here. Yes, here it is.
⌜(*He reads.*)⌝ *They have pressed a power, but it is not known*
*Whether for east or west. The dearth is great.*
*The people mutinous; and, it is rumored,*
*Cominius, Martius your old enemy,*
*Who is of Rome worse hated than of you,*
*And Titus Lartius, a most valiant Roman,*
*These three lead on this preparation*
*Whither 'tis bent. Most likely 'tis for you.*
*Consider of it.*
FIRST SENATOR Our army's in the field.
We never yet made doubt but Rome was ready
To answer us.
AUFIDIUS Nor did you think it folly
To keep your great pretenses veiled till when
They needs must show themselves, which, in the hatching,
It seemed, appeared to Rome. By the discovery
We shall be shortened in our aim, which was
To take in many towns ere almost Rome
Should know we were afoot.
SECOND SENATOR Noble Aufidius,
Take your commission; hie you to your bands.
Let us alone to guard Corioles.
If they set down before 's, for the remove
Bring up your army. But I think you'll find
They've not prepared for us.
AUFIDIUS O, doubt not that;
I speak from certainties. Nay, more,

39. **parcels:** portions

41. **we:** i.e., I

**1.3** Volumnia, Martius's mother, and Virgilia, his wife, are visited by Valeria, who brings news of Martius at Corioles.

---

0 SD. **set them down:** sit **down**

2. **comfortable:** cheerful; **sort:** way

6. **tender-bodied:** i.e., easily hurt

7. **comeliness:** handsomeness, beauty

9. **should not sell him:** i.e., would **not** give **him** up

10–11. **become . . . person:** i.e., suit a man of such an appearance

14. **like:** i.e., likely

16. **oak:** i.e., the garland of **oak** awarded for valor in battle (See picture, page 124, and longer note to 2.1.154–55, pages 285–86.)

Women doing needlework. (1.3.0 SD)
From Jan van der Straet, [. . . *The celebrated Roman women*] (1543).

Some parcels of their power are forth already,
And only hitherward. I leave your Honors.
If we and Caius Martius chance to meet,
'Tis sworn between us we shall ever strike
Till one can do no more.

ALL The gods assist you!

AUFIDIUS And keep your Honors safe!

FIRST SENATOR Farewell.

SECOND SENATOR Farewell.

ALL Farewell.

*All exit.*

## ⌜Scene 3⌝

*Enter Volumnia and Virgilia, mother and wife to Martius. They set them down on two low stools and sew.*

VOLUMNIA I pray you, daughter, sing, or express yourself in a more comfortable sort. If my son were my husband, I should freelier rejoice in that absence wherein he won honor than in the embracements of his bed where he would show most love. When yet he was but tender-bodied and the only son of my womb, when youth with comeliness plucked all gaze his way, when for a day of kings' entreaties a mother should not sell him an hour from her beholding, I, considering how honor would become such a person—that it was no better than picture-like to hang by th' wall, if renown made it not stir—was pleased to let him seek danger where he was like to find fame. To a cruel war I sent him, from whence he returned, his brows bound with oak. I tell thee, daughter, I sprang not more in joy at first hearing he was a man-child than now in first seeing he had proved himself a man.

21. **report:** reputation

22. **issue:** offspring

26. **surfeit:** indulge himself

27. **action:** combat

27 SD. **Gentlewoman:** a woman of superior rank serving Volumnia

30. **retire myself:** withdraw

32. **Methinks:** it seems to me; **hither:** i.e., approaching

34. **shunning him:** seeking safety away from him

36. **got:** begotten, conceived

38. **mailed hand: hand** gloved with metal

39. **harvestman:** reaper; **tasked:** forced, required

39–40. **to mow . . . hire:** i.e., either **to mow all or lose his** wages

41. **Jupiter:** king of the Roman gods (also known as "Jove") See picture, page 146.

43. **gilt:** a thin layer of gold; **trophy:** memorial of victory in war; **Hecuba:** queen of Troy

44. **Hector:** eldest of the sons of **Hecuba** and King Priam, and leader of the Trojan army against the Greeks in the Trojan War (See picture, page 204.)

46. **contemning:** scorning, disdaining

47. **fit:** inclined, ready

VIRGILIA But had he died in the business, madam, how then?

VOLUMNIA Then his good report should have been my son; I therein would have found issue. Hear me profess sincerely: had I a dozen sons, each in my love alike and none less dear than thine and my good Martius, I had rather had eleven die nobly for their country than one voluptuously surfeit out of action.

*Enter a Gentlewoman.*

GENTLEWOMAN Madam, the Lady Valeria is come to visit you.

VIRGILIA
Beseech you, give me leave to retire myself.

VOLUMNIA Indeed you shall not.
Methinks I hear hither your husband's drum,
See him pluck Aufidius down by th' hair;
As children from a bear, the Volsces shunning him.
Methinks I see him stamp thus and call thus:
"Come on, you cowards! You were got in fear,
Though you were born in Rome." His bloody brow
With his mailed hand then wiping, forth he goes
Like to a harvestman ⌜that's⌝ tasked to mow
Or all or lose his hire.

VIRGILIA
His bloody brow? O Jupiter, no blood!

VOLUMNIA
Away, you fool! It more becomes a man
Than gilt his trophy. The breasts of Hecuba,
When she did suckle Hector, looked not lovelier
Than Hector's forehead when it spit forth blood
At Grecian sword, contemning.—Tell Valeria
We are fit to bid her welcome. *Gentlewoman exits.*

48. **fell:** fierce, cruel

50 SD. **Usher:** male attendant on a lady

54. **manifest:** obvious

54–55. **housekeepers:** (1) women engaged in domestic tasks; (2) those who stay at home, or keep to their houses

55. **spot:** piece of embroidery

60, 61. **O' my word, O' my troth:** very mild oaths (Valeria is given such ladylike expressions—e.g., **Indeed, la; Fie; In truth, la; Verily; In earnest**—throughout the scene.)

62. **H'as:** i.e., he has

62–63. **confirmed:** settled, determined

63. **countenance:** expression

65. **over and over:** i.e., rolling **over and over,** or head **over** heels

66. **catched:** caught; **Or whether:** i.e., **whether**

67. **how 'twas:** i.e., however it was; **set:** clenched

68. **mammocked it:** tore it to pieces

69. **on 's:** i.e., of his

71. **crack:** lively child

73. **huswife:** housewife

74. **not out:** i.e., **not** go **out**

77. **by your patience:** i.e., with your indulgence; with your permission

VIRGILIA
Heavens bless my lord from fell Aufidius!

VOLUMNIA
He'll beat Aufidius' head below his knee
And tread upon his neck.

*Enter Valeria with an Usher and a Gentlewoman.*

VALERIA My ladies both, good day to you.

VOLUMNIA Sweet madam.

VIRGILIA I am glad to see your Ladyship.

VALERIA How do you both? You are manifest housekeepers. What are you sewing here? A fine spot, in good faith. How does your little son?

VIRGILIA I thank your Ladyship; well, good madam.

VOLUMNIA He had rather see the swords and hear a drum than look upon his schoolmaster.

VALERIA O' my word, the father's son! I'll swear 'tis a very pretty boy. O' my troth, I looked upon him o' Wednesday half an hour together. H'as such a confirmed countenance. I saw him run after a gilded butterfly, and when he caught it, he let it go again, and after it again, and over and over he comes, and up again, catched it again. Or whether his fall enraged him or how 'twas, he did so set his teeth and tear it. O, I warrant how he mammocked it!

VOLUMNIA One on 's father's moods.

VALERIA Indeed, la, 'tis a noble child.

VIRGILIA A crack, madam.

VALERIA Come, lay aside your stitchery. I must have you play the idle huswife with me this afternoon.

VIRGILIA No, good madam, I will not out of doors.

VALERIA Not out of doors?

VOLUMNIA She shall, she shall.

VIRGILIA Indeed, no, by your patience. I'll not over the threshold till my lord return from the wars.

80. **lies in:** is confined, about to give birth or having just given birth

84. **want love:** lack charity

85–87. **You . . . moths: Penelope,** wife of Ulysses, king of **Ithaca**, used her weaving as a strategy to put off persistent suitors during his twenty-year absence. (See longer note, page 284, and picture, below.)

87. **cambric:** fine linen

88. **sensible:** sensitive

98. **In earnest:** i.e., honestly

101. **power:** army

102. **set down before:** i.e., laying siege to

103. **nothing doubt:** do not at all **doubt**

106. **Give me excuse:** i.e., excuse me, release me (from this obligation)

109. **disease:** trouble; **mirth:** amusement

Penelope. (1.3.85)

From [Guillaume Rouillé,] . . . *Promptuarii iconum* . . . (1553).

VALERIA Fie, you confine yourself most unreasonably. Come, you must go visit the good lady that lies in.

VIRGILIA I will wish her speedy strength and visit her with my prayers, but I cannot go thither.

VOLUMNIA Why, I pray you?

⌜VIRGILIA⌝ 'Tis not to save labor, nor that I want love.

VALERIA You would be another Penelope. Yet they say all the yarn she spun in Ulysses' absence did but fill Ithaca full of moths. Come, I would your cambric were sensible as your finger, that you might leave pricking it for pity. Come, you shall go with us.

VIRGILIA No, good madam, pardon me; indeed, I will not forth.

VALERIA In truth, la, go with me, and I'll tell you excellent news of your husband.

VIRGILIA O, good madam, there can be none yet.

VALERIA Verily, I do not jest with you. There came news from him last night.

VIRGILIA Indeed, madam!

VALERIA In earnest, it's true. I heard a senator speak it. Thus it is: the Volsces have an army forth, against whom Cominius the General is gone with one part of our Roman power. Your lord and Titus Lartius are set down before their city Corioles. They nothing doubt prevailing, and to make it brief wars. This is true, on mine honor, and so, I pray, go with us.

VIRGILIA Give me excuse, good madam. I will obey you in everything hereafter.

VOLUMNIA Let her alone, lady. As she is now, she will but disease our better mirth.

VALERIA In troth, I think she would.—Fare you well, then.—Come, good sweet lady.—Prithee, Virgilia, turn thy solemness out o' door, and go along with us.

114. **at a word:** in **a word,** briefly

**1.4** Before the Romans can besiege Corioles, the Volscians emerge to attack them. Martius rallies the troops to beat the Volscians back through their city gates. He then goes through the gates with them and is shut in to fight them alone. Covered in blood, he reopens the gates and admits the Romans.

---

0 SD. **Drum:** drummer; **Colors:** standard-bearers; **as:** i.e., **as** if

1. **met:** i.e., **met** in battle, fought

6. **spoke:** i.e., fought

9. **nor sell:** neither **sell**

10. **Summon the town:** i.e., signal a parley with the leaders of Corioles

13. **'larum:** call to arms

14. **Mars:** Roman god of war (See picture, page 190.)

17. **fielded friends: friends** already on the battlefield

17 SD. **sound:** signal

VIRGILIA No, at a word, madam. Indeed, I must not. I wish you much mirth.

VALERIA Well, then, farewell.

*Ladies exit.*

⌜Scene 4⌝

*Enter Martius, Titus Lartius, with ⌜Trumpet,⌝ Drum, and Colors, with Captains and Soldiers, as before the city ⌜of⌝ Corioles. To them a Messenger.*

MARTIUS
Yonder comes news. A wager they have met.

LARTIUS
My horse to yours, no.

MARTIUS 'Tis done.

LARTIUS Agreed.

MARTIUS, ⌜*to Messenger*⌝
Say, has our general met the enemy?

MESSENGER
They lie in view but have not spoke as yet.

LARTIUS
So the good horse is mine.

MARTIUS I'll buy him of you.

LARTIUS
No, I'll nor sell nor give him. Lend you him I will
For half a hundred years.—Summon the town.

MARTIUS How far off lie these armies?

MESSENGER Within this mile and half.

MARTIUS
Then shall we hear their 'larum and they ours.
Now, Mars, I prithee, make us quick in work,
That we with smoking swords may march from hence
To help our fielded friends!—Come, blow thy blast.

*They sound a parley.*

19–20. **less, lesser, little:** The language here is confusing, but the sense is that the Volscian soldiers, like Aufidius, have no fear of Martius.

23. **pound us up:** shut **us up** (as if we were cattle in a pound)

24. **pinned:** fastened shut

28. **List:** listen to

29. **cloven:** divided (with one part attacking Corioles, and the other on the battlefield); or, perhaps, split into pieces (under the Volsces' attack)

31. **Ladders:** i.e., scaling **ladders** for soldiers to climb the city walls (The **ladders** may or may not be brought onstage. Because the Volsces enter immediately, the **ladders** are unnecessary to the action.)

34. **proof:** strong, impervious

40. **edge:** i.e., sword

Neptune. (3.1.327)
From Johann Basilius Herold, *Heydenweldt* . . . [1554].

*Enter two Senators with others on the walls of Corioles.*

Tullus Aufidius, is he within your walls?

FIRST SENATOR

No, nor a man that fears you less than he:
That's lesser than a little. *Drum afar off.*
Hark, our drums
Are bringing forth our youth. We'll break our walls
Rather than they shall pound us up. Our gates,
Which yet seem shut, we have but pinned with
rushes.
They'll open of themselves. *Alarum far off.*
Hark you, far off!
There is Aufidius. List what work he makes
Amongst your cloven army.
⌜*They exit from the walls.*⌝

MARTIUS O, they are at it!

LARTIUS

Their noise be our instruction.—Ladders, ho!

*Enter the Army of the Volsces ⌜as through the city gates.⌝*

MARTIUS

They fear us not but issue forth their city.—
Now put your shields before your hearts, and fight
With hearts more proof than shields.—Advance,
brave Titus.
They do disdain us much beyond our thoughts,
Which makes me sweat with wrath.—Come on, my
fellows!
He that retires, I'll take him for a Volsce,
And he shall feel mine edge.

*Alarum. The Romans are beat back to their trenches.*
⌜*They exit, with the Volsces following.*⌝

*Enter Martius cursing, ⌜with Roman soldiers.⌝*

41. **contagion of the south:** i.e., the contagious diseases thought to be borne on the south wind

44. **abhorred:** i.e., because of your smell

46. **Against . . . mile:** i.e., the distance of **a mile,** even **against** the direction of **the wind**

48. **slaves:** a general term of contempt; **Pluto:** god of the underworld (See picture, below.)

49. **hurt behind:** i.e., wounded in the back (a clear sign of cowardice)

50. **agued:** fevered, shaking; **Mend:** improve; **home:** to the point aimed at

52. **Look to ’t:** beware

55. **ope:** open

56. **seconds:** supporters

57. **widens:** opens

58. **fliers:** those who avoid battle; **Mark:** observe; **like:** same

62. **pot:** i.e., cooking **pot**

Pluto at the entrance to hell. (1.4.48)
From Philippe Galle, *De deis gentium imagines* . . . (1581).

MARTIUS

All the contagion of the south light on you,
You shames of Rome! You herd of—Boils and
plagues
Plaster you o'er, that you may be abhorred
Farther than seen, and one infect another
Against the wind a mile! You souls of geese,
That bear the shapes of men, how have you run
From slaves that apes would beat! Pluto and hell!
All hurt behind. Backs red, and faces pale
With flight and agued fear! Mend, and charge home,
Or, by the fires of heaven, I'll leave the foe
And make my wars on you. Look to 't. Come on!
If you'll stand fast, we'll beat them to their wives,
As they us to our trenches. Follow 's!

*Another alarum.* ⌜*The Volsces re-enter and are driven back to the gates of Corioles, which open to admit them.*⌝

So, now the gates are ope. Now prove good
seconds!
'Tis for the followers fortune widens them,
Not for the fliers. Mark me, and do the like.

*Martius follows* ⌜*the fleeing Volsces through*⌝ *the gates, and is shut in.*

FIRST SOLDIER Foolhardiness, not I.

SECOND SOLDIER Nor I.

FIRST SOLDIER See they have shut him in.

*Alarum continues.*

ALL To th' pot, I warrant him.

*Enter Titus Lartius.*

LARTIUS

What is become of Martius?

ALL Slain, sir, doubtless.

65. **fliers:** i.e., Volsces who fled

66. **upon the sudden:** suddenly

67. **Clapped to:** shut

68. **answer:** encounter, fight

70. **sensibly:** as a living being; **senseless:** incapable of sensation

71. **left:** (1) abandoned; (2) alone, without rival

73. **carbuncle:** red precious stone; **entire:** perfect

75. **Even to Cato's wish:** i.e., exactly of the kind that Cato wanted (Marcus Porcius Cato, or Cato the Censor [234–149 B.C.E.], supported *mos maiorum* [ancestral custom] and was a valiant but notoriously severe military man. He lived several centuries after the time of Coriolanus.) **terrible:** terrifying

82. **fetch him off:** rescue **him; make remain alike:** i.e., stay, just as he does

**1.5** Leaving Lartius to secure Corioles, Martius goes to the aid of the Roman general Cominius on the battlefield near the city.

---

3. **A murrain on 't:** may a pestilence fall on it; **took this for:** thought **this** was

4. **movers:** those who incite others to action (ironic); **prize:** value

5. **drachma:** Greek silver coin of little worth

FIRST SOLDIER
Following the fliers at the very heels,
With them he enters, who upon the sudden
Clapped to their gates. He is himself alone,
To answer all the city.

LARTIUS O, noble fellow,
Who sensibly outdares his senseless sword,
And when it bows, stand'st up! Thou art left,
Martius.
A carbuncle entire, as big as thou art,
Were not so rich a jewel. Thou wast a soldier
Even to ⌜Cato's⌝ wish, not fierce and terrible
Only in strokes, but with thy grim looks and
The thunderlike percussion of thy sounds
Thou mad'st thine enemies shake, as if the world
Were feverous and did tremble.

*Enter Martius, bleeding, ⌜as if from Corioles,⌝ assaulted by the enemy.*

FIRST SOLDIER Look, sir.

LARTIUS O, 'tis Martius!
Let's fetch him off or make remain alike.
*They fight, and all enter the city, ⌜exiting the stage.⌝*

## ⌜Scene 5⌝

*Enter certain Romans, with spoils.*

FIRST ROMAN This will I carry to Rome.

SECOND ROMAN And I this.

THIRD ROMAN A murrain on 't! I took this for silver.

*Enter Martius, and Titus ⌜Lartius⌝ with a Trumpet.*

MARTIUS
See here these movers that do prize their hours
At a cracked drachma. Cushions, leaden spoons,

6. **Irons:** iron weapons, tools, or utensils; **of a doit:** i.e., worth nothing (**A doit** was a Dutch copper coin of small value.)

6–7. **doublets . . . them:** Executioners (**hangmen**) had the right to claim the clothes of their victims. **doublets:** tight-fitting coats for males

7. **slaves:** contemptuous term

8. **Ere:** before; **pack up:** put up in packs; **Down:** away

12. **make good:** secure

17. **second course of fight:** i.e., **second** battle (with wordplay on a **second course** at a banquet) See longer note, page 284.

20. **drop:** let fall, shed; **physical:** medicinal (Barber-surgeons drew **blood** from patients to improve their health.)

23. **fair:** beautiful; **Fortune: the goddess** who determined who succeeded and who failed

26. **Prosperity:** success; **be thy page:** i.e., accompany and serve you

27. **Thy friend:** i.e., may **the goddess Fortune** be **thy friend**

28. **those:** i.e., she is the friend of **those; placeth highest:** perhaps, raises to the top of her wheel (See picture, page 176.)

30. **sound:** i.e., issue a summons with

32. **know our mind:** i.e., hear me speak plainly

Irons of a doit, doublets that hangmen would
Bury with those that wore them, these base slaves,
Ere yet the fight be done, pack up. Down with them!
⌜*The Romans with spoils*⌝ *exit.*
*Alarum continues still afar off.*
And hark, what noise the General makes! To him!
There is the man of my soul's hate, Aufidius,
Piercing our Romans. Then, valiant Titus, take
Convenient numbers to make good the city,
Whilst I, with those that have the spirit, will haste
To help Cominius.

LARTIUS Worthy sir, thou bleed'st.
Thy exercise hath been too violent
For a second course of fight.

MARTIUS Sir, praise me not.
My work hath yet not warmed me. Fare you well.
The blood I drop is rather physical
Than dangerous to me. To Aufidius thus
I will appear and fight.

LARTIUS Now the fair goddess Fortune
Fall deep in love with thee, and her great charms
Misguide thy opposers' swords! Bold gentleman,
Prosperity be thy page!

MARTIUS Thy friend no less
Than those she placeth highest! So farewell.

LARTIUS Thou worthiest Martius! ⌜*Martius exits.*⌝
Go sound thy trumpet in the marketplace.
Call thither all the officers o' th' town,
Where they shall know our mind. Away!
*They exit.*

**1.6** Martius joins Cominius and inspires the Roman troops to further combat.

---

0 SD. **as . . . retire: as** if **in** retreat; **Soldiers:** See picture, page 22.

1. **Breathe:** pause, rest

1–2. **are come off:** have left the battlefield

3. **foolish:** i.e., foolhardy; **our stands:** in holding **our** ground against the enemy

5. **struck:** fought

6. **By interims:** at intervals; **conveying gusts:** i.e., **gusts** of wind **conveying** sound

7. **The Roman:** i.e., may **the Roman**

8. **Lead:** manage; **their successes:** i.e., **our friends'** fortunes

9. **powers:** armies; **fronts:** (1) faces; (2) foremost ranks of men

11. **you: the Roman gods** (line 7)

13. **issued:** emerged, come forth

15. **party:** side

18. **Methinks:** it seems to me

21. **briefly:** i.e., just now

22. **confound:** waste, spend

25. **that:** i.e., so **that**

## ⌜Scene 6⌝

*Enter Cominius as it were in retire, with Soldiers.*

COMINIUS
Breathe you, my friends. Well fought! We are come off
Like Romans, neither foolish in our stands
Nor cowardly in retire. Believe me, sirs,
We shall be charged again. Whiles we have struck,
By interims and conveying gusts we have heard
The charges of our friends. The Roman gods
Lead their successes as we wish our own,
That both our powers, with smiling fronts encount'ring,
May give you thankful sacrifice!

*Enter a Messenger.*

Thy news?

MESSENGER
The citizens of Corioles have issued
And given to Lartius and to Martius battle.
I saw our party to their trenches driven,
And then I came away.

COMINIUS Though thou speakest truth,
Methinks thou speak'st not well. How long is 't since?

MESSENGER Above an hour, my lord.

COMINIUS
'Tis not a mile; briefly we heard their drums.
How couldst thou in a mile confound an hour
And bring thy news so late?

MESSENGER Spies of the Volsces
Held me in chase, that I was forced to wheel

26. **else:** otherwise

29. **as:** i.e., **as** if

30. **stamp:** cast, appearance

31. **Before-time:** previously

33. **knows not:** i.e., cannot distinguish; **tabor:** small drum

35. **meaner man:** i.e., person inferior to him

39. **clip:** embrace

41. **our . . . done:** i.e., mine and my wife's wedding day was over

42. **to bedward:** toward bed (to lead the newly married couple there)

43. **Flower:** best, choicest

46. **Ransoming . . . pitying:** i.e., freeing a captive either because he pays for his release or because he is pitied by Titus **Ransoming:** setting free on payment of a sum

48. **Even:** just; **fawning:** cringing; **in the leash:** i.e., on a **leash**

49. **let him slip:** i.e., unleash it

51. **Which:** i.e., who

54. **inform:** tell

Three or four miles about; else had I, sir,
Half an hour since brought my report. ⌜*He exits.*⌝

*Enter Martius,* ⌜*bloody.*⌝

COMINIUS Who's yonder,
That does appear as he were flayed? O gods,
He has the stamp of Martius, and I have
Before-time seen him thus.

MARTIUS Come I too late?

COMINIUS
The shepherd knows not thunder from a tabor
More than I know the sound of Martius' tongue
From every meaner man.

MARTIUS Come I too late?

COMINIUS
Ay, if you come not in the blood of others,
But mantled in your own.

MARTIUS O, let me clip you
In arms as sound as when I wooed, in heart
As merry as when our nuptial day was done
And tapers burnt to bedward! ⌜*They embrace.*⌝

COMINIUS
Flower of warriors, how is 't with Titus Lartius?

MARTIUS
As with a man busied about decrees,
Condemning some to death and some to exile;
Ransoming him or pitying, threat'ning th' other;
Holding Corioles in the name of Rome
Even like a fawning greyhound in the leash,
To let him slip at will.

COMINIUS Where is that slave
Which told me they had beat you to your trenches?
Where is he? Call him hither.

MARTIUS Let him alone.
He did inform the truth. But for our gentlemen,

55. **The common file:** i.e., the masses, "**the common** herd"

56. **budge:** flinch

57. **rascals:** rabble

58. **how prevailed you: how** did **you** win

59. **think:** i.e., **think** so

64. **battle:** army, i.e., battle formation

68. **bands:** troops; **vaward:** vanguard; **Antiates:** men of Antium

69. **Of their best trust:** i.e., whom they trust most; **o'er them:** i.e., commanding them

77. **delay:** postpone; **present:** present time

78. **advanced:** raised; **darts:** spears (perhaps with catapults) See picture, page 114.

79. **prove:** i.e., put ourselves to the test

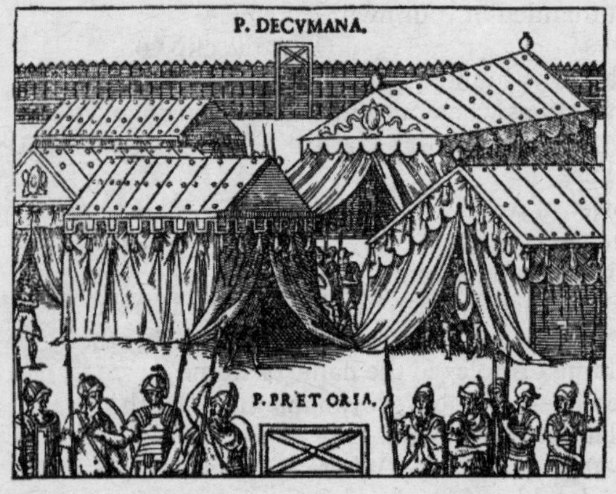


A Roman military camp. (1.7.8–9)
From Guillaume Du Choul, *Los discursos de la religion . . .* (1579).

The common file—a plague! Tribunes for them!—
The mouse ne'er shunned the cat as they did budge
From rascals worse than they.

COMINIUS But how prevailed you?

MARTIUS
Will the time serve to tell? I do not think.
Where is the enemy? Are you lords o' th' field?
If not, why cease you till you are so?

COMINIUS
Martius, we have at disadvantage fought
And did retire to win our purpose.

MARTIUS
How lies their battle? Know you on which side
They have placed their men of trust?

COMINIUS As I guess,
Martius,
Their bands i' th' vaward are the ⌜Antiates,⌝
Of their best trust; o'er them Aufidius,
Their very heart of hope.

MARTIUS I do beseech you,
By all the battles wherein we have fought,
By th' blood we have shed together, by th' vows we
have made
To endure friends, that you directly set me
Against Aufidius and his Antiates,
And that you not delay the present, but,
Filling the air with swords advanced and darts,
We prove this very hour.

COMINIUS Though I could wish
You were conducted to a gentle bath
And balms applied to you, yet dare I never
Deny your asking. Take your choice of those
That best can aid your action.

MARTIUS Those are they
That most are willing. If any such be here—

87. **this painting:** i.e., blood

88–89. **fear . . . report:** is less apprehensive about **his** body **than** about a bad reputation

92. **him alone:** only that man

95. **O, me alone:** These words have occasioned much debate. Martius perhaps expresses delight that the soldiers see him as having no equal.

96. **shows:** displays; **outward:** external, rather than indicative of mind or thought

97. **But is:** i.e., **is** not equivalent to

102. **cause will be obeyed:** i.e., conditions will require

103. **draw out:** select; **command:** the troops I will command

106. **ostentation:** display

107. **Divide . . . us:** obtain a share of the military glory (or of the booty) equal to ours

**1.7** Having secured Corioles, Lartius leaves to join Cominius.

---

0 SD. **Drum:** i.e., drummer; **Trumpet:** i.e., trumpeter

1. **ports:** gates; **Keep:** maintain

2. **send: send** a message

3. **centuries:** divisions (originally, companies of a hundred men)

As it were sin to doubt—that love this painting
Wherein you see me smeared; if any fear
⌜Lesser⌝ his person than an ill report;
If any think brave death outweighs bad life,
And that his country's dearer than himself;
Let him alone, or so many so minded,
Wave thus to express his disposition
And follow Martius. *⌜He waves his sword.⌝*

*They all shout and wave their swords, take him up in their arms, and cast up their caps.*

O, me alone! Make you a sword of me?
If these shows be not outward, which of you
But is four Volsces? None of you but is
Able to bear against the great Aufidius
A shield as hard as his. A certain number,
Though thanks to all, must I select from all.
The rest shall bear the business in some other fight,
As cause will be obeyed. Please you to march,
And ⌜I⌝ shall quickly draw out my command,
Which men are best inclined.

COMINIUS March on, my fellows.
Make good this ostentation, and you shall
Divide in all with us.

*They exit.*

## ⌜Scene 7⌝

*Titus Lartius, having set a guard upon Corioles, going with Drum and Trumpet toward Cominius and Caius Martius, enters with a Lieutenant, other Soldiers, and a Scout.*

LARTIUS
So, let the ports be guarded. Keep your duties
As I have set them down. If I do send, dispatch
Those centuries to our aid; the rest will serve

6. **Fear:** doubt
7. **upon 's:** i.e., upon us

**1.8** Martius defeats Aufidius and his Volscian supporters.

---

0 SD. **several:** separate
4. **Afric:** Africa
5. **fame and envy:** i.e., (1) envied **fame** (hendiadys); (2) renown **and** malice; (3) renown **and** the **envy** it provokes in me; **Fix thy foot:** take a sure foothold
6. **budger:** one who flinches
8. **fly:** flee
9. **Hollo:** i.e., hunt (literally, call after, in hunting)
12. **in:** within
15. **Wrench:** force, jerk
17. **Hector:** See note to 1.3.44.
18. **whip of:** scourge belonging to; **your bragged progeny:** the lineage of which you boast (The Romans traced their ancestry to the Trojans.)

For a short holding. If we lose the field,
We cannot keep the town.

LIEUTENANT Fear not our care, sir.

LARTIUS Hence, and shut your gates upon 's.
⌜(*To the Scout.*)⌝ Our guider, come. To th' Roman
camp conduct us.

⌜*They*⌝ *exit,* ⌜*the Lieutenant one way, Lartius another.*⌝

## ⌜Scene 8⌝

*Alarum, as in battle.*
*Enter Martius and Aufidius at several doors.*

MARTIUS
I'll fight with none but thee, for I do hate thee
Worse than a promise-breaker.

AUFIDIUS We hate alike.
Not Afric owns a serpent I abhor
More than thy fame and envy. Fix thy foot.

MARTIUS
Let the first budger die the other's slave,
And the gods doom him after!

AUFIDIUS If I fly, Martius,
Hollo me like a hare.

MARTIUS Within these three hours,
Tullus,
Alone I fought in your Corioles' walls
And made what work I pleased. 'Tis not my blood
Wherein thou seest me masked. For thy revenge,
Wrench up thy power to th' highest.

AUFIDIUS Wert thou the
Hector
That was the whip of your bragged progeny,
Thou shouldst not scape me here.

*Here they fight, and certain Volsces come in the aid of Aufidius.*

20. **Officious:** meddlesome

22. **In . . . seconds:** i.e., by your damned assistance

22 SD. **driven in: driven** offstage

**1.9** Cominius awards Martius the name *Coriolanus* for his service at Corioles.

---

0 SD. **scarf:** sling

1. **tell thee o'er:** i.e., give you an account of

2. **Thou 't:** i.e., you would

4. **attend:** listen; **shrug:** move their bodies in gestures of joy

5. **admire:** marvel

6. **quaked:** made to tremble; **dull:** foolish, gloomy

8. **fusty:** musty-smelling

9. **against:** in opposition to

11. **morsel:** bite, mouthful (the **feast** [i.e., battle] being nearly over) See longer note to 1.5.17, page 284.

12 SD. **power:** army

14. **Here:** with reference to Martius; **caparison:** cloth spread over the saddle or harness of a horse

17. **charter:** privilege, right; **blood:** members of her family

18. **grieves:** vexes, troubles

21. **effected:** accomplished; **will:** intention, purpose

22. **overta'en:** i.e., exceeded (See longer note, page 284.)

⌜(*To the Volsces.*)⌝ Officious and not valiant, you have shamed me
In your condemnèd seconds.

*Martius fights till they be driven in breathless.*
⌜*Aufidius and Martius exit, separately.*⌝

## ⌜Scene 9⌝

*Alarum. A retreat is sounded. Flourish. Enter, at one door, Cominius with the Romans; at another door Martius, with his arm in a scarf.*

COMINIUS, ⌜*to Martius*⌝
If I should tell thee o'er this thy day's work,
Thou 't not believe thy deeds. But I'll report it
Where senators shall mingle tears with smiles;
Where great patricians shall attend and shrug,
I' th' end admire; where ladies shall be frighted
And, gladly quaked, hear more; where the dull tribunes,
That with the fusty plebeians hate thine honors,
Shall say against their hearts "We thank the gods
Our Rome hath such a soldier."
Yet cam'st thou to a morsel of this feast,
Having fully dined before.

*Enter Titus ⌜Lartius⌝ with his power, from the pursuit.*

LARTIUS O general,
Here is the steed, we the caparison.
Hadst thou beheld—

MARTIUS Pray now, no more. My mother,
Who has a charter to extol her blood,
When she does praise me grieves me. I have done
As you have done—that's what I can;
Induced as you have been—that's for my country.
He that has but effected his good will
Hath overta'en mine act.

24. **deserving:** deserts

26. **traducement:** defamation, slander

28. **spire and top:** summit, highest point; **vouched:** affirmed, attested

29. **modest:** moderate, not excessive

30. **In sign:** as an indication

35. **'gainst:** in the presence of

36. **tent . . . death:** i.e., use **death** as a remedy (Literally, to **tent wounds** was to probe them with a tent, a roll of soft absorbent cloth, often medicated, to keep them open so that they would heal.)

37. **good:** i.e., **good** ones; **good store:** a great many

40. **the common distribution:** i.e., its division among all the soldiers

41. **At your only choice: at your choice** alone

45. **stand:** insist; **my common part:** i.e., a share for me in common

46 SD. **bare:** i.e., bareheaded

50. **Made all:** entirely constituted; **false-faced soothing:** flattery, feigned approval; **steel:** i.e., weapons, armor

51. **the parasite's silk:** i.e., the fine clothes of a courtier who earns his meals by flattery

52. **ovator:** one who receives an ovation, or the public acclamation of his whole city, upon returning successfully from a military campaign (See longer note, page 284.)

53. **For that:** because

54. **foiled:** defeated; **debile:** feeble; **note:** regard, notice

COMINIUS You shall not be
The grave of your deserving. Rome must know
The value of her own. 'Twere a concealment
Worse than a theft, no less than a traducement,
To hide your doings and to silence that
Which, to the spire and top of praises vouched,
Would seem but modest. Therefore, I beseech you—
In sign of what you are, not to reward
What you have done—before our army hear me.

MARTIUS
I have some wounds upon me, and they smart
To hear themselves remembered.

COMINIUS Should they not,
Well might they fester 'gainst ingratitude
And tent themselves with death. Of all the horses—
Whereof we have ta'en good and good store—of all
The treasure in this field achieved and city,
We render you the tenth, to be ta'en forth
Before the common distribution
At your only choice.

MARTIUS I thank you, general,
But cannot make my heart consent to take
A bribe to pay my sword. I do refuse it
And stand upon my common part with those
That have beheld the doing.

*A long flourish. They all cry "Martius, Martius!"*
⌜*and*⌝ *cast up their caps and lances.*
*Cominius and Lartius stand bare.*

May these same instruments, which you profane,
Never sound more! When drums and trumpets shall
I' th' field prove flatterers, let courts and cities be
Made all of false-faced soothing! When steel grows
Soft as the parasite's silk, let him be made
An ⌜ovator⌝ for th' wars! No more, I say.
For that I have not washed my nose that bled,
Or foiled some debile wretch—which, without note,

55. **Here's . . . done:** i.e., **many** others here **have done**

57. **I loved my little should be:** i.e., it pleased me to have my small accomplishments

57–58. **dieted / In . . . lies:** i.e., fed with **praises** seasoned with falsehoods

61. **give:** represent; **By your patience:** with your forbearance

63. **means:** intends; **his proper harm:** i.e., **harm** to himself

66. **Wears . . . garland:** See note to 1.3.16.

68. **trim:** fine; **belonging:** i.e., trappings

71. **Martius Caius Coriolanus:** If the Folio text followed Roman custom, the name would be given as **Caius Martius Coriolanus** (the family name following the first name). Martius is, in fact, sometimes called "Caius Martius" earlier in the play.

72. **addition:** title

75. **fair:** clean

77. **stride:** bestride, straddle

78. **undercrest:** support as on a crest (as if the new title were an **addition**—a mark of honor added to a coat of arms); i.e., live up to

79. **To th' fairness of my power:** i.e., "as becomingly as I can" (Arden 1)

80. **to our:** i.e., let's go **to our**

83. **back:** i.e., go **back**

84. **The best:** i.e., **the best** (i.e., highest-ranking) men of **Corioles; articulate:** come to terms

Here's many else have done—you shout me forth
In acclamations hyperbolical,
As if I loved my little should be dieted
In praises sauced with lies.

COMINIUS Too modest are you,
More cruel to your good report than grateful
To us that give you truly. By your patience,
If 'gainst yourself you be incensed, we'll put you,
Like one that means his proper harm, in manacles,
Then reason safely with you. Therefore be it known,
As to us to all the world, that Caius Martius
Wears this war's garland, in token of the which
My noble steed, known to the camp, I give him,
With all his trim belonging. And from this time,
For what he did before Corioles, call him,
With all th' applause and clamor of the host,
Martius Caius Coriolanus! Bear
Th' addition nobly ever!

*Flourish. Trumpets sound, and drums.*

ALL
Martius Caius Coriolanus!

CORIOLANUS I will go wash;
And when my face is fair, you shall perceive
Whether I blush or no. Howbeit, I thank you.
I mean to stride your steed and at all times
To undercrest your good addition
To th' fairness of my power.

COMINIUS So, to our tent,
Where, ere we do repose us, we will write
To Rome of our success.—You, Titus Lartius,
Must to Corioles back. Send us to Rome
The best, with whom we may articulate
For their own good and ours.

LARTIUS I shall, my lord.

88. **bound:** obliged; about

91. **sometime:** once; formerly; at one time; **lay:** resided

92. **used:** treated

93. **cried:** i.e., **cried** out

106 SD. **cornets:** wind instruments made of horn

**1.10** Aufidius vows to destroy Coriolanus by any means possible

---

2. **on good condition:** i.e., according to favorable terms or conditions of a treaty (Aufidius [line 6] treats **good condition** as meaning "state of well-being.")

4. **would:** wish

5. **that:** i.e., **that** which

Coriolanus.
From [Guillaume Rouillé,]
... *Promptuarii iconum* ... (1553).

CORIOLANUS
The gods begin to mock me. I, that now
Refused most princely gifts, am bound to beg
Of my lord general.

COMINIUS Take 't, 'tis yours. What is 't?

CORIOLANUS
I sometime lay here in Corioles
At a poor man's house; he used me kindly.
He cried to me; I saw him prisoner;
But then Aufidius was within my view,
And wrath o'erwhelmed my pity. I request you
To give my poor host freedom.

COMINIUS O, well begged!
Were he the butcher of my son, he should
Be free as is the wind.—Deliver him, Titus.

LARTIUS
Martius, his name?

CORIOLANUS By Jupiter, forgot!
I am weary; yea, my memory is tired.
Have we no wine here?

COMINIUS Go we to our tent.
The blood upon your visage dries; 'tis time
It should be looked to. Come.

*A flourish ⌜of⌝ cornets. They exit.*

## ⌜Scene 10⌝

*Enter Tullus Aufidius bloody, with two or three Soldiers.*

AUFIDIUS The town is ta'en.

SOLDIER
'Twill be delivered back on good condition.

AUFIDIUS Condition?
I would I were a Roman, for I cannot,
Being a Volsce, be that I am. Condition?
What good condition can a treaty find

7. **part . . . mercy:** side or party that has surrendered

12. **emulation:** ambitious rivalry

13. **where:** whereas

14. **in an equal force:** i.e., fairly

15. **potch:** stab, poke (a vulgar word)

16. **Or:** either; **craft:** cunning, guile

19. **only suff'ring stain:** suffering nothing but disgrace

19–20. **for . . . itself:** i.e., because of him, my valor will no longer be itself

20. **Nor sleep:** i.e., neither his being asleep; **sanctuary:** i.e., (his being protected from harm in) a sacred place

21. **naked:** without weapons or armor; **nor fane:** neither temple

23. **Embarquements all of fury:** all embargos against or impediments to **fury**

24. **rotten:** decayed, corrupt with age

26. **upon my brother's guard:** under **my brother's** protection

27. **hospitable canon:** law of hospitality

29. **what:** i.e., who

32. **attended:** waited for

33. **south the city mills: south** of **the city mills** (See longer note, page 285.)

34. **that to:** i.e., so **that** in accordance with

I' th' part that is at mercy? Five times, Martius,
I have fought with thee; so often hast thou beat me
And wouldst do so, I think, should we encounter
As often as we eat. By th' elements,
If e'er again I meet him beard to beard,
He's mine, or I am his. Mine emulation
Hath not that honor in 't it had; for where
I thought to crush him in an equal force,
True sword to sword, I'll potch at him some way
Or wrath or craft may get him.

SOLDIER
He's the devil.

AUFIDIUS
Bolder, though not so subtle. My valor's poisoned
With only suff'ring stain by him; for him
Shall fly out of itself. Nor sleep nor sanctuary,
Being naked, sick, nor fane nor Capitol,
The prayers of priests nor times of sacrifice,
Embarquements all of fury, shall lift up
Their rotten privilege and custom 'gainst
My hate to Martius. Where I find him, were it
At home, upon my brother's guard, even there,
Against the hospitable canon, would I
Wash my fierce hand in 's heart. Go you to th' city;
Learn how 'tis held and what they are that must
Be hostages for Rome.

SOLDIER
Will not you go?

AUFIDIUS
I am attended at the cypress grove. I pray you—
'Tis south the city mills—bring me word thither
How the world goes, that to the pace of it
I may spur on my journey.

SOLDIER
I shall, sir.

⌜*They exit, Aufidius through one door,*
*Soldiers through another.*⌝

# CORIOLANUS

## ACT 2

**2.1** Coriolanus is welcomed back to Rome by his family and Menenius, and is expected to be elected consul. (Coriolanus's entry into Rome has often been staged as a great spectacle; see John Ripley, "*Coriolanus*'s Stage Imagery," in Further Reading.)

---

1. **augurer:** soothsayer, Roman priest who predicts the future and gives advice on public affairs by interpreting the behavior of birds, the entrails of sacrificed animals, and other portents (See picture, page 126.)

4. **according to:** in accordance with, answering to

6. **Nature . . . friends:** See Ecclesiasticus 13.16, 17: "Every beast loveth his like. . . . How can **the wolf** [line 7] agree with **the lamb** [line 8]?"

13. **old men:** with the implication that they should also be wise (Proverbial: "Older and wiser.")

16. **In . . . in:** i.e., through **what** wickedness **is Martius** morally inferior **enormity:** extreme wickedness; abnormality **poor in:** i.e., morally inferior by virtue of

18. **stored:** stocked, supplied

22. **censured:** criticized, judged

23. **right-hand file:** roll of those who take precedence (military language, here referring to the patricians)

# ACT 2

## ⌜Scene 1⌝

*Enter Menenius with the two Tribunes of the people, Sicinius and Brutus.*

MENENIUS The augurer tells me we shall have news tonight.

BRUTUS Good or bad?

MENENIUS Not according to the prayer of the people, for they love not Martius.

SICINIUS Nature teaches beasts to know their friends.

MENENIUS Pray you, who does the wolf love?

SICINIUS The lamb.

MENENIUS Ay, to devour him, as the hungry plebeians would the noble Martius.

BRUTUS He's a lamb indeed, that baas like a bear.

MENENIUS He's a bear indeed, that lives like a lamb. You two are old men; tell me one thing that I shall ask you.

BOTH Well, sir.

MENENIUS In what enormity is Martius poor in, that you two have not in abundance?

BRUTUS He's poor in no one fault, but stored with all.

SICINIUS Especially in pride.

BRUTUS And topping all others in boasting.

MENENIUS This is strange now. Do you two know how you are censured here in the city, I mean of us o' th' right-hand file, do you?

28–29. **a very little thief of occasion:** i.e., the smallest excuse or pretext (Syntactically, **thief of occasion** is an example of the genitive of definition, where **occasion** is a specific kind of **thief.**)

37. **wondrous:** wonderfully; **single:** slight, poor (playing on **single** as **alone** [line 35])

43. **brace:** pair

47. **humorous:** whimsical, moody

48. **hot:** i.e., mulled

49. **allaying Tiber:** i.e., water **allaying:** diluting **Tiber:** i.e., the **Tiber** River, which flows through Rome (See picture, page 2.) **said:** i.e., **I am said; something:** somewhat

50. **complaint:** i.e., the plaintiff in court, speaking before his adversary, the defendant

50–51. **tinderlike:** i.e., quickly heated with anger

51. **motion:** cause, case at law; **converses:** keeps company

54. **spend:** exhaust; **breath:** i.e., words

55. **wealsmen:** men devoted to the public good (with possible wordplay on the tribunes' habit of repeatedly saying "well")

56. **Lycurguses:** wise lawgivers (Lycurgus is traditionally credited with founding the institutions and creating the constitution of ancient Sparta.)

56–57. **if . . . adversely:** i.e., **if** I don't like what **you** say

58. **your Worships:** the title of magistrates; **delivered:** stated

59. **ass:** fool; **in compound:** i.e., combined

BOTH Why, how are we censured?

MENENIUS Because you talk of pride now, will you not be angry?

BOTH Well, well, sir, well?

MENENIUS Why, 'tis no great matter; for a very little thief of occasion will rob you of a great deal of patience. Give your dispositions the reins, and be angry at your pleasures, at the least, if you take it as a pleasure to you in being so. You blame Martius for being proud.

BRUTUS We do it not alone, sir.

MENENIUS I know you can do very little alone, for your helps are many, or else your actions would grow wondrous single. Your abilities are too infantlike for doing much alone. You talk of pride. O, that you could turn your eyes toward the napes of your necks and make but an interior survey of your good selves! O, that you could!

BOTH What then, sir?

MENENIUS Why, then you should discover a brace of unmeriting, proud, violent, testy magistrates, alias fools, as any in Rome.

SICINIUS Menenius, you are known well enough, too.

MENENIUS I am known to be a humorous patrician and one that loves a cup of hot wine with not a drop of allaying Tiber in 't; said to be something imperfect in favoring the first complaint, hasty and tinderlike upon too trivial motion; one that converses more with the buttock of the night than with the forehead of the morning. What I think I utter, and spend my malice in my breath. Meeting two such wealsmen as you are—I cannot call you Lycurguses—if the drink you give me touch my palate adversely, I make a crooked face at it. I ⌜cannot⌝ say your Worships have delivered the matter well when I find the ass in compound with the

63. **good:** adequately attractive; **this:** i.e., **this** description of my nature, or **this character** (line 66)

63–64. **map of my microcosm:** i.e., my face **microcosm:** little world of the individual person, regarded as the epitome of the universe

65. **bisson:** blind; **conspectuities:** faculties of sight; visions

66. **this character:** i.e., **this** description of my **character**

70–71. **caps and legs:** i.e., doffing **caps** and making curtsies (as signs of deference)

71–72. **forenoon:** morning

72. **cause:** case at law; **orange-wife:** woman who sells oranges

73. **faucet-seller:** one who sells pegs or spigots for casks; **rejourn:** adjourn, postpone

74. **of threepence:** concerning **threepence** (a trifling amount); **audience:** judicial hearing

75, 76. **party:** litigant

77. **mummers:** actors in dumb shows (alluding to their grimaces)

77–78. **set . . . patience:** i.e., lose **patience** completely (To **set up the bloody flag** is to declare war or, perhaps, to signal that no quarter will be given.)

79. **bleeding:** raw, i.e., unresolved

80. **hearing:** the trial you presided over

84. **giber:** one who taunts and jeers; **for the table:** i.e., at dinner; **necessary:** indispensable

85. **bencher:** senator

87. **subjects:** (1) subordinates; (2) topics for conversation

91. **a botcher's cushion:** the **cushion** of a mender of old clothes

*(continued)*

major part of your syllables. And though I must be content to bear with those that say you are reverend grave men, yet they lie deadly that tell you have good faces. If you see this in the map of my microcosm, follows it that I am known well enough too? What harm can your bisson conspectuities glean out of this character, if I be known well enough, too?

BRUTUS Come, sir, come; we know you well enough.

MENENIUS You know neither me, yourselves, nor anything. You are ambitious for poor knaves' caps and legs. You wear out a good wholesome forenoon in hearing a cause between an orange-wife and a faucet-seller, and then rejourn the controversy of threepence to a second day of audience. When you are hearing a matter between party and party, if you chance to be pinched with the colic, you make faces like mummers, set up the bloody flag against all patience, and, in roaring for a chamber pot, dismiss the controversy bleeding, the more entangled by your hearing. All the peace you make in their cause is calling both the parties knaves. You are a pair of strange ones.

BRUTUS Come, come. You are well understood to be a perfecter giber for the table than a necessary bencher in the Capitol.

MENENIUS Our very priests must become mockers if they shall encounter such ridiculous subjects as you are. When you speak best unto the purpose, it is not worth the wagging of your beards, and your beards deserve not so honorable a grave as to stuff a botcher's cushion or to be entombed in an ass's packsaddle. Yet you must be saying Martius is proud, who, in a cheap estimation, is worth all your predecessors since Deucalion, though peradventure some of the best of 'em were hereditary

93. **in a cheap estimation:** i.e., at low estimated value

94. **Deucalion:** in Greek mythology, the sole human male to survive Zeus's flooding of the earth (He and his wife repopulated the earth by throwing stones over their shoulders. See picture, page 174.)

94–95. **peradventure:** perhaps

95–96. **hereditary hangmen:** executioners who inherited the job

96. **Good e'en:** i.e., goodbye (literally, **good** evening)

97. **conversation:** talk; company; **being:** i.e., you **being**

100. **How now:** a greeting that inquires about one's well-being; **fair:** beautiful

101. **moon:** goddess Diana

101–2. **whither . . . fast:** i.e., where are **you** going **so fast** to see something

104. **Juno:** queen of the Roman gods (See picture, page 188.)

106–7. **prosperous approbation:** i.e., approval for (his) success

109. **Hoo:** exclamation, here of delight

113. **state:** government

117. **certain:** i.e., certainly

118. **estate of:** i.e., legal right to, or title to

119. **make a lip:** poke fun

120. **sovereign:** efficacious, powerful

121. **Galen:** second-century Greek physician whose writing was still authoritative in Shakespeare's time (See picture, page 212.) **empiricutic:** empirical (based on distrusted experimentation, not

*(continued)*

hangmen. Good e'en to your Worships. More of your conversation would infect my brain, being the herdsmen of the beastly plebeians. I will be bold to take my leave of you.

⌜*He begins to exit.*⌝ *Brutus and Sicinius* ⌜*stand*⌝ *aside.*

*Enter Volumnia, Virgilia, and Valeria.*

How now, my as fair as noble ladies—and the moon, were she earthly, no nobler—whither do you follow your eyes so fast?

VOLUMNIA Honorable Menenius, my boy Martius approaches. For the love of Juno, let's go!

MENENIUS Ha? Martius coming home?

VOLUMNIA Ay, worthy Menenius, and with most prosperous approbation.

MENENIUS Take my cap, Jupiter, and I thank thee! ⌜(*He throws his cap in the air.*)⌝ Hoo! Martius coming home?

⌜VALERIA, VIRGILIA⌝ Nay, 'tis true.

VOLUMNIA Look, here's a letter from him. ⌜*She produces a paper.*⌝ The state hath another, his wife another, and I think there's one at home for you.

MENENIUS I will make my very house reel tonight. A letter for me?

VIRGILIA Yes, certain, there's a letter for you; I saw 't.

MENENIUS A letter for me? It gives me an estate of seven years' health, in which time I will make a lip at the physician. The most sovereign prescription in Galen is but empiricutic and, to this preservative, of no better report than a horse drench. Is he not wounded? He was wont to come home wounded.

VIRGILIA O no, no, no!

VOLUMNIA O, he is wounded, I thank the gods for 't.

MENENIUS So do I too, if it be not too much. Brings he victory in his pocket, the wounds become him.

on authorities like **Galen**); **to this preservative:** i.e., in comparison to this **letter** (line 118)

122. **report:** reputation, repute; **horse drench:** medicine for **a horse**

123. **wont:** accustomed

126. **Brings he:** i.e., if **he brings**

127. **become:** look well on

128. **On 's brows:** i.e., not **in his pocket** (line 127)

129. **oaken garland:** See note to 1.3.16.

130. **disciplined:** thrashed

132. **got off:** escaped, **got** away

134. **An he:** i.e., if Aufidius

135. **'fidiused:** beaten as Aufidius should be (the word is presented as Menenius's creation, based on Aufidius's name)

136. **possessed:** informed

140. **name:** i.e., glory, honor

141. **action:** fight

145. **true purchasing:** truly earning

147. **Pow waw:** expression of derision

153. **cicatrices:** scars

154. **stand . . . place:** i.e., **stand for** election to **his** office (i.e., the consulship)

154–55. **repulse of Tarquin:** i.e., battle in which **Tarquin** was overcome (See 2.2.103–14, below, and longer note, page 285. See also picture, page 104.)

157. **nine:** Editors have noted the "discrepant arithmetic" here (Brockbank) and "the competitive insensitivity of their gloating" (Parker).

VOLUMNIA On 's brows, Menenius. He comes the third time home with the oaken garland.

MENENIUS Has he disciplined Aufidius soundly?

VOLUMNIA Titus Lartius writes they fought together, but Aufidius got off.

MENENIUS And 'twas time for him too, I'll warrant him that. An he had stayed by him, I would not have been so 'fidiused for all the chests in Corioles and the gold that's in them. Is the Senate possessed of this?

VOLUMNIA Good ladies, let's go.—Yes, yes, yes. The Senate has letters from the General, wherein he gives my son the whole name of the war. He hath in this action outdone his former deeds doubly.

VALERIA In troth, there's wondrous things spoke of him.

MENENIUS Wondrous? Ay, I warrant you, and not without his true purchasing.

VIRGILIA The gods grant them true.

VOLUMNIA True? Pow waw!

MENENIUS True? I'll be sworn they are true. Where is he wounded? ⌜(*To the Tribunes.*)⌝ God save your good Worships! Martius is coming home; he has more cause to be proud.—Where is he wounded?

VOLUMNIA I' th' shoulder and i' th' left arm. There will be large cicatrices to show the people when he shall stand for his place. He received in the repulse of Tarquin seven hurts i' th' body.

MENENIUS One i' th' neck and two i' th' thigh—there's nine that I know.

VOLUMNIA He had, before this last expedition, twenty-five wounds upon him.

MENENIUS Now it's twenty-seven. Every gash was an enemy's grave. (*A shout and flourish.*) Hark, the trumpets!

163. **ushers:** harbingers, precursors

165. **nervy:** sinewy

166. **advanced:** raised; **declines:** falls

166 SD. **sennet:** trumpet signal to accompany a ceremonial entrance; **Enter:** See headnote to this scene, page 70, above. **Titus Lartius:** See longer note, page 286.

169. **With fame:** i.e., together **with fame; a name to:** i.e., **a name** in addition **to; these:** i.e., **Martius Caius**

181. **deed-achieving honor:** i.e., **honor** acquired by achieving feats

184. **gracious:** lovely

Bringing home "hostages for Rome." (1.10.30)
From Onofrio Panvinio, . . . *De lvdis circensibvs, libri II. De trivmphis* . . . (1642).

VOLUMNIA These are the ushers of Martius: before him he carries noise, and behind him he leaves tears.
Death, that dark spirit, in 's nervy arm doth lie,
Which, being advanced, declines, and then men die.
*A sennet.*

*Enter Cominius the General and Titus Lartius, between them Coriolanus crowned with an oaken garland, with Captains and Soldiers and a Herald. Trumpets sound.*

HERALD
Know, Rome, that all alone Martius did fight
Within Corioles' gates, where he hath won,
With fame, a name to Martius Caius; these
In honor follows "Coriolanus."
Welcome to Rome, renownèd Coriolanus.
*Sound flourish.*

ALL
Welcome to Rome, renownèd Coriolanus!

CORIOLANUS
No more of this. It does offend my heart.
Pray now, no more.

COMINIUS Look, sir, your mother.

CORIOLANUS O,
You have, I know, petitioned all the gods
For my prosperity. *Kneels.*

VOLUMNIA Nay, my good soldier, up.
⌜*He stands.*⌝
My gentle Martius, worthy Caius, and
By deed-achieving honor newly named—
What is it? Coriolanus must I call thee?
But, O, thy wife—

CORIOLANUS My gracious silence, hail.
Wouldst thou have laughed had I come coffined home,
That weep'st to see me triumph? Ah, my dear,

197. **light:** cheerful; **heavy:** i.e., emotional (literally, sorrowful)

198. **on 's heart:** i.e., of his **heart**

199. **You are three:** presumably referring to Cominius, Titus Lartius, and Coriolanus (See longer note to 2.1.166 SD, page 286.)

201. **old crab trees:** bad-tempered **old** men (literally, **old** wild apple **trees**)

203. **grafted . . . relish:** i.e., altered as through grafting so as to like you (See longer note, page 287.) **relish:** liking

204–5. **We call . . . folly:** See Proverbs 14.24: "The **folly of fools** is foolishness." **nettle:** See picture, page 202.

208. **Give . . . on:** presumably a command to the crowd to move aside and to the soldiers to prepare to march forward

214. **change of honors:** i.e., new **honors** (by analogy with **change of** clothes)

216. **see inherited:** i.e., **see** you inherit, or **see** you come into possession of; **my very wishes:** exactly what I wished for

217. **fancy:** imagination

218. **wanting:** lacking

Such eyes the widows in Corioles wear
And mothers that lack sons.

MENENIUS Now the gods crown
thee!

⌜CORIOLANUS⌝
And live you yet? ⌜(*To Valeria.*)⌝ O, my sweet lady,
pardon.

VOLUMNIA
I know not where to turn. O, welcome home!—
And, welcome, general.—And you're welcome all.

MENENIUS
A hundred thousand welcomes! I could weep,
And I could laugh; I am light and heavy. Welcome.
A curse begin at very root on 's heart
That is not glad to see thee! ⌜You⌝ are three
That Rome should dote on; yet, by the faith of men,
We have some old crab trees here at home that will
not
Be grafted to your relish. Yet welcome, warriors!
We call a nettle but a nettle, and
The faults of fools but folly.

COMINIUS Ever right.

CORIOLANUS Menenius ever, ever.

HERALD
Give way there, and go on!

CORIOLANUS, ⌜*to Volumnia and Virgilia*⌝ Your hand
and yours.
Ere in our own house I do shade my head,
The good patricians must be visited,
From whom I have received not only greetings,
But with them change of honors.

VOLUMNIA I have lived
To see inherited my very wishes
And the buildings of my fancy. Only
There's one thing wanting, which I doubt not but
Our Rome will cast upon thee.

222. **sway with:** (1) rule or govern **with;** (2) i.e., go along **with**

223 SD. **in state:** with great pomp and solemnity

224–25. **the blearèd . . . spectacled:** i.e., those with dim vision put on spectacles or eyeglasses (an anachronism)

225. **Your:** i.e., the; **nurse:** one who suckles infants or cares for young children

226. **rapture:** fit

227. **chats:** i.e., chatters about; **kitchen malkin:** untidy **kitchen** servant

228. **lockram:** piece of linen; **reechy:** dirty

229. **Stalls:** benches in front of shops used to display goods; **bulks:** frameworks projecting from shop fronts

231. **smothered up:** crowded (literally, densely covered); **leads:** roofs (literally, roofs covered with sheets or strips of lead); **ridges:** crests of roofs; **horsed:** straddled, bestrode (as if they were horses)

232. **variable complexions:** i.e., people of various temperaments (See longer note, page 287.)

233. **Seld-shown flamens:** priests who seldom appear in public

234. **press:** push their way; **popular throngs:** plebeian crowds; **puff:** breathe hard

235. **vulgar station:** place to stand among the common people (with possible wordplay on **station** as social standing); **veiled dames:** i.e., ladies who usually wear veils

236–37. **war . . . cheeks:** i.e., their complexions **damask:** pink **nicely-gauded:** carefully made-up

237. **wanton:** rude, violent; **spoil:** injury

*(continued)*

CORIOLANUS Know, good mother,
I had rather be their servant in my way
Than sway with them in theirs.

COMINIUS On, to the Capitol.

*Flourish ⌜of⌝ cornets. They exit in state, as before.*

*Brutus and Sicinius ⌜come forward.⌝*

BRUTUS
All tongues speak of him, and the blearèd sights
Are spectacled to see him. Your prattling nurse
Into a rapture lets her baby cry
While she chats him. The kitchen malkin pins
Her richest lockram 'bout her reechy neck,
Clamb'ring the walls to eye him. Stalls, bulks, windows
Are smothered up, leads filled, and ridges horsed
With variable complexions, all agreeing
In earnestness to see him. Seld-shown flamens
Do press among the popular throngs and puff
To win a vulgar station. Our veiled dames
Commit the war of white and damask in
Their nicely-gauded cheeks to th' wanton spoil
Of Phoebus' burning kisses. Such a pother
As if that whatsoever god who leads him
Were slyly crept into his human powers
And gave him graceful posture.

SICINIUS On the sudden
I warrant him consul.

BRUTUS Then our office may,
During his power, go sleep.

SICINIUS
He cannot temp'rately transport his honors
From where he should begin and end, but will
Lose those he hath won.

BRUTUS In that there's comfort.

238. **Phoebus':** Phoebus Apollo is the sun god. **pother:** commotion

239. **As . . . him: "as if that god who leads him, whatsoever god that** be" (Samuel Johnson, 1765)

242. **On the sudden:** without delay

243. **warrant:** predict

244. **office:** position of authority, function

247. **and end:** i.e., to where he **should end**

250–52. **Doubt not . . . they:** i.e., do not **doubt but** that **the commoners, for whom we** do our duty

254. **which:** i.e., **which cause**

256. **As:** i.e., **as** that

258. **stand for: stand for** election as

260. **napless:** threadbare; **vesture:** garment (See longer note, page 287.)

261. **manner:** custom

264. **miss it:** i.e., lose the consulship

265. **carry:** win; **but:** i.e., in any way except; **suit:** petition, entreaty

270. **like:** i.e., likely

271. **our good: our** advantage; **wills:** requires

272. **sure:** certain

274. **for an end:** i.e., bound to come to **an end**

275. **suggest the people:** insinuate into the minds of **the people**

276. **still:** always; **to 's:** i.e., to the extent of his

277. **mules:** i.e., pack animals (with a possible allusion to the mule's inability to procreate)

278. **Dispropertied:** i.e., dispossessed them of

281. **their war:** i.e., the patricians' **war; who:** which; **provand:** provender, food

282. **sore:** severe

SICINIUS Doubt
not
The commoners, for whom we stand, but they
Upon their ancient malice will forget
With the least cause these his new honors—which
That he will give them make I as little question
As he is proud to do 't.

BRUTUS I heard him swear,
Were he to stand for consul, never would he
Appear i' th' marketplace nor on him put
The napless vesture of humility,
Nor showing, as the manner is, his wounds
To th' people, beg their stinking breaths.

SICINIUS 'Tis right.

BRUTUS
It was his word. O, he would miss it rather
Than carry it but by the suit of the gentry to him
And the desire of the nobles.

SICINIUS I wish no better
Than have him hold that purpose and to put it
In execution.

BRUTUS 'Tis most like he will.

SICINIUS
It shall be to him then as our good wills,
A sure destruction.

BRUTUS So it must fall out
To him, or our authority's for an end.
We must suggest the people in what hatred
He still hath held them; that to 's power he would
Have made them mules, silenced their pleaders, and
Dispropertied their freedoms; holding them
In human action and capacity
Of no more soul nor fitness for the world
Than camels in their war, who have their provand
Only for bearing burdens, and sore blows
For sinking under them.

286. **touch:** vex; **want:** be lacking
287. **put upon 't:** incited to it
296. **maids:** maidens, young unmarried women
298. **Jove's statue:** the **statue** of Jupiter, king of the Roman gods (See picture, page 112.)
302. **time:** occasion
303. **event:** outcome
304. **Have with you:** i.e., I am **with you**

**2.2** The Senate meets to hear Cominius praise Coriolanus in a formal oration and then to choose Coriolanus as its nominee for consul.

---

0 SD. **cushions:** In this play, **cushions** serve to suggest the Senate. The **cushions,** when placed onstage, may be large enough to be used as seats. **Capitol:** Historically, the Senate met not **in the Capitol** but near the Roman Forum.
2. **stand for:** i.e., present themselves to the Senate, which will select its nominee
3–4. **of everyone:** i.e., by **everyone**
4. **carry it:** i.e., win

SICINIUS This, as you say, suggested
At some time when his soaring insolence
Shall ⌜touch⌝ the people—which time shall not want
If he be put upon 't, and that's as easy
As to set dogs on sheep—will be his fire
To kindle their dry stubble, and their blaze
Shall darken him forever.

*Enter a Messenger.*

BRUTUS What's the matter?

MESSENGER
You are sent for to the Capitol. 'Tis thought
That Martius shall be consul. I have seen
The dumb men throng to see him, and the blind
To hear him speak; matrons flung gloves,
Ladies and maids their scarves and handkerchiefs,
Upon him as he passed; the nobles bended
As to Jove's statue, and the Commons made
A shower and thunder with their caps and shouts.
I never saw the like.

BRUTUS Let's to the Capitol,
And carry with us ears and eyes for th' time,
But hearts for the event.

SICINIUS Have with you.

*They exit.*

⌜Scene 2⌝

*Enter two Officers, to lay cushions, as it were in the Capitol.*

FIRST OFFICER Come, come. They are almost here. How many stand for consulships?

SECOND OFFICER Three, they say; but 'tis thought of everyone Coriolanus will carry it.

5–6. **vengeance:** extremely, intensely

8–9. **who ne'er loved them:** The pronouns here are ambiguous. The lines may mean either "**the people** never **loved** the flattering **great men**" or "The **great men** never **loved the people.**"

14. **in their:** i.e., of **their**

17. **waved:** i.e., would waver, vacillate; **indifferently:** neutrally

17–18. **'twixt . . . harm:** a mixing of two constructions: (1) between **good** and **harm;** (2) **doing them neither good nor harm**

20. **discover him:** show him to be

21. **opposite:** adversary; **affect:** be fond of, show preference for

25. **degrees:** steps (literally, rungs of a ladder)

26. **supple:** artfully accommodating

27. **bonneted:** i.e., uncovered their heads as a mark of respect for the people

28. **have them:** lead or convey themselves (i.e., the **supple** politicians [line 26]); **their estimation and report:** the people's esteem and commendation

32. **ingrateful:** ungrateful

33. **giving itself the lie:** demonstrating its own falsity

36 SD. **Lictors:** magistrates' attendants, carrying the magistrates' symbols of authority, the fasces (See picture, page 106.)

FIRST OFFICER That's a brave fellow, but he's vengeance proud and loves not the common people.

SECOND OFFICER 'Faith, there hath been many great men that have flattered the people who ne'er loved them; and there be many that they have loved they know not wherefore; so that, if they love they know not why, they hate upon no better a ground. Therefore, for Coriolanus neither to care whether they love or hate him manifests the true knowledge he has in their disposition and, out of his noble carelessness, lets them plainly see 't.

FIRST OFFICER If he did not care whether he had their love or no, he waved indifferently 'twixt doing them neither good nor harm; but he seeks their hate with greater devotion than they can render it him and leaves nothing undone that may fully discover him their opposite. Now, to seem to affect the malice and displeasure of the people is as bad as that which he dislikes, to flatter them for their love.

SECOND OFFICER He hath deserved worthily of his country, and his ascent is not by such easy degrees as those who, having been supple and courteous to the people, bonneted, without any further deed to have them at all into their estimation and report; but he hath so planted his honors in their eyes and his actions in their hearts that for their tongues to be silent and not confess so much were a kind of ingrateful injury. To report otherwise were a malice that, giving itself the lie, would pluck reproof and rebuke from every ear that heard it.

FIRST OFFICER No more of him; he's a worthy man. Make way. They are coming.

*A sennet. Enter the Patricians and the Tribunes of the people, Lictors before them; Coriolanus, Menenius, Cominius the consul.* ⌜*The Patricians sit.*⌝ *Sicinius*

37. **determined of:** i.e., decided what to do about

39. **after-meeting:** subsequent meeting

40. **gratify:** show gratitude for; reward

41. **stood for:** defended, supported

43. **desire:** request

44. **last:** latest, most recent

45. **well-found:** valued; commendable

47. **whom:** the object of **thank and remember** (line 48)

48. **met here:** i.e., are **here** assembled

49. **like himself:** suitable to him

51. **for length:** i.e., because your speech takes a long time

52. **state's:** government is; **defective for requital:** lacking means to reward adequately

53. **we . . . out:** i.e., we are unwilling to strain our means in order to reward suitably

55. **after:** afterward

56. **motion toward:** i.e., prompting of; **common body:** i.e., **common** people

57. **yield:** allow, grant; **passes:** is transacted, is decided

58. **convented:** gathered

59. **treaty:** discussion of terms

60. **Inclinable:** favorably disposed

63. **blest:** happy

63–64. **remember . . . value:** i.e., bear in mind a higher estimate

65. **hereto:** up to this time, hitherto

66. **off:** i.e., not pertinent

*and Brutus take their places by themselves.*
*Coriolanus stands.*

MENENIUS
Having determined of the Volsces and
To send for Titus Lartius, it remains,
As the main point of this our after-meeting,
To gratify his noble service that
Hath thus stood for his country. Therefore please you,
Most reverend and grave elders, to desire
The present consul and last general
In our well-found successes to report
A little of that worthy work performed
By Martius Caius Coriolanus, whom
We met here both to thank and to remember
With honors like himself. ⌜*Coriolanus sits.*⌝

FIRST SENATOR Speak, good Cominius.
Leave nothing out for length, and make us think
Rather our state's defective for requital,
Than we to stretch it out. ⌜(*To the Tribunes.*)⌝ Masters o' th' people,
We do request your kindest ears and, after,
Your loving motion toward the common body
To yield what passes here.

SICINIUS We are convented
Upon a pleasing treaty and have hearts
Inclinable to honor and advance
The theme of our assembly.

BRUTUS Which the rather
We shall be blest to do if he remember
A kinder value of the people than
He hath hereto prized them at.

MENENIUS That's off, that's off!
I would you rather had been silent. Please you
To hear Cominius speak?

72. **your people:** (1) the **people** you represent; (2) the **people** you speak of

73. **tie:** bind, constrain

76. **shame:** be ashamed

82. **disbenched you:** forced you from your seat

85. **soothed:** flattered

87. **as they weigh:** according to their value

90. **alarum:** call to arms; **struck:** sounded on a drum

91. **monstered:** pointed out as wonderful

92. **Masters of the people:** i.e., tribunes

94. **thousand:** i.e., a **thousand** plebeians

97. **on 's:** i.e., of his

98. **voice:** i.e., the capacity to speak adequately

"The senators of Rome." (1.1.157)
From Livy, *Decades* . . . [1511].

BRUTUS Most willingly,
But yet my caution was more pertinent
Than the rebuke you give it.

MENENIUS He loves your people,
But tie him not to be their bedfellow.—
Worthy Cominius, speak.

*Coriolanus rises and offers to go away.*

Nay, keep your place.

⌜FIRST⌝ SENATOR
Sit, Coriolanus. Never shame to hear
What you have nobly done.

CORIOLANUS Your Honors, pardon.
I had rather have my wounds to heal again
Than hear say how I got them.

BRUTUS Sir, I hope
My words disbenched you not?

CORIOLANUS No, sir. Yet oft,
When blows have made me stay, I fled from words.
You soothed not, therefore hurt not; but your people,
I love them as they weigh.

MENENIUS Pray now, sit down.

CORIOLANUS
I had rather have one scratch my head i' th' sun
When the alarum were struck than idly sit
To hear my nothings monstered. *Coriolanus exits.*

MENENIUS Masters of the people,
Your multiplying spawn how can he flatter—
That's thousand to one good one—when you now see
He had rather venture all his limbs for honor
Than one on 's ears to hear it.—Proceed, Cominius.

COMINIUS
I shall lack voice. The deeds of Coriolanus
Should not be uttered feebly. It is held
That valor is the chiefest virtue and

101. **haver:** one who has it

103. **singly counterpoised:** counterbalanced by any single man

104. **made a head for:** raised an army against; **he:** Coriolanus (For Plutarch's account of the action described in 2.2.103–14, see longer note to 2.1.154–55, page 285.) See also picture, page 104.

105. **mark:** limit; **dictator:** official elected to exercise absolute authority only during a time of national crisis, like a war

106. **Whom . . . at:** an English version of a familiar phrase in Latin speeches of praise

107. **Amazonian:** i.e., beardless (Amazons were women warriors.) See picture, page 186.

108. **bristled lips:** i.e., bearded opponents

109. **o'erpressed:** overthrown

110. **met:** encountered

111. **on his knee:** i.e., to his knees

112. **act . . . scene:** As boys acted the women's parts on Shakespeare's stage, so young Martius was entitled to **act** as if he were a **woman** (by crying or retreating) **in that day's feats** (line 111) **scene:** drama, play

113. **meed:** reward

114. **brow-bound with the oak:** For **the oak** garland, see note to 1.3.16 and picture, page 124.

114–15. **His pupil . . . Man-entered:** i.e., having already at the age of a **pupil** behaved as if a full-grown man

116. **brunt:** shock, violence

117. **lurched:** robbed; **swords:** i.e., fellow combatants; **garland:** i.e., oak **garland; For:** i.e., as **for; last:** i.e., most recent battle

*(continued)*

Most dignifies the haver; if it be,
The man I speak of cannot in the world
Be singly counterpoised. At sixteen years,
When Tarquin made a head for Rome, he fought
Beyond the mark of others. Our then dictator,
Whom with all praise I point at, saw him fight
When with his Amazonian chin he drove
The bristled lips before him. He bestrid
An o'erpressed Roman and i' th' Consul's view
Slew three opposers. Tarquin's self he met
And struck him on his knee. In that day's feats,
When he might act the woman in the scene,
He proved best man i' th' field and for his meed
Was brow-bound with the oak. His pupil age
Man-entered thus, he waxèd like a sea,
And in the brunt of seventeen battles since
He lurched all swords of the garland. For this last,
Before and in Corioles, let me say,
I cannot speak him home. He stopped the flyers
And by his rare example made the coward
Turn terror into sport. As weeds before
A vessel under sail, so men obeyed
And fell below his stem. His sword, Death's stamp,
Where it did mark, it took; from face to foot
He was a thing of blood, whose every motion
Was timed with dying cries. Alone he entered
The mortal gate o' th' city, which he painted
With shunless destiny; aidless came off
And with a sudden reinforcement struck
Corioles like a planet. Now all's his,
When by and by the din of war gan pierce
His ready sense; then straight his doubled spirit
Requickened what in flesh was fatigate,
And to the battle came he, where he did
Run reeking o'er the lives of men as if
'Twere a perpetual spoil; and till we called

119. **speak him home:** i.e., describe the full extent of his achievements; **flyers:** i.e., those Romans fleeing from battle

123. **stem:** bow (literally, the main timber of a ship's bow); **stamp:** stamping tool for marking things

124. **took: took** possession (i.e., killed)

126. **Was timed:** was accompanied, was synchronous

127. **mortal:** deadly

127–28. **painted . . . destiny:** i.e., covered in the blood of those fated to be killed **shunless:** unavoidable

128. **came off:** extricated himself

129. **reinforcement:** fresh assault

130. **like a planet:** (1) with the force of **a planet;** (2) with the devastating influence then attributed to an angry or plague-bearing **planet; Now:** i.e., for a moment

131. **by and by:** soon; **gan pierce:** began to **pierce**

132. **ready:** prompt; **sense:** i.e., **sense** of hearing; **straight:** immediately; **doubled:** redoubled

133. **Requickened:** revived; **fatigate:** weary

135. **reeking:** steaming with fresh blood

136. **spoil:** destruction

137. **field:** battlefield; **stood: stood** still, stopped

140. **cannot but:** i.e., surely will; **with measure fit:** i.e., measure up to

141. **devise:** i.e., assign to

142. **spoils:** booty, plunder; **kicked at:** scorned

145. **misery:** extreme poverty

*(continued)*

Both field and city ours, he never stood
To ease his breast with panting.

MENENIUS Worthy man!

⌜FIRST⌝ SENATOR
He cannot but with measure fit the honors
Which we devise him.

COMINIUS Our spoils he kicked at
And looked upon things precious as they were
The common muck of the world. He covets less
Than misery itself would give, rewards
His deeds with doing them, and is content
To spend the time to end it.

MENENIUS He's right noble.
Let him be called for.

⌜FIRST⌝ SENATOR Call Coriolanus.

OFFICER He doth appear.

*Enter Coriolanus.*

MENENIUS
The Senate, Coriolanus, are well pleased
To make thee consul.

CORIOLANUS I do owe them still
My life and services.

MENENIUS It then remains
That you do speak to the people.

CORIOLANUS I do beseech you,
Let me o'erleap that custom, for I cannot
Put on the gown, stand naked, and entreat them
For my wounds' sake to give their suffrage. Please you
That I may pass this doing.

SICINIUS Sir, the people
Must have their voices; neither will they bate
One jot of ceremony.

MENENIUS, ⌜*to Coriolanus*⌝ Put them not to 't.
Pray you, go fit you to the custom, and

146–47. **is content . . . it:** "**is content** that **the time** [well] spent be an end in itself" (Brockbank)

148. **right:** very

154. **still:** always

159. **o'erleap:** omit

160. **naked:** i.e., with no tunic under his toga (See longer note to 2.1.260, page 287.)

163. **pass:** avoid

165. **voices:** votes; **bate:** abate, leave out

167. **Put them not to 't:** do **not** challenge **them**

168. **fit you:** conform yourself

170. **form:** observance of due ceremony

178. **breath:** i.e., voices or votes

179. **stand upon 't:** i.e., insist on it

180. **recommend:** commend, commit

181. **purpose:** intention (i.e., to make Coriolanus consul); **them:** i.e., the people

185. **perceive 's:** i.e., **perceive** his; **require:** request

186. **did contemn what:** i.e., was contemptuous that **what**

190. **attend:** wait for

**2.3** According to custom, Coriolanus asks a number of individual plebeians for their votes. Although he mocks them, they consent to his election. Later meeting with the tribunes, the plebeians reflect on Coriolanus's mockery and decide, with the tribunes' encouragement, to revoke their votes for him.

---

1. **Once:** first; in short

Take to you, as your predecessors have,
Your honor with your form.

CORIOLANUS It is a part
That I shall blush in acting, and might well
Be taken from the people.

BRUTUS, ⌜*to Sicinius*⌝ Mark you that?

CORIOLANUS
To brag unto them "Thus I did, and thus!"
Show them th' unaching scars, which I should hide,
As if I had received them for the hire
Of their breath only!

MENENIUS Do not stand upon 't.—
We recommend to you, tribunes of the people,
Our purpose to them, and to our noble consul
Wish we all joy and honor.

SENATORS
To Coriolanus come all joy and honor!

*Flourish cornets. Then they exit. Sicinius and Brutus remain.*

BRUTUS
You see how he intends to use the people.

SICINIUS
May they perceive 's intent! He will require them
As if he did contemn what he requested
Should be in them to give.

BRUTUS Come, we'll inform them
Of our proceedings here. On th' marketplace
I know they do attend us.

⌜*They exit.*⌝

## ⌜Scene 3⌝

*Enter seven or eight Citizens.*

FIRST CITIZEN Once, if he do require our voices, we ought not to deny him.

3. **will:** wish

4. **power:** legal authority

5. **no power: no** liberty, **no** permission

14. **thought of:** i.e., by the patricians

15. **once:** i.e., **once** when; **stood up:** engaged in confrontation

16. **corn:** wheat (See 1.1.178–215.) **stuck:** hesitated

16–17. **many-headed multitude:** proverbial, denoting the fickleness of the populace

18. **of many:** i.e., by **many**

20. **abram:** auburn (which, in Shakespeare's day, meant a yellowish-white color); **wits:** minds

23. **consent of:** agreement about

24. **to all:** i.e., **to** go to **all**

27. **out:** issue **out**

29. **sure:** i.e., surely go

32–33. **To lose . . . dews:** England associated the south with moisture (**fog**) and contagion. (See note to 1.4.41.)

34. **return:** i.e., to the **blockhead** (lines 28–29)

36–37. **You may:** i.e., you win

SECOND CITIZEN We may, sir, if we will.

THIRD CITIZEN We have power in ourselves to do it, but it is a power that we have no power to do; for, if he show us his wounds and tell us his deeds, we are to put our tongues into those wounds and speak for them. So, if he tell us his noble deeds, we must also tell him our noble acceptance of them. Ingratitude is monstrous, and for the multitude to be ingrateful were to make a monster of the multitude, of the which, we being members, should bring ourselves to be monstrous members.

FIRST CITIZEN And to make us no better thought of, a little help will serve; for once we stood up about the corn, he himself stuck not to call us the many-headed multitude.

THIRD CITIZEN We have been called so of many; not that our heads are some brown, some black, some abram, some bald, but that our wits are so diversely colored; and truly I think if all our wits were to issue out of one skull, they would fly east, west, north, south, and their consent of one direct way should be at once to all the points o' th' compass.

SECOND CITIZEN Think you so? Which way do you judge my wit would fly?

THIRD CITIZEN Nay, your wit will not so soon out as another man's will; 'tis strongly wedged up in a blockhead. But if it were at liberty, 'twould sure southward.

SECOND CITIZEN Why that way?

THIRD CITIZEN To lose itself in a fog, where, being three parts melted away with rotten dews, the fourth would return for conscience' sake, to help to get thee a wife.

SECOND CITIZEN You are never without your tricks. You may, you may.

39. **greater part:** majority; **carries it:** wins the day

40. **incline to:** favor

41 SD. **gown of humility:** See longer note to 2.1.260, page 287.

45–46. **by particulars:** i.e., of each of us in particular

46. **single:** individual

54. **plague upon 't:** an exclamation of impatience

55. **pace:** regulated gait (like that of a trained horse)

61. **think upon:** consider, remember

63. **virtues:** displays of moral excellence (i.e., in sermons)

64. **divines:** priests; **lose:** waste; **by:** because of

67. **wholesome:** beneficial (Coriolanus's response plays on **wholesome** as "promoting or conducive to health.")

The expulsion of Tarquin. (2.1.154–55; 2.2.104)
From Livy, *Historicus duobus libris auctos* . . . (1520).

THIRD CITIZEN Are you all resolved to give your voices? But that's no matter; the greater part carries it. I say, if he would incline to the people, there was never a worthier man.

*Enter Coriolanus in a gown of humility, with Menenius.*

Here he comes, and in the gown of humility. Mark his behavior. We are not to stay all together, but to come by him where he stands, by ones, by twos, and by threes. He's to make his requests by particulars, wherein every one of us has a single honor in giving him our own voices with our own tongues. Therefore follow me, and I'll direct you how you shall go by him.

ALL Content, content. ⌜*Citizens exit.*⌝

MENENIUS
O sir, you are not right. Have you not known
The worthiest men have done 't?

CORIOLANUS What must I say?
"I pray, sir?"—plague upon 't! I cannot bring
My tongue to such a pace. "Look, sir, my wounds!
I got them in my country's service when
Some certain of your brethren roared and ran
From th' noise of our own drums."

MENENIUS O me, the gods!
You must not speak of that. You must desire them
To think upon you.

CORIOLANUS Think upon me? Hang 'em!
I would they would forget me, like the virtues
Which our divines lose by 'em.

MENENIUS You'll mar all.
I'll leave you. Pray you, speak to 'em, I pray you,
In wholesome manner. *He exits.*

CORIOLANUS Bid them wash their faces
And keep their teeth clean.

70. **brace:** pair, couple

73. **desert:** merit

83. **kindly:** good-naturedly, agreeably

86. **voice:** vote

88. **A match:** agreed, done, it's a deal

89. **alms:** See lines 77–78, where Coriolanus describes himself as a beggar.

90–91. **something:** somewhat

92. **An 'twere:** if it were

94. **stand:** agree, accord

Roman lictors. (2.2.36 SD)

From Onofrio Panvinio, . . . *De lvdis circensibvs, libri II. De trivmphis* . . . (1642).

*Enter three of the Citizens.*

So, here comes a brace.—
You know the cause, sir, of my standing here.

THIRD CITIZEN
We do, sir. Tell us what hath brought you to 't.

CORIOLANUS Mine own desert.

SECOND CITIZEN Your own desert?

CORIOLANUS Ay, but ⌜not⌝ mine own desire.

THIRD CITIZEN How, not your own desire?

CORIOLANUS No, sir, 'twas never my desire yet to trouble the poor with begging.

THIRD CITIZEN You must think if we give you anything, we hope to gain by you.

CORIOLANUS Well then, I pray, your price o' th' consulship?

FIRST CITIZEN The price is to ask it kindly.

CORIOLANUS Kindly, sir, I pray, let me ha 't. I have wounds to show you, which shall be yours in private.—Your good voice, sir. What say you?

SECOND CITIZEN You shall ha 't, worthy sir.

CORIOLANUS A match, sir. There's in all two worthy voices begged. I have your alms. Adieu.

THIRD CITIZEN, ⌜*to the other Citizens*⌝ But this is something odd.

SECOND CITIZEN An 'twere to give again—but 'tis no matter. ⌜*These citizens*⌝ *exit.*

*Enter two other Citizens.*

CORIOLANUS Pray you now, if it may stand with the tune of your voices that I may be consul, I have here the customary gown.

⌜FOURTH CITIZEN⌝ You have deserved nobly of your country, and you have not deserved nobly.

CORIOLANUS Your enigma?

101. **rod:** punishment

104. **common in:** indiscriminate **in**

105. **sworn brother:** i.e., close friend

106. **dearer:** higher; **estimation of:** valuation from; **'tis a condition:** perhaps, flattery is a qualification; or perhaps, the flatterer is a person

107. **gentle:** noble

108. **my hat:** i.e., **my hat** doffed to them as a sign of deference

109. **insinuating:** ingratiating; **be off:** i.e., take **my hat off**

110. **counterfeitly:** feignedly, hypocritically; **counterfeit:** imitate

110–11. **bewitchment:** charm

111. **popular man:** (1) common **man,** plebeian; (2) **man** anxious to win the favor of the people

111–12. **bountiful:** bountifully, generously

118. **seal:** ratify (as if by affixing a seal)

124. **crave:** beg for; **hire:** reward; **first . . . deserve:** i.e., we already deserved **first:** before

125. **woolvish:** (1) woolly (and therefore the garment of the plebeians or "woolen vassals" [3.2.10]); (2) wolfish (as if Coriolanus is a wolf in sheep's clothing); **toge:** toga

126. **Hob . . . appear:** whatever fellows present themselves **Hob:** variation of *Rob* (for *Robert* or *Robin*), and, like **Dick,** a typical name for a commoner

127. **needless:** unnecessary (i.e., because only the Senate's approval ought to be necessary, according to Coriolanus); **vouches:** attestations

131. **o'erpeer:** look over; **fool it so:** (1) act like such a fool; (2) thus act like a fool

134. **suffered:** endured

⌜FOURTH CITIZEN⌝ You have been a scourge to her enemies; you have been a rod to her friends. You have not indeed loved the common people.

CORIOLANUS You should account me the more virtuous that I have not been common in my love. I will, sir, flatter my sworn brother, the people, to earn a dearer estimation of them; 'tis a condition they account gentle. And since the wisdom of their choice is rather to have my hat than my heart, I will practice the insinuating nod and be off to them most counterfeitly. That is, sir, I will counterfeit the bewitchment of some popular man and give it bountiful to the desirers. Therefore, beseech you, I may be consul.

⌜FIFTH CITIZEN⌝ We hope to find you our friend, and therefore give you our voices heartily.

⌜FOURTH CITIZEN⌝ You have received many wounds for your country.

CORIOLANUS I will not seal your knowledge with showing them. I will make much of your voices and so trouble you no farther.

BOTH The gods give you joy, sir, heartily.

*⌜Citizens exit.⌝*

CORIOLANUS Most sweet voices!
Better it is to die, better to starve,
Than crave the ⌜hire⌝ which first we do deserve.
Why in this woolvish ⌜toge⌝ should I stand here
To beg of Hob and Dick that does appear
Their needless vouches? Custom calls me to 't.
What custom wills, in all things should we do 't?
The dust on antique time would lie unswept
And mountainous error be too highly heaped
For truth to o'erpeer. Rather than fool it so,
Let the high office and the honor go
To one that would do thus. I am half through;
The one part suffered, the other will I do.

137. **Watched:** stayed awake (e.g., on guard duty)

150. **limitation:** allotted time

151. **Endue:** endow; **Remains:** i.e., it **remains**

152. **official marks:** insignia of your office

153. **Anon:** immediately

156. **admit you:** allow you to enter into office; **are summoned:** i.e., **the Senate** (line 153) is **summoned**

157. **upon your approbation:** i.e., in order to confirm their **approbation** of you

Fame. (1.1.301)
From August Casimir Redel,
*Apophtegmata symbolica* . . . [n.d.].

*Enter three Citizens more.*

Here come more voices.—
Your voices! For your voices I have fought;
Watched for your voices; for your voices bear
Of wounds two dozen odd. Battles thrice six
I have seen and heard of; for your voices have
Done many things, some less, some more. Your
voices!
Indeed, I would be consul.

⌜SIXTH⌝ CITIZEN He has done nobly, and cannot go without any honest man's voice.

⌜SEVENTH⌝ CITIZEN Therefore let him be consul. The gods give him joy, and make him good friend to the people!

ALL Amen, amen. God save thee, noble consul.
⌜*Citizens exit.*⌝

CORIOLANUS Worthy voices!

*Enter Menenius, with Brutus and Sicinius.*

MENENIUS
You have stood your limitation, and the Tribunes
Endue you with the people's voice. Remains
That in th' official marks invested, you
Anon do meet the Senate.

CORIOLANUS Is this done?

SICINIUS
The custom of request you have discharged.
The people do admit you, and are summoned
To meet anon upon your approbation.

CORIOLANUS
Where? At the Senate House?

SICINIUS There, Coriolanus.

CORIOLANUS
May I change these garments?

SICINIUS You may, sir.

162. **straight:** straightaway, immediately
167. **methinks:** it seems to me
170. **weeds:** clothes
171. **How now:** i.e., **how** is it **now; chose:** i.e., chosen
176. **flouted:** insulted
177. **kind:** characteristic manner

The Temple of Jupiter, housing "Jove's statue." (2.1.298)
From Guillaume Du Choul, *Los discursos de la religion* . . . (1579).

CORIOLANUS
That I'll straight do and, knowing myself again,
Repair to th' Senate House.

MENENIUS
I'll keep you company.—Will you along?

BRUTUS
We stay here for the people.

SICINIUS
Fare you well.
*Coriolanus and Menenius exit.*
He has it now; and by his looks, methinks,
'Tis warm at 's heart.

BRUTUS
With a proud heart he wore
His humble weeds. Will you dismiss the people?

*Enter the Plebeians.*

SICINIUS
How now, my masters, have you chose this man?

FIRST CITIZEN He has our voices, sir.

BRUTUS
We pray the gods he may deserve your loves.

SECOND CITIZEN
Amen, sir. To my poor unworthy notice,
He mocked us when he begged our voices.

THIRD CITIZEN
Certainly, he flouted us downright.

FIRST CITIZEN
No, 'tis his kind of speech. He did not mock us.

SECOND CITIZEN
Not one amongst us, save yourself, but says
He used us scornfully. He should have showed us
His marks of merit, wounds received for 's country.

SICINIUS Why, so he did, I am sure.

ALL No, no. No man saw 'em.

THIRD CITIZEN
He said he had wounds, which he could show in
private,

192. **no further:** i.e., nothing **further**

193. **were . . . see 't:** i.e., did **you** lack the skill to notice **this mockery** (line 192)

197. **lessoned:** instructed

200. **charters:** publicly conceded rights

201. **weal:** commonweal, state; **arriving:** i.e., reaching

202. **place:** office; **sway:** rule

210. **Standing:** acting the part of

212. **fore-advised:** advised beforehand; **touched:** tested the fineness of (as if rubbing gold against a touchstone)

213. **tried:** tested

215. **As . . . called you up:** i.e., when (or if) occasion stirred you

216. **surly:** arrogant

217. **article:** provision, condition

A catapult. (1.6.78)

From Guillaume Du Choul, *Los discursos de la religion* . . . (1579).

And with his hat, thus waving it in scorn,
"I would be consul," says he. "Agèd custom,
But by your voices, will not so permit me;
Your voices therefore." When we granted that,
Here was "I thank you for your voices. Thank you.
Your most sweet voices! Now you have left your
voices,
I have no further with you." Was not this mockery?

SICINIUS
Why either were you ignorant to see 't
Or, seeing it, of such childish friendliness
To yield your voices?

BRUTUS Could you not have told him
As you were lessoned? When he had no power,
But was a petty servant to the state,
He was your enemy, ever spake against
Your liberties and the charters that you bear
I' th' body of the weal; and, now arriving
A place of potency and sway o' th' state,
If he should still malignantly remain
Fast foe to th' plebeii, your voices might
Be curses to yourselves. You should have said
That as his worthy deeds did claim no less
Than what he stood for, so his gracious nature
Would think upon you for your voices, and
Translate his malice towards you into love,
Standing your friendly lord.

SICINIUS Thus to have said,
As you were fore-advised, had touched his spirit
And tried his inclination; from him plucked
Either his gracious promise, which you might,
As cause had called you up, have held him to;
Or else it would have galled his surly nature,
Which easily endures not article
Tying him to aught. So putting him to rage,

222. **free:** unrestrained

227. **heart:** spirit, intellect; **cry:** raise your voice in protest

228. **rectorship:** rule, government

229. **ere:** before

230. **of him:** i.e., on him

231. **sued-for:** sought-after; **tongues:** voices, votes

236. **piece:** join

238. **chose:** i.e., chosen

241. **therefor:** for that reason

243. **safer:** more sane or sound

244. **election:** choice, selection; **Enforce:** urge, lay stress on

246. **weed:** garment

247. **suit:** petition (with possible wordplay on *garment*)

249. **apprehension:** perception; **present portance:** conduct at that moment

250. **gibingly:** sneeringly; **ungravely:** without dignity or seriousness

You should have ta'en th' advantage of his choler
And passed him unelected.

BRUTUS Did you perceive
He did solicit you in free contempt
When he did need your loves, and do you think
That his contempt shall not be bruising to you
When he hath power to crush? Why, had your bodies
No heart among you? Or had you tongues to cry
Against the rectorship of judgment?

SICINIUS
Have you ere now denied the asker? And now
Again, of him that did not ask but mock,
Bestow your sued-for tongues?

THIRD CITIZEN He's not confirmed.
We may deny him yet.

SECOND CITIZEN And will deny him.
I'll have five hundred voices of that sound.

FIRST CITIZEN
I twice five hundred, and their friends to piece 'em.

BRUTUS
Get you hence instantly, and tell those friends
They have chose a consul that will from them take
Their liberties, make them of no more voice
Than dogs that are as often beat for barking
As therefor kept to do so.

SICINIUS Let them assemble
And, on a safer judgment, all revoke
Your ignorant election. Enforce his pride
And his old hate unto you. Besides, forget not
With what contempt he wore the humble weed,
How in his suit he scorned you; but your loves,
Thinking upon his services, took from you
Th' apprehension of his present portance,
Which most gibingly, ungravely, he did fashion
After the inveterate hate he bears you.

254. **No impediment between:** i.e., without regard for any obstruction in the way

257. **after:** as a consequence of

258. **affections:** inclinations, feelings

261. **voice:** elect

265. **Martians:** those named Martius

266–72. **Ancus . . . ancestor:** See longer note, page 288. **censor:** magistrate responsible for drawing up the census of citizens and for supervising public morals

274. **in his person:** personally; **wrought:** worked

275. **place:** office

277. **Scaling:** weighing (as if in scales) See picture, below.

279. **sudden:** hasty

281. **putting on:** urging

282. **presently:** immediately; **drawn:** gathered, collected; **number:** multitude

Scales. (2.3.277)
From Silvestro Pietrasanta,
. . . *Symbola heroica* . . . (1682).

BRUTUS Lay
A fault on us, your tribunes, that we labored,
No impediment between, but that you must
Cast your election on him.

SICINIUS Say you chose him
More after our commandment than as guided
By your own true affections, and that your minds,
Preoccupied with what you rather must do
Than what you should, made you against the grain
To voice him consul. Lay the fault on us.

BRUTUS
Ay, spare us not. Say we read lectures to you,
How youngly he began to serve his country,
How long continued, and what stock he springs of,
The noble house o' th' Martians, from whence came
That Ancus Martius, Numa's daughter's son,
Who after great Hostilius here was king,
Of the same house Publius and Quintus were,
That our best water brought by conduits hither;
⌜And Censorinus, that was so surnamed,⌝
And nobly namèd so, twice being censor,
Was his great ancestor.

SICINIUS One thus descended,
That hath besides well in his person wrought
To be set high in place, we did commend
To your remembrances; but you have found,
Scaling his present bearing with his past,
That he's your fixèd enemy, and revoke
Your sudden approbation.

BRUTUS Say you ne'er had done 't—
Harp on that still—but by our putting on.
And presently, when you have drawn your number,
Repair to th' Capitol.

ALL We will so. Almost all
Repent in their election. *Plebeians exit.*

BRUTUS Let them go on.

287. **mutiny:** rebellion; **put in hazard: put** at risk

288. **stay . . . greater:** "wait **for** a **greater** one that undoubtedly would come later" (Bliss)

290–91. **answer / The vantage of:** i.e., respond to the advantage provided by

The Capitol. (1.1.48, 275; 2.1.85)
From Bartolommeo Marliani, *Urbis Romae topographia* . . . (1588).

This mutiny were better put in hazard
Than stay, past doubt, for greater.
If, as his nature is, he fall in rage
With their refusal, both observe and answer
The vantage of his anger.

SICINIUS To th' Capitol, come.
We will be there before the stream o' th' people,
And this shall seem, as partly 'tis, their own,
Which we have goaded onward.

*They exit.*

# CORIOLANUS

## ACT 3

**3.1** Learning that the plebeians have revoked their votes, Coriolanus publicly attacks the decision that had given the people tribunes. Accusing him of treason, the tribunes attempt to have him arrested and executed, but he is rescued by his fellow patricians, who, to avoid civil war with the plebeians, agree to bring him to the marketplace to face the tribunes.

---

1. **made new head:** raised another army

3. **swifter composition:** i.e., more quickly arriving at terms for a truce

5. **road:** raid, incursion

7. **worn:** exhausted, enfeebled; **lord consul:** Note that here Cominius assumes that Coriolanus has already been named **consul.** Coriolanus may, in fact, already wear the clothing of a **consul.**

8. **ages:** lives

11. **safeguard:** guarantee of safe passage

12. **for:** because; **vilely:** ignominiously, basely

13. **is retired:** has withdrawn

An "oaken garland." (2.1.129; see also 1.3.16 and 2.2.114)
From Claude Guichard, *Funerailles et diverses manieres* . . . (1581).

## ACT 3

### ⌜Scene 1⌝

*Cornets. Enter Coriolanus, Menenius, all the Gentry, Cominius, Titus Lartius, and other Senators.*

CORIOLANUS
Tullus Aufidius then had made new head?

LARTIUS
He had, my lord, and that it was which caused
Our swifter composition.

CORIOLANUS
So then the Volsces stand but as at first,
Ready, when time shall prompt them, to make road
Upon 's again.

COMINIUS They are worn, lord consul, so,
That we shall hardly in our ages see
Their banners wave again.

CORIOLANUS Saw you Aufidius?

LARTIUS
On safeguard he came to me, and did curse
Against the Volsces, for they had so vilely
Yielded the town. He is retired to Antium.

CORIOLANUS
Spoke he of me?

LARTIUS He did, my lord.

CORIOLANUS How? What?

LARTIUS
How often he had met you sword to sword;

20. **hopeless restitution:** i.e., without hope of ever recovering them; **so:** on condition that

29. **prank them:** dress themselves up

30. **noble sufferance:** toleration by the nobility

35. **matter:** i.e., (1) subject of contention or dispute; or (2) what is intended or desired

36. **passed:** been ratified or approved by

42. **broil:** turmoil

44. **voices:** votes; **yield:** give, offer; **now:** i.e., at one moment

An augurer reading the entrails of a bull. (2.1.1)
From Conrad Lycosthenes, *Prodigiorum* . . . [1557].

That of all things upon the earth he hated
Your person most; that he would pawn his fortunes
To hopeless restitution, so he might
Be called your vanquisher.

CORIOLANUS At Antium lives he?

LARTIUS At Antium.

CORIOLANUS
I wish I had a cause to seek him there,
To oppose his hatred fully. Welcome home.

*Enter Sicinius and Brutus.*

Behold, these are the tribunes of the people,
The tongues o' th' common mouth. I do despise
them,
For they do prank them in authority
Against all noble sufferance.

SICINIUS Pass no further.

CORIOLANUS Ha? What is that?

BRUTUS
It will be dangerous to go on. No further.

CORIOLANUS What makes this change?

MENENIUS The matter?

COMINIUS
Hath he not passed the noble and the common?

BRUTUS
Cominius, no.

CORIOLANUS Have I had children's voices?

⌜FIRST⌝ SENATOR
Tribunes, give way. He shall to th' marketplace.

BRUTUS
The people are incensed against him.

SICINIUS Stop,
Or all will fall in broil.

CORIOLANUS Are these your herd?
Must these have voices, that can yield them now

45. **straight:** immediately

46. **offices:** duties, functions

49. **set them on:** urged them to attack (language applied to attack animals and thus connected to the phrase **their teeth** [lines 47–48])

51. **purposed thing:** design, i.e., a crafty scheme

53. **Suffer:** permit; **live:** i.e., you will have to **live**

56. **cry:** protest; **of late:** lately, recently

57. **corn:** wheat; **gratis:** free; **repined:** complained

58. **Scandaled:** defamed

62. **sithence:** since

65 SP. COMINIUS: Editors often reassign this speech to Coriolanus, arguing that the exchange at lines 66–67 depends on this reassignment.

65. **like:** i.e., likely

66. **Not unlike:** i.e., I am **not** unlikely; **each way:** i.e., in every **way; to better yours:** i.e., to do better than you

67. **By yond clouds:** a mild oath

68. **so ill:** as badly

70. **that:** i.e., **that** quality

71. **stir:** rise in revolt

72. **where you are bound:** literally, to the marketplace; figuratively, to the consulship

And straight disclaim their tongues? What are your offices?
You being their mouths, why rule you not their teeth?
Have you not set them on?

MENENIUS Be calm, be calm.

CORIOLANUS
It is a purposed thing, and grows by plot,
To curb the will of the nobility.
Suffer 't, and live with such as cannot rule
Nor ever will be ruled.

BRUTUS Call 't not a plot.
The people cry you mocked them; and, of late,
When corn was given them gratis, you repined,
Scandaled the suppliants for the people, called them
Timepleasers, flatterers, foes to nobleness.

CORIOLANUS
Why, this was known before.

BRUTUS Not to them all.

CORIOLANUS
Have you informed them sithence?

BRUTUS How? I inform them?

COMINIUS You are like to do such business.

BRUTUS
Not unlike, each way, to better yours.

CORIOLANUS
Why then should I be consul? By yond clouds,
Let me deserve so ill as you, and make me
Your fellow tribune.

SICINIUS You show too much of that
For which the people stir. If you will pass
To where you are bound, you must inquire your way,

74. **are out of:** stray from

78. **abused:** deceived, imposed on; **set on:** incited; **palt'ring:** equivocation, trifling

79. **Becomes not:** is **not** appropriate to

80. **dishonored:** dishonorable; **rub:** impediment (The term is from lawn bowling, where the **rub** is an obstacle on the bowling green that knocks the ball off its course or out of its **plain way** [line 81].) **laid falsely:** treacherously placed

83. **was my speech:** is what I said

87. **For:** i.e., as **for**

88. **mutable:** changeable; **meiny:** common herd, masses

89. **Regard me:** wordplay on (1) pay attention to me; and (2) look at me; **as:** since, because

90. **Therein:** i.e., in my unflattering words

91. **soothing:** humoring, flattering

92. **cockle:** a destructive weed that grows in wheat fields (See longer note, page 288.) **insolence:** arrogance

95. **honored:** honorable

103. **their decay:** the **decay** of **my lungs** (line 102); **measles:** pustules (The metaphor of disease introduced here continues with **tetter** [line 104] and **catch** [line 105].)

104. **tetter:** affect with eruptions of the skin

Which you are out of, with a gentler spirit,
Or never be so noble as a consul,
Nor yoke with him for tribune.

MENENIUS Let's be calm.

COMINIUS
The people are abused, set on. This palt'ring
Becomes not Rome, nor has Coriolanus
Deserved this so dishonored rub, laid falsely
I' th' plain way of his merit.

CORIOLANUS Tell me of corn?
This was my speech, and I will speak 't again.

MENENIUS
Not now, not now.

⌜FIRST⌝ SENATOR Not in this heat, sir, now.

CORIOLANUS Now, as I live, I will.
My nobler friends, I crave their pardons. For
The mutable, rank-scented meiny, let them
Regard me, as I do not flatter, and
Therein behold themselves. I say again,
In soothing them, we nourish 'gainst our senate
The cockle of rebellion, insolence, sedition,
Which we ourselves have plowed for, sowed, and
  scattered
By mingling them with us, the honored number,
Who lack not virtue, no, nor power, but that
Which they have given to beggars.

MENENIUS Well, no more.

⌜FIRST⌝ SENATOR
No more words, we beseech you.

CORIOLANUS How? No more?
As for my country I have shed my blood,
Not fearing outward force, so shall my lungs
Coin words till their decay against those measles
Which we disdain should tetter us, yet sought
The very way to catch them.

108. **of their infirmity:** i.e., sharing universal human **infirmity**

111. **His choler:** i.e., **his** (words spoken in) anger

114. **my mind:** i.e., what I think (Sicinius responds as if the phrase were meant literally.)

119. **Triton:** the sea deity who trumpeted the approach of Neptune, god of the sea

120. **absolute "shall": "Shall"** expresses a speaker's determination to bring something about, and suggests that the speaker has power to make it happen.

121. **from the canon:** i.e., exceeding the tribune's legal authority **canon:** law

125. **Given:** allowed; **Hydra:** i.e., "the many-headed multitude" (2.3.16–17) **Hydra** was, in mythology, a many-headed water serpent. When one of its heads was cut off, two more grew. (See picture, page 142.) **officer:** i.e., tribune

127. **horn and noise:** i.e., noisy **horn** (hendiadys), alluding perhaps to **Triton** (line 119); **th' monster's:** Hydra's

130. **vail your ignorance:** "abase your ignorant selves in submission" (Brockbank); **awake:** i.e., **awake** from

133. **them:** the tribunes; **cushions:** i.e., places to sit in the Senate (See 2.2.0 SD and note.)

134. **no less:** i.e., **no less** than **senators**

135. **both your voices:** the **voices** of **both senators** and tribunes

135–36. **the great'st taste / Most palates theirs:** i.e., in the blend of **voices,** the predominant flavor will be what tastes best to them (i.e., the **plebeians**)

136. **magistrate:** i.e., tribune

*(continued)*

BRUTUS You speak o' th' people
As if you were a god to punish, not
A man of their infirmity.
SICINIUS 'Twere well
We let the people know 't.
MENENIUS What, what? His choler?
CORIOLANUS Choler?
Were I as patient as the midnight sleep,
By Jove, 'twould be my mind.
SICINIUS It is a mind
That shall remain a poison where it is,
Not poison any further.
CORIOLANUS "Shall remain"?
Hear you this Triton of the minnows? Mark you
His absolute "shall"?
COMINIUS 'Twas from the canon.
CORIOLANUS "Shall"?
O ⌜good⌝ but most unwise patricians, why,
You grave but reckless senators, have you thus
Given Hydra here to choose an officer,
That with his peremptory "shall," being but
The horn and noise o' th' monster's, wants not spirit
To say he'll turn your current in a ditch
And make your channel his? If he have power,
Then vail your ignorance; if none, awake
Your dangerous lenity. If you are learned,
Be not as common fools; if you are not,
Let them have cushions by you. You are plebeians,
If they be senators; and they are no less
When, both your voices blended, the great'st taste
Most palates theirs. They choose their magistrate,
And such a one as he, who puts his "shall,"
His popular "shall," against a graver bench
Than ever frowned in Greece. By Jove himself,
It makes the consuls base! And my soul aches
To know, when two authorities are up,

137. **he:** i.e., Sicinius

138. **popular:** plebeian; **against:** in opposition to; **bench:** judiciary

141. **up:** i.e., in revolt against each other

142. **confusion:** destruction

143–44. **take . . . by th' other:** attack **one** through the agency of **th' other**

147. **'twas used:** it was the custom

148. **Sometime:** formerly

151. **they:** i.e., **whoever gave that counsel** (line 146)

158. **recompense:** reward; **resting:** remaining

159. **service:** i.e., military **service; pressed to:** i.e., impressed for, forced to serve in

160. **navel:** center; **touched:** affected

161. **thread the gates:** i.e., pass through Rome's **gates** (to go to war)

165. **spoke . . . them:** did **not** speak well of **them**

165–66. **accusation . . . Senate:** For such an **accusation,** see, e.g., 1.1.81–88, especially the charge that the senators "Suffer us to famish, and their storehouses crammed with grain" (lines 82–83).

167. **All cause unborn:** i.e., without any justification; **native:** original; i.e., origin

168. **frank donation:** generous gift

169. **bosom multiplied:** many-stomached monster (i.e., the multitude) **bosom:** (1) stomach; (2) seat of thought; **digest:** (1) absorb as food; (2) understand

170. **deeds:** For such **deeds,** see the acts described in lines 176–77 below.

171. **What's like:** i.e., what are likely

*(continued)*

Neither supreme, how soon confusion
May enter 'twixt the gap of both and take
The one by th' other.

COMINIUS Well, on to th' marketplace.

CORIOLANUS
Whoever gave that counsel to give forth
The corn o' th' storehouse gratis, as 'twas used
Sometime in Greece—

MENENIUS Well, well, no more of that.

CORIOLANUS
Though there the people had more absolute power,
I say they nourished disobedience, fed
The ruin of the state.

BRUTUS Why shall the people give
One that speaks thus their voice?

CORIOLANUS I'll give my reasons,
More worthier than their voices. They know the corn
Was not our recompense, resting well assured
They ne'er did service for 't. Being pressed to th' war,
Even when the navel of the state was touched,
They would not thread the gates. This kind of service
Did not deserve corn gratis. Being i' th' war,
Their mutinies and revolts, wherein they showed
Most valor, spoke not for them. Th' accusation
Which they have often made against the Senate,
All cause unborn, could never be the native
Of our so frank donation. Well, what then?
How shall this bosom multiplied digest
The Senate's courtesy? Let deeds express
What's like to be their words: "We did request it;
We are the greater poll, and in true fear
They gave us our demands." Thus we debase
The nature of our seats and make the rabble
Call our cares fears, which will in time

172. **poll:** number of persons; **true:** genuine

174. **seats:** positions in the Senate

175. **cares:** concerns; **which:** i.e., **the rabble** (line 174)

177. **crows:** carrion birds (but with an allusion to crowbars in "Break ope the locks" [line 176])

179. **over-measure:** excess

182. **Seal:** confirm, ratify; **withal:** with; **double worship:** i.e., the "two authorities" (line 141 above) **worship:** title of honor for a magistrate

183. **part:** party, faction

184. **gentry:** rank by birth

186. **conclude:** come to decisions

187. **general:** common; **it:** i.e., **this double worship** (line 182); **omit:** neglect

188. **the while:** in the meantime

189. **slightness:** triviality, trifling

190. **beseech:** i.e., I entreat

192. **discreet:** prudent, judicious

193. **state:** all that concerns the government

194. **doubt:** fear; **on 't:** i.e., of it

196. **jump:** hazard, risk; **physic:** medicine

198. **multitudinous tongue:** i.e., **tongue** of the multitude (i.e., the tribunes)

199. **sweet:** i.e., sweet dish; **Your dishonor:** perhaps, **your** disgrace (i.e., in having made concessions to the plebeians); or, perhaps, the **dishonor** shown you

200. **bereaves:** robs

201. **integrity:** wholeness; soundness of moral principle; **become 't:** be appropriate to it

203. **For th' ill:** i.e., because of the evil; **control:** overpower

*(continued)*

Break ope the locks o' th' Senate and bring in
The crows to peck the eagles.

MENENIUS Come, enough.

BRUTUS
Enough, with over-measure.

CORIOLANUS No, take more!
What may be sworn by, both divine and human,
Seal what I end withal! This double worship—
⌜Where one⌝ part does disdain with cause, the other
Insult without all reason, where gentry, title,
wisdom
Cannot conclude but by the yea and no
Of general ignorance—it must omit
Real necessities and give way the while
To unstable slightness. Purpose so barred, it follows
Nothing is done to purpose. Therefore, beseech
you—
You that will be less fearful than discreet,
That love the fundamental part of state
More than you doubt the change on 't, that prefer
A noble life before a long, and wish
To jump a body with a dangerous physic
That's sure of death without it—at once pluck out
The multitudinous tongue; let them not lick
The sweet which is their poison. Your dishonor
Mangles true judgment and bereaves the state
Of that integrity which should become 't,
Not having the power to do the good it would
For th' ill which doth control 't.

BRUTUS 'Has said enough.

SICINIUS
'Has spoken like a traitor and shall answer
As traitors do.

CORIOLANUS Thou wretch, despite o'erwhelm thee!
What should the people do with these bald tribunes,
On whom depending, their obedience fails

204. **’Has:** i.e., he has

205. **answer:** suffer the consequences

207. **despite:** contempt, scorn

208. **What . . . do with:** i.e., why **should the people** have, **what** is their business with; **bald:** For other references to the tribunes’ age, see, e.g., “Hence, old goat” and “Agèd sir,” lines 223, 225.

210. **greater bench:** more important magistrates or legislators (i.e., the Senate)

211. **meet:** fitting, appropriate

212. **they:** i.e., the tribunes

217. **aediles:** municipal officers

220. **Attach:** arrest; **innovator:** revolutionary

221. **weal:** welfare

222. **answer:** defense (i.e., of yourself against these charges)

224. **surety:** take responsibility for

To' th' greater bench? In a rebellion,
When what's not meet but what must be was law,
Then were they chosen. In a better hour,
Let what is meet be said it must be meet,
And throw their power i' th' dust.

BRUTUS Manifest treason.

SICINIUS This a consul? No.

BRUTUS The aediles, ho! Let him be apprehended.

*Enter an Aedile.*

SICINIUS
Go, call the people; ⌜*Aedile exits.*⌝ in whose name myself
Attach thee as a traitorous innovator,
A foe to' th' public weal. Obey, I charge thee,
And follow to thine answer.

CORIOLANUS Hence, old goat.

ALL ⌜PATRICIANS⌝
We'll surety him.

COMINIUS, ⌜*to Sicinius*⌝ Agèd sir, hands off.

CORIOLANUS, ⌜*to Sicinius*⌝
Hence, rotten thing, or I shall shake thy bones
Out of thy garments.

SICINIUS Help, you citizens!

*Enter a rabble of Plebeians with the Aediles.*

MENENIUS On both sides more respect!

SICINIUS
Here's he that would take from you all your power.

BRUTUS Seize him, aediles.

ALL ⌜PLEBEIANS⌝ Down with him, down with him!

SECOND SENATOR Weapons, weapons, weapons!
*They all bustle about Coriolanus.*
Tribunes, patricians, citizens, what ho!
Sicinius, Brutus, Coriolanus, citizens!

238. **Confusion's:** destruction is

239. **patience:** i.e., be calm

243. **at point:** just about; **liberties:** rights

245. **late:** just now

255. **like:** likely

258. **yet:** as yet; **distinctly ranges:** i.e., extends as a line of separate buildings

260. **This:** Coriolanus's proposal to abolish the office of tribune (lines 197–98, 214) and his comment on their disastrous effect on Rome (lines 256–59)

261. **Or:** either; **stand to:** maintain

Patience. (1.1.132)
From Cesare Ripa, *Iconologia* . . . (1603).

ALL Peace, peace, peace! Stay, hold, peace!

MENENIUS
What is about to be? I am out of breath.
Confusion's near. I cannot speak. You, tribunes
To th' people!—Coriolanus, patience!—
Speak, good Sicinius.

SICINIUS Hear me, people! Peace!

ALL ⌜PLEBEIANS⌝
Let's hear our tribune. Peace! Speak, speak, speak.

SICINIUS
You are at point to lose your liberties.
Martius would have all from you, Martius,
Whom late you have named for consul.

MENENIUS Fie, fie, fie!
This is the way to kindle, not to quench.

⌜FIRST⌝ SENATOR
To unbuild the city and to lay all flat.

SICINIUS
What is the city but the people?

ALL ⌜PLEBEIANS⌝ True,
The people are the city.

BRUTUS
By the consent of all, we were established
The people's magistrates.

ALL ⌜PLEBEIANS⌝ You so remain.

MENENIUS And so are like to do.

⌜CORIOLANUS⌝
That is the way to lay the city flat,
To bring the roof to the foundation
And bury all which yet distinctly ranges
In heaps and piles of ruin.

SICINIUS This deserves death.

BRUTUS
Or let us stand to our authority
Or let us lose it. We do here pronounce,
Upon the part o' th' people, in whose power

265. **present:** immediate

267. **rock Tarpeian:** cliff from which Roman traitors were thrown to their deaths

274. **that:** i.e., **that** which

277. **cold:** deliberate, unimpassioned

278. **helps:** remedies, cures

283. **seen me:** i.e., **seen me** do in war

288 SD. **mutiny:** brawl; **beat in:** driven offstage

290. **naught:** i.e., brought to nothing; **else:** otherwise

The Hydra. (3.1.125)
From Claude François Menestrier, *L'art des emblemes* . . . (1684).

We were elected theirs, Martius is worthy
Of present death.

SICINIUS Therefore lay hold of him,
Bear him to th' rock Tarpeian, and from thence
Into destruction cast him.

BRUTUS Aediles, seize him!

ALL PLEBEIANS
Yield, Martius, yield!

MENENIUS Hear me one word.
Beseech you, tribunes, hear me but a word.

AEDILES Peace, peace!

MENENIUS
Be that you seem, truly your country's friend,
And temp'rately proceed to what you would
Thus violently redress.

BRUTUS Sir, those cold ways,
That seem like prudent helps, are very poisonous
Where the disease is violent.—Lay hands upon him,
And bear him to the rock.

*Coriolanus draws his sword.*

CORIOLANUS No, I'll die here.
There's some among you have beheld me fighting.
Come, try upon yourselves what you have seen me.

MENENIUS
Down with that sword!—Tribunes, withdraw awhile.

BRUTUS
Lay hands upon him!

MENENIUS Help Martius, help!
You that be noble, help him, young and old!

ALL ⌜PLEBEIANS⌝ Down with him, down with him!

*In this mutiny, the Tribunes, the Aediles, and the People are beat in.*

MENENIUS, ⌜*to Coriolanus*⌝
Go, get you to ⌜your⌝ house. Begone, away.
All will be naught else.

297. **cause:** sickness, disease

299. **tent:** treat, remedy (See note to 1.9.36.)

301. **would:** wish; **barbarians:** foreigners; wild, uncivilized people

302, 304. **littered, calved:** born (terms used for animals, thus derogatory here)

307. **One . . . another:** i.e., **another** occasion will make up for this **one**

308. **fair:** even

311. **Take . . . brace:** i.e., **take** on a pair

313. **'tis odds:** i.e., the **odds** against us are; **arithmetic:** computation, counting

314. **manhood:** courage, manliness; **foolery:** i.e., foolhardiness; **stands:** holds its ground

315. **fabric:** building

317. **tag:** rabble, mob

317–19. **rend . . . bear:** The image is of rushing **waters** that, blocked or obstructed, burst and overwhelm the banks that normally hold them. **o'erbear:** overwhelm **bear:** sustain the pressure of

321. **wit:** discretion, good judgment; **in request:** in fashion, sought after

SECOND SENATOR Get you gone.

⌜CORIOLANUS⌝ Stand fast!
We have as many friends as enemies.

MENENIUS
Shall it be put to that?

⌜FIRST⌝ SENATOR The gods forbid!—
I prithee, noble friend, home to thy house;
Leave us to cure this cause.

MENENIUS For 'tis a sore upon us
You cannot tent yourself. Begone, beseech you.

⌜COMINIUS⌝ Come, sir, along with us.

⌜CORIOLANUS⌝
I would they were barbarians, as they are,
Though in Rome littered; not Romans, as they are not,
Though calved i' th' porch o' th' Capitol.

MENENIUS Begone!
Put not your worthy rage into your tongue.
One time will owe another.

CORIOLANUS On fair ground
I could beat forty of them.

MENENIUS I could myself
Take up a brace o' th' best of them, yea, the two tribunes.

COMINIUS
But now 'tis odds beyond arithmetic,
And manhood is called foolery when it stands
Against a falling fabric. ⌜*To Coriolanus.*⌝ Will you hence,
Before the tag return, whose rage doth rend
Like interrupted waters and o'erbear
What they are used to bear?

MENENIUS, ⌜*to Coriolanus*⌝ Pray you, begone.
I'll try whether my old wit be in request
With those that have but little. This must be patched
With cloth of any color.

327. **trident:** three-pronged spear

328–29. **His . . . mouth:** Proverbial: "What the **heart** thinks the tongue speaks." See also Ecclesiasticus 21.26: "The **heart** of fools is in their **mouth:** but the **mouth** of the wise is in their **heart.**"

330. **vent:** express

335. **What the vengeance:** an expression used to strengthen the question it introduces

336. **speak 'em fair: speak** to them courteously

342. **rigorous:** severe, harsh

343. **scorn:** i.e., disdain to offer

349. **sure on 't:** i.e., certainly

Jove throwing a thunderbolt. (3.1.328)
From Vincenzo Cartari, *Le vere e noue imagini* . . . (1615).

COMINIUS Nay, come away.

*Coriolanus and Cominius exit.*

PATRICIAN This man has marred his fortune.

MENENIUS
His nature is too noble for the world.
He would not flatter Neptune for his trident
Or Jove for 's power to thunder. His heart's his
mouth;
What his breast forges, that his tongue must vent,
And, being angry, does forget that ever
He heard the name of death. *A noise within.*
Here's goodly work.

PATRICIAN I would they were abed!

MENENIUS
I would they were in Tiber. What the vengeance,
Could he not speak 'em fair?

*Enter Brutus and Sicinius with the rabble again.*

SICINIUS Where is this viper
That would depopulate the city and
Be every man himself?

MENENIUS You worthy tribunes—

SICINIUS
He shall be thrown down the Tarpeian rock
With rigorous hands. He hath resisted law,
And therefore law shall scorn him further trial
Than the severity of the public power
Which he so sets at naught.

FIRST CITIZEN He shall well know
The noble tribunes are the people's mouths
And we their hands.

ALL ⌜PLEBEIANS⌝ He shall, sure on 't.

MENENIUS Sir, sir—

SICINIUS Peace!

352. **cry havoc:** The cry of "**Havoc**!" was the signal given an army to pillage.

352–53. **hunt . . . warrant:** i.e., pursue your prey with license to use moderate, not excessive, force or ferocity **modest:** moderate **warrant:** authorization

355. **holp:** helped; **rescue:** forcible release of a person from legal custody

363. **leave:** permission

365. **turn:** put

368. **peremptory:** absolutely determined (accent on first and third syllables); **dispatch:** kill

370. **one danger:** perhaps, the **danger** of Coriolanus's violent return (But see longer note, page 288.)

375. **deservèd:** deserving

376. **Jove's own book:** There is no agreement about the specific reference here. **dam:** mother (a term for animals)

380. **Mortal:** fatal

A sieve separating "meal" from "bran." (3.1.410)
From Geoffrey Whitney, *A choice of emblemes* . . . (1586).

MENENIUS
Do not cry havoc where you should but hunt
With modest warrant.
SICINIUS Sir, how com'st that you
Have holp to make this rescue?
MENENIUS Hear me speak.
As I do know the Consul's worthiness,
So can I name his faults.
SICINIUS Consul? What consul?
MENENIUS The consul Coriolanus.
BRUTUS He consul?
ALL ⌜PLEBEIANS⌝ No, no, no, no, no!
MENENIUS
If, by the Tribunes' leave, and yours, good people,
I may be heard, I would crave a word or two,
The which shall turn you to no further harm
Than so much loss of time.
SICINIUS Speak briefly then,
For we are peremptory to dispatch
This viperous traitor. To eject him hence
Were but one danger, and to keep him here
Our certain death. Therefore it is decreed
He dies tonight.
MENENIUS Now the good gods forbid
That our renownèd Rome, whose gratitude
Towards her deservèd children is enrolled
In Jove's own book, like an unnatural dam
Should now eat up her own.
SICINIUS
He's a disease that must be cut away.
MENENIUS
O, he's a limb that has but a disease—
Mortal to cut it off; to cure it easy.
What has he done to Rome that's worthy death?
Killing our enemies, the blood he hath lost—
Which I dare vouch is more than that he hath

384. **dropped it:** let it fall

385. **by his:** i.e., **by** the hands of **his**

386. **suffer:** allow

387. **brand:** mark of infamy

388. **clean:** completely; **cam:** crooked (Welsh)

389. **Merely:** entirely

391. **service:** use

396. **his infection:** probably alludes to the **disease** of line 378; **catching:** contagious

399. **tiger-footed:** i.e., fast-moving

400. **unscanned:** unexamined, unconsidered

401. **pounds:** i.e., weights; **to 's:** i.e., to its; **process:** legal action

402. **parties:** factions

405. **What:** why

408. **bred:** brought up, trained

410. **bolted:** choice, carefully selected (To *bolt* is to sift the **meal** or flour from the **bran** or husk. See picture, page 148.)

411. **leave:** permission

413. **answer:** defend himself from the charges against him

414. **to . . . peril:** taking responsibility for the consequences of any disobedience of the law

By many an ounce—he dropped it for his country;
And what is left, to lose it by his country
Were to us all that do 't and suffer it
A brand to th' end o' th' world.

SICINIUS This is clean cam.

BRUTUS
Merely awry. When he did love his country,
It honored him.

⌜SICINIUS⌝ The service of the foot,
Being once gangrened, is not then respected
For what before it was.

BRUTUS We'll hear no more.
Pursue him to his house, and pluck him thence,
Lest his infection, being of catching nature,
Spread further.

MENENIUS One word more, one word!
This tiger-footed rage, when it shall find
The harm of unscanned swiftness, will too late
Tie leaden pounds to 's heels. Proceed by process,
Lest parties—as he is beloved—break out
And sack great Rome with Romans.

BRUTUS If it were so—

SICINIUS What do you talk?
Have we not had a taste of his obedience?
Our aediles smote! Ourselves resisted! Come.

MENENIUS
Consider this: he has been bred i' th' wars
Since he could draw a sword, and is ill schooled
In bolted language; meal and bran together
He throws without distinction. Give me leave,
I'll go to him and undertake to bring him
Where he shall answer by a lawful form,
In peace, to his utmost peril.

FIRST SENATOR Noble tribunes,
It is the humane way: the other course

424. **attend:** wait for

**3.2** The patricians and Volumnia persuade Coriolanus to pretend to tolerate the plebeians and their tribunes.

---

1. **pull: pull** down

2. **on the wheel:** i.e., tied to **the** executioner's **wheel** and tortured to death as my bones are broken; **at wild horses' heels:** i.e., with my limbs each tied to a **wild** horse, and the horses made to run off in different directions

4. **precipitation:** steepness of the descent

5. **Below . . . sight:** further than can be seen (The phrase **the beam of sight** reflects the belief that the eye illuminated what it saw.)

8. **muse:** wonder that

9. **further:** more

10. **woolen vassals:** base people wearing coarse **woolen** clothes

11. **groats:** English coins worth only four pennies; **show bare heads:** doff their caps in deference to their social superiors

12. **congregations:** gatherings; **yawn:** gape; **wonder:** marvel, be struck with astonishment

Will prove too bloody, and the end of it
Unknown to the beginning.

SICINIUS Noble Menenius,
Be you then as the people's officer.—
Masters, lay down your weapons.

BRUTUS Go not home.

SICINIUS
Meet on the marketplace. ⌜*To Menenius.*⌝ We'll
attend you there,
Where if you bring not Martius, we'll proceed
In our first way.

MENENIUS I'll bring him to you.
⌜*To Senators.*⌝ Let me desire your company. He must
come,
Or what is worst will follow.

⌜FIRST⌝ SENATOR Pray you, let's to him.

*All exit.*

## ⌜Scene 2⌝

*Enter Coriolanus with Nobles.*

CORIOLANUS
Let them pull all about mine ears, present me
Death on the wheel or at wild horses' heels,
Or pile ten hills on the Tarpeian rock,
That the precipitation might down stretch
Below the beam of sight, yet will I still
Be thus to them.

NOBLE You do the nobler.

CORIOLANUS I muse my mother
Does not approve me further, who was wont
To call them woolen vassals, things created
To buy and sell with groats, to show bare heads
In congregations, to yawn, be still, and wonder

13. **ordinance:** rank

20. **put . . . on:** i.e., dressed yourself securely in your power

22. **Let go:** leave off, stop

27. **Ere:** before; **cross:** oppose

30. **something:** somewhat

37. **apt:** i.e., compliant (literally, ready, prepared)

39. **better vantage:** greater advantage

41. **stoop:** humble himself, condescend

42. **fit:** bout of illness; **physic:** medicine

A Roman matron. (2.1.295)
From Cesare Vecellio, *Degli habiti antichi et moderni . . .* (1590).

When one but of my ordinance stood up
To speak of peace or war.

*Enter Volumnia.*

I talk of you.
Why did you wish me milder? Would you have me
False to my nature? Rather say I play
The man I am.

VOLUMNIA O sir, sir, sir,
I would have had you put your power well on
Before you had worn it out.

CORIOLANUS Let go.

VOLUMNIA
You might have been enough the man you are
With striving less to be so. Lesser had been
The ⌜thwartings⌝ of your dispositions if
You had not showed them how you were disposed
Ere they lacked power to cross you.

CORIOLANUS Let them hang!

VOLUMNIA Ay, and burn too.

*Enter Menenius with the Senators.*

MENENIUS, ⌜*to Coriolanus*⌝
Come, come, you have been too rough, something too rough.
You must return and mend it.

⌜FIRST⌝ SENATOR There's no remedy,
Unless, by not so doing, our good city
Cleave in the midst and perish.

VOLUMNIA Pray be counseled.
I have a heart as little apt as yours,
But yet a brain that leads my use of anger
To better vantage.

MENENIUS Well said, noble woman.
Before he should thus stoop to th' ⌜herd⌝—but that
The violent fit o' th' time craves it as physic

51. **absolute:** decided (and therefore inflexible)

53. **extremities:** conditions of extreme urgency; **speak:** i.e., announce themselves

54. **policy:** crafty device, dissimulation; **unsevered:** inseparable

57. **there:** i.e., in peace

60. **demand:** question

64. **it shall:** i.e., **policy** (line 54) **shall**

65. **to both:** i.e., **in** both **war** and **peace**

66. **stands in like request:** i.e., is equally in demand or sought after

67. **force:** urge

68. **lies you on:** is obligatory for you

69. **by:** according to; **instruction:** direction

70. **matter:** subject **matter**

71. **roted:** rattled off from memory

72. **bastards:** i.e., **words** (line 71) you do not claim as your own

73. **Of no allowance to:** i.e., that win **no** approval or praise from; **your bosom's truth:** i.e., **your** true, secret thought

For the whole state—I would put mine armor on,
Which I can scarcely bear.
CORIOLANUS What must I do?
MENENIUS
Return to th' Tribunes.
CORIOLANUS Well, what then? What then?
MENENIUS Repent what you have spoke.
CORIOLANUS
For them? I cannot do it to the gods.
Must I then do 't to them?
VOLUMNIA You are too absolute,
Though therein you can never be too noble
But when extremities speak. I have heard you say
Honor and policy, like unsevered friends,
I' th' war do grow together. Grant that, and tell me
In peace what each of them by th' other lose
That they combine not there?
CORIOLANUS Tush, tush!
MENENIUS A good
demand.
VOLUMNIA
If it be honor in your wars to seem
The same you are not, which for your best ends
You adopt your policy, how is it less or worse
That it shall hold companionship in peace
With honor as in war, since that to both
It stands in like request?
CORIOLANUS Why force you this?
VOLUMNIA
Because that now it lies you on to speak
To th' people, not by your own instruction,
Nor by th' matter which your heart prompts you,
But with such words that are but roted in
Your tongue, though but bastards and syllables
Of no allowance to your bosom's truth.

75. **take in:** capture

76. **else:** otherwise; **put:** force, require; **to your fortune:** i.e., to take **your** chances in battle

79. **at stake:** at risk

82. **general louts:** common boors

83. **fawn:** flattering courtesy

84. **inheritance:** possession

85. **that want:** i.e., the lack of **their loves** (line 84)

87. **fair:** courteously

88. **Not . . . present:** i.e., **not** only **what is dangerous** now; **but:** i.e., **but** also

91. **this bonnet in thy hand:** as a sign of deference **bonnet:** hat

92. **thus far . . . it:** Volumnia's speech is designed to be accompanied by action demonstrating to Coriolanus how to play the humble supplicant to the people.

92–93. **here be with them:** perhaps, do what they expect, go along **with them**

94. **bussing:** kissing

96. **waving thy head:** moving your **head** up and down (perhaps to acknowledge the presence of each plebeian individually)

97. **stout:** proud

98. **ripest mulberry:** proverbially associated with a yielding disposition

99. **hold:** endure, bear (Ripe mulberries are so soft that they are crushed as they are picked.)

100. **bred:** raised, trained; **broils:** tumults

102. **fit:** appropriate

103. **frame:** fashion, construct

104. **forsooth:** truly

*(continued)*

Now, this no more dishonors you at all
Than to take in a town with gentle words,
Which else would put you to your fortune and
The hazard of much blood.
I would dissemble with my nature where
My fortunes and my friends at stake required
I should do so in honor. I am in this
Your wife, your son, these senators, the nobles;
And you will rather show our general louts
How you can frown than spend a fawn upon 'em
For the inheritance of their loves and safeguard
Of what that want might ruin.

MENENIUS Noble lady!—
Come, go with us; speak fair. You may salve so,
Not what is dangerous present, but the loss
Of what is past.

VOLUMNIA I prithee now, my son,
Go to them with this bonnet in thy hand,
And thus far having stretched it—here be with
them—
Thy knee bussing the stones—for in such business
Action is eloquence, and the eyes of th' ignorant
More learnèd than the ears—waving thy head,
Which often thus correcting thy stout heart,
Now humble as the ripest mulberry
That will not hold the handling. Or say to them
Thou art their soldier and, being bred in broils,
Hast not the soft way, which thou dost confess
Were fit for thee to use as they to claim,
In asking their good loves; but thou wilt frame
Thyself, forsooth, hereafter theirs, so far
As thou hast power and person.

MENENIUS This but done
Even as she speaks, why, their hearts were yours;
For they have pardons, being asked, as free
As words to little purpose.

105. **person:** capacity

107. **Even:** just, exactly; **were:** would be

108–9. **they have . . . purpose:** i.e., **they** grant requested **pardons** as generously **as they** gratuitously or readily use **words** **free:** wordplay on (1) lavishly, generously; (2) gratuitously, readily

112. **gulf:** abyss

113. **bower:** (1) boudoir; (2) arbor

116. **make strong party:** i.e., proceed with many supporters

118. **fair:** courteous

120. **frame:** adjust

123. **unbarbèd:** (1) uncovered (as a mark of respect); (2) unarmed; **sconce:** head

124. **base:** lowly; **noble:** (1) admirable; (2) patrician

126. **single plot:** i.e., individual body (A **plot** is, literally, a small piece of earth, as is the human body, said to be formed of earth or **dust** [line 127]. See Genesis 2.7.)

127. **mold:** wordplay on (1) earth regarded as the material of the body; (2) bodily form; **should:** used here to express a desire, command, or request

129. **put me now to:** i.e., forced **me now** to play

130. **discharge:** perform; **to th' life:** with lifelike presentation

139. **harlot's:** (1) beggar's; (2) prostitute's; (3) perhaps, actor's

VOLUMNIA Prithee now,
Go, and be ruled; although I know thou hadst rather
Follow thine enemy in a fiery gulf
Than flatter him in a bower.

*Enter Cominius.*

Here is Cominius.

COMINIUS
I have been i' th' marketplace; and, sir, 'tis fit
You make strong party or defend yourself
By calmness or by absence. All's in anger.

MENENIUS
Only fair speech.

COMINIUS I think 'twill serve, if he
Can thereto frame his spirit.

VOLUMNIA He must, and will.—
Prithee, now, say you will, and go about it.

CORIOLANUS
Must I go show them my unbarbèd sconce? Must I
With my base tongue give to my noble heart
A lie that it must bear? Well, I will do 't.
Yet, were there but this single plot to lose,
This mold of Martius, they to dust should grind it
And throw 't against the wind. To th' marketplace!
You have put me now to such a part which never
I shall discharge to th' life.

COMINIUS Come, come, we'll prompt
you.

VOLUMNIA
I prithee now, sweet son, as thou hast said
My praises made thee first a soldier, so,
To have my praise for this, perform a part
Thou hast not done before.

CORIOLANUS Well, I must do 't.
Away, my disposition, and possess me
Some harlot's spirit! My throat of war be turned,

140. **choirèd:** sang; **pipe:** i.e., **throat** (line 139) issuing a piping voice

141. **Small:** soft

142. **babies lull asleep:** i.e., lulls **babies asleep**

143. **Tent:** encamp; **take up:** obstruct

144. **The . . . sight:** i.e., my vision

146. **Who:** i.e., which

148. **surcease to honor:** stop honoring

150. **inherent:** fixed, permanently indwelling

154. **thy pride:** i.e., the outcome of your **pride**

155. **stoutness:** stubbornness

156. **list:** please

158. **owe:** own

161. **mountebank their loves:** prevail over **their loves** by using the tricks of a charlatan

162. **Cog:** obtain by flattery

165. **Commend me to:** remember me kindly to

169. **attend:** wait for

Volumnia.
From [Guillaume Rouillé,]
. . . *Promptuarii iconum* . . . (1553).



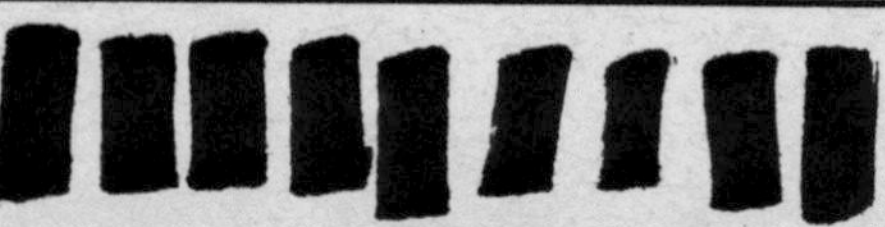

Which choirèd with my drum, into a pipe
Small as an eunuch or the virgin voice
That babies lull asleep! The smiles of knaves
Tent in my cheeks, and schoolboys' tears take up
The glasses of my sight! A beggar's tongue
Make motion through my lips, and my armed knees,
Who bowed but in my stirrup, bend like his
That hath received an alms. I will not do 't,
Lest I surcease to honor mine own truth
And, by my body's action, teach my mind
A most inherent baseness.

VOLUMNIA At thy choice, then.
To beg of thee, it is my more dishonor
Than thou of them. Come all to ruin. Let
Thy mother rather feel thy pride than fear
Thy dangerous stoutness, for I mock at death
With as big heart as thou. Do as thou list.
Thy valiantness was mine; thou suck'st it from me,
But owe thy pride thyself.

CORIOLANUS Pray be content.
Mother, I am going to the marketplace.
Chide me no more. I'll mountebank their loves,
Cog their hearts from them, and come home
  beloved
Of all the trades in Rome. Look, I am going.
Commend me to my wife. I'll return consul,
Or never trust to what my tongue can do
I' th' way of flattery further.

VOLUMNIA Do your will.

*Volumnia exits.*

COMINIUS
Away! The Tribunes do attend you. Arm yourself
To answer mildly, for they are prepared
With accusations, as I hear, more strong
Than are upon you yet.

173. **word:** password

174. **accuse . . . invention:** i.e., make up false charges against me

**3.3** When the tribunes call Coriolanus a traitor, he angrily insults them, and they first impose a death sentence and then commute that to banishment.

---

1. **In:** i.e., on; **charge him home:** attack him with all force (military language); **affects:** seeks to obtain

3. **Enforce him with:** i.e., urge against him; **envy:** malice

4. **got on:** i.e., **got** from

6. **What:** an interjection introducing a question

12. **voices:** votes

13. **th' poll:** the counting of heads (a method of tabulating votes that favors the people because it is not weighted by class or wealth)

15. **tribes:** political divisions of the Roman people

17. **presently:** immediately

CORIOLANUS
The word is "mildly." Pray you, let us go.
Let them accuse me by invention, I
Will answer in mine honor.

MENENIUS Ay, but mildly.

CORIOLANUS Well, mildly be it, then. Mildly.

*They exit.*

## ⌜Scene 3⌝

*Enter Sicinius and Brutus.*

BRUTUS
In this point charge him home, that he affects
Tyrannical power. If he evade us there,
Enforce him with his envy to the people,
And that the spoil got on the Antiates
Was ne'er distributed.

*Enter an Aedile.*

What, will he come?

AEDILE He's coming.

BRUTUS How accompanied?

AEDILE
With old Menenius, and those senators
That always favored him.

SICINIUS Have you a catalogue
Of all the voices that we have procured,
Set down by th' poll?

AEDILE I have. 'Tis ready.

SICINIUS
Have you collected them by tribes?

AEDILE I have.

SICINIUS
Assemble presently the people hither;
And when they hear me say "It shall be so

19. **commons:** common people, plebeians

22. **old:** long-established; **prerogative:** right, privilege

27. **Enforce:** urge; **present:** immediate; **execution:** putting into effect

31. **hap:** happen

33. **Put . . . straight:** i.e., make him angry right away

34–35. **worth / Of contradiction:** (1) pennyworth of contrariness; (2) fame for prevailing through fighting back

37. **looks:** promises, looks likely

38. **With us:** i.e., with our help

42. **hostler:** groom, stableman; **piece:** i.e., of money

43. **bear:** endure; **the knave by th' volume:** i.e., being called **knave** often enough to fill a book

A "casque," or helmet. (4.7.45)
From Louis de Gaya, *Traité des armes, des machines de guerre* . . . (1678).

I' th' right and strength o' th' commons," be it either
For death, for fine, or banishment, then let them
If I say "Fine," cry "Fine," if "Death," cry "Death,"
Insisting on the old prerogative
And power i' th' truth o' th' cause.

AEDILE I shall inform them.

BRUTUS
And when such time they have begun to cry,
Let them not cease, but with a din confused
Enforce the present execution
Of what we chance to sentence.

AEDILE Very well.

SICINIUS
Make them be strong and ready for this hint
When we shall hap to give 't them.

BRUTUS Go about it.
⌜*Aedile exits.*⌝

Put him to choler straight. He hath been used
Ever to conquer and to have his worth
Of contradiction. Being once chafed, he cannot
Be reined again to temperance; then he speaks
What's in his heart, and that is there which looks
With us to break his neck.

*Enter Coriolanus, Menenius, and Cominius, with others* ⌜*(Senators).*⌝

SICINIUS Well, here he comes.

MENENIUS, ⌜*aside to Coriolanus*⌝ Calmly, I do beseech
you.

CORIOLANUS, ⌜*aside to Menenius*⌝
Ay, as an hostler that ⌜for th'⌝ poorest piece
Will bear the knave by th' volume.—Th' honored
gods
Keep Rome in safety and the chairs of justice
Supplied with worthy men! Plant love among 's!

47. **shows:** spectacles, pageants

52. **List:** listen; **Audience:** attention

55. **Shall . . . this present:** i.e., will **I be charged** in future with anything else

56. **determine:** come to an end, conclude

59. **Allow:** acknowledge

74. **become:** are appropriate to

75. **envy:** i.e., ill will against

237

THE LIFE OF CAIVS
*Martius Coriolanus.*

A THE houſe of the *Martians* at ROME was of the number of the *Patricians*, out of the which hath ſprong many noble perſonages: whereof *Ancus Martius* was one, king *Numaes* daughters ſonne, who was king of ROME after *Tullus Hoſtilius*. Of the ſame houſe were *Publius*, and *Quintus*, who brought to ROME their beſt water they had by conducts. *Cenſorinus* alſo came of that familie, that was ſo ſurnamed, bicauſe the people had choſen him *Cenſor* twiſe. Through whoſe perſuaſion they made a lawe, that no man from thenceforth might require, or enioye the *Cenſorſhippe* twiſe. *Caius Martius*, whoſe life we intend now to write, being left an orphan by his father, was brought vp vnder his mother a
B widowe, who taught vs by experience, that orphanage bringeth many diſcommodities to a childe, but doth not hinder him to become an honeſt man, and to excell in vertue aboue the common ſorte: as they that are meanely borne, wrongfully doe complayne, that it is the occaſion of their caſting awaye, for that no man in their youth taketh any care of them to ſee them well brought vp, and taught that were meete. This man alſo is a good proofe to confirme ſome mens opinions. That a rare and excellent witte vntaught, doth bring forth many good and euill things together: like as a fat ſoile bringeth forth herbes & weedes that lieth vnmanured. For this *Martius* naturall wit and great harte dyd marueilouſly ſturre vp his corage, to doe and attempt notable actes. But on the other ſide for lacke of education, he was ſo chol- lericke and impacient, that he would yeld to no liuing creature: which made him churliſhe,
C vnciuill, and altogether vnfit for any mans conuerſation. Yet men marueling much at his conſtancy, that he was neuer ouercome with pleaſure, nor money, and howe he would endure eaſely all manner of paynes and trauailles: thereupon they well liked and commended his ſtowtnes and temperancie. But for all that, they could not be acquainted with him, as one cittizen vſeth to be with another in the cittie. His behauiour was ſo vnpleaſaunt to them, by reaſon of a certaine inſolent and ſterne manner he had, which bicauſe it was to lordly, was diſliked. And to ſaye truely, the greateſt benefit that learning bringeth men vnto, is this: that it teacheth men that be rude and rough of nature, by compaſſe and rule of reaſon, to be ciuill and

*The familie of the Martians.*

*Publius and Quintus Martius, brought the water by conducts to Rome. Cenſorinus lawe.*

*Coriolanus wit.*

*The benefit of learning.*

Plutarch's "Life" of Caius Martius Coriolanus.
From Plutarch, *The Lives of the Noble Grecians and Romanes* (1579).

⌜Throng⌝ our large temples with the shows of peace
And not our streets with war!

FIRST SENATOR Amen, amen.

MENENIUS A noble wish.

*Enter the Aedile with the Plebeians.*

SICINIUS Draw near, you people.

AEDILE
List to your tribunes. Audience! Peace, I say!

CORIOLANUS First, hear me speak.

BOTH TRIBUNES Well, say.—Peace, ho!

CORIOLANUS
Shall I be charged no further than this present?
Must all determine here?

SICINIUS I do demand
If you submit you to the people's voices,
Allow their officers, and are content
To suffer lawful censure for such faults
As shall be proved upon you.

CORIOLANUS I am content.

MENENIUS
Lo, citizens, he says he is content.
The warlike service he has done, consider. Think
Upon the wounds his body bears, which show
Like graves i' th' holy churchyard.

CORIOLANUS Scratches with briars,
Scars to move laughter only.

MENENIUS Consider further,
That when he speaks not like a citizen,
You find him like a soldier. Do not take
His rougher ⌜accents⌝ for malicious sounds,
But, as I say, such as become a soldier
Rather than envy you.

COMINIUS Well, well, no more.

81. **Answer to us:** i.e., defend yourself against our charges (rather than laying charges against us)

82. **Say:** i.e., speak

84. **seasoned:** moderate; tempered (as opposed to **tyrannical** [line 85]); **office:** officeholders; **wind:** insinuate

89. **fold in:** envelop

90. **their traitor: traitor** to them; **injurious:** insulting

91. **Within:** i.e., if within

94. **free:** frank, unreserved

95. **pray:** i.e., **pray** to

96. **Mark:** observe

99. **matter:** allegations; **his charge:** i.e., the charges against him

102. **strokes:** i.e., of his sword (drawn but not used by Coriolanus in 3.1)

104. **capital:** punishable by death

"His sword, Death's stamp." (2.2.123; see also 2.1.165)
From *Todten-Tantz* (1696).

CORIOLANUS What is the matter,
That, being passed for consul with full voice,
I am so dishonored that the very hour
You take it off again?
SICINIUS Answer to us.
CORIOLANUS Say then. 'Tis true, I ought so.
SICINIUS
We charge you that you have contrived to take
From Rome all seasoned office and to wind
Yourself into a power tyrannical,
For which you are a traitor to the people.
CORIOLANUS
How? Traitor?
MENENIUS Nay, temperately! Your promise.
CORIOLANUS
The fires i' th' lowest hell fold in the people!
Call me their traitor? Thou injurious tribune!
Within thine eyes sat twenty thousand deaths,
In thy hands clutched as many millions, in
Thy lying tongue both numbers, I would say
"Thou liest" unto thee with a voice as free
As I do pray the gods.
SICINIUS Mark you this, people?
ALL ⌜PLEBEIANS⌝ To' th' rock, to' th' rock with him!
SICINIUS Peace!
We need not put new matter to his charge.
What you have seen him do and heard him speak,
Beating your officers, cursing yourselves,
Opposing laws with strokes, and here defying
Those whose great power must try him—even this,
So criminal and in such capital kind,
Deserves th' extremest death.
BRUTUS But since he hath
Served well for Rome—
CORIOLANUS What do you prate of service?
BRUTUS I talk of that that know it.

115. **pent:** i.e., **pent** up, imprisoned; **linger:** "remain long in languor and pain" (Samuel Johnson)

118. **courage:** heart, spirit

119. **To have 't with:** i.e., if I could **have** it by

120. **For that:** because

122. **Envied:** felt a grudge (It is possible that this word should be *Inveighed* [railed loudly], which was sometimes spelled "Enveid" and thus could be misread as **Envied.**)

124. **Given:** i.e., (he) has **given; not:** i.e., **not** only

125. **dreaded:** awe-inspiring; feared; **justice:** judicial authority (i.e., "those whose great power must try him" [line 103]); **but:** i.e., **but** also; **ministers:** officers entrusted with the administration of the law (i.e., officers of the law)

129. **precipitation:** being hurled down headlong

135. **common:** commoner, plebeian

CORIOLANUS You?
MENENIUS
Is this the promise that you made your mother?
COMINIUS Know, I pray you—
CORIOLANUS I'll know no further.
Let them pronounce the steep Tarpeian death,
Vagabond exile, flaying, pent to linger
But with a grain a day, I would not buy
Their mercy at the price of one fair word,
Nor check my courage for what they can give,
To have 't with saying "Good morrow."
SICINIUS For that he has,
As much as in him lies, from time to time
Envied against the people, seeking means
To pluck away their power, as now at last
Given hostile strokes, and that not in the presence
Of dreaded justice, but on the ministers
That doth distribute it, in the name o' th' people
And in the power of us the Tribunes, we,
Even from this instant, banish him our city
In peril of precipitation
From off the rock Tarpeian, never more
To enter our Rome gates. I' th' people's name,
I say it shall be so.
ALL ⌜PLEBEIANS⌝
It shall be so, it shall be so! Let him away!
He's banished, and it shall be so.
COMINIUS
Hear me, my masters and my common friends—
SICINIUS
He's sentenced. No more hearing.
COMINIUS Let me speak.
I have been consul and can show ⌜for⌝ Rome
Her enemies' marks upon me. I do love
My country's good with a respect more tender,
More holy and profound, than mine own life,

142. **estimate:** reputation

142–43. **her womb's . . . loins:** i.e., our children

150. **cry:** pack

151. **reek:** vapor; **fens:** swamps

154. **And here:** i.e., **and** may you **here**

156. **Your enemies:** i.e., may **your enemies; plumes:** feathers on their soldiers' helmets

157. **Have:** i.e., may you **have; still:** always

159. **finds:** comes to knowledge; **feels:** experiences

160. **Making . . . of:** excepting only

162. **abated:** beaten, subdued

164. **For you:** because of you

169. **despite:** scorn

Deucalion and Pyrrha repopulating the earth. (2.1.94)
From Lodovico Dolce, *Le trasformationi* . . . (1570).

My dear wife's estimate, her womb's increase,
And treasure of my loins. Then if I would
Speak that—

SICINIUS We know your drift. Speak what?

BRUTUS
There's no more to be said, but he is banished
As enemy to the people and his country.
It shall be so.

ALL ⌜PLEBEIANS⌝ It shall be so, it shall be so!

CORIOLANUS
You common cry of curs, whose breath I hate
As reek o' th' rotten fens, whose loves I prize
As the dead carcasses of unburied men
That do corrupt my air, I banish you!
And here remain with your uncertainty;
Let every feeble rumor shake your hearts;
Your enemies, with nodding of their plumes,
Fan you into despair! Have the power still
To banish your defenders, till at length
Your ignorance—which finds not till it feels,
Making but reservation of yourselves,
Still your own foes—deliver you
As most abated captives to some nation
That won you without blows! Despising
For you the city, thus I turn my back.
There is a world elsewhere.

*Coriolanus, Cominius, with others ⌜(Senators)⌝ exit.*

AEDILE
The people's enemy is gone, is gone.

ALL ⌜PLEBEIANS⌝
Our enemy is banished; he is gone. Hoo, hoo!

*They all shout and throw up their caps.*

SICINIUS
Go see him out at gates, and follow him,
As he hath followed you, with all despite.

170. **vexation:** harassment
171. **Attend:** accompany

"Goddess Fortune," turning her wheel. (1.5.23, 27–28)
From Gregor Reisch, *Margarita philosophica* . . . [1503].

Give him deserved vexation. Let a guard
Attend us through the city.

ALL ⌜PLEBEIANS⌝

Come, come, let's see him out at gates! Come!
The gods preserve our noble tribunes! Come!

*They exit.*

# CORIOLANUS

ACT 4

**4.1** Coriolanus says goodbye to his family and closest supporters.

---

1–2. **beast . . . heads:** See notes to 2.3.16–17 and 3.1.125.

3. **ancient:** former; **used:** accustomed

4. **extremities:** greatest adversities; **was:** were

5. **common chances:** ordinary mishaps

8. **struck home:** i.e., **struck** most directly or effectively; **being gentle wounded:** perhaps, bearing one's wounds as is fitting for one who is a wellborn

10. **cunning:** skill, ability

12. **conned:** memorized

16. **pestilence:** plague (The **red pestilence** might be typhus, a symptom of which is red skin eruptions. The calling down of **pestilence** on one's enemies is a conventional curse.)

17. **occupations:** handicrafts

19. **lacked:** missed, noticed to be absent

21. **Hercules:** Greek hero famous for carrying out twelve apparently impossible **labors** (line 22) See picture, page 184.

# ACT 4

## ⌜Scene 1⌝

*Enter Coriolanus, Volumnia, Virgilia, Menenius, Cominius, with the young nobility of Rome.*

CORIOLANUS
Come, leave your tears. A brief farewell. The beast
With many heads butts me away. Nay, mother,
Where is your ancient courage? You were used
To say extremities was the trier of spirits;
That common chances common men could bear;
That when the sea was calm, all boats alike
Showed mastership in floating; fortune's blows
When most struck home, being gentle wounded
craves
A noble cunning. You were used to load me
With precepts that would make invincible
The heart that conned them.

VIRGILIA O heavens! O heavens!

CORIOLANUS Nay, I prithee,
woman—

VOLUMNIA
Now the red pestilence strike all trades in Rome,
And occupations perish!

CORIOLANUS What, what, what!
I shall be loved when I am lacked. Nay, mother,
Resume that spirit when you were wont to say
If you had been the wife of Hercules,

26. **salter:** more salty

27. **venomous:** harmful; **sometime:** former

31. **'Tis fond . . . strokes:** proverbial **fond:** i.e., **as** foolish

32. **wot:** know

33. **still:** always

35. **fen:** marsh

38. **or:** i.e., either; **the common:** perhaps, the deeds of ordinary men; or, perhaps, the ordinary deeds of men

39. **cautelous:** deceitful, crafty; **practice:** intrigue

40. **first son:** It was established at 1.3.6–7 that Coriolanus is Volumnia's only **son.**

43. **exposure to:** i.e., defenselessness in the face of

44. **starts:** springs up

49. **cause:** motive; **thy repeal:** i.e., the **repeal** of your banishment

51. **advantage:** opportunity

55. **Of the wars' surfeits:** i.e., from excessive indulgence in war, as if it were food (See **full** [line 54] and longer note to 1.5.17, page 284.)

56. **at gate:** i.e., **at** the **gate**

Six of his labors you'd have done and saved
Your husband so much sweat.—Cominius,
Droop not. Adieu.—Farewell, my wife, my mother.
I'll do well yet.—Thou old and true Menenius,
Thy tears are salter than a younger man's
And venomous to thine eyes.—My sometime
  general,
I have seen thee stern, and thou hast oft beheld
Heart-hard'ning spectacles. Tell these sad women
'Tis fond to wail inevitable strokes
As 'tis to laugh at 'em.—My mother, you wot well
My hazards still have been your solace, and—
Believe 't not lightly—though I go alone,
Like to a lonely dragon that his fen
Makes feared and talked of more than seen, your
  son
Will or exceed the common or be caught
With cautelous baits and practice.

VOLUMNIA My first son,
Whither ⌜wilt⌝ thou go? Take good Cominius
With thee awhile. Determine on some course
More than a wild exposure to each chance
That starts i' th' way before thee.

⌜VIRGILIA⌝ O the gods!

COMINIUS
I'll follow thee a month, devise with thee
Where thou shalt rest, that thou mayst hear of us
And we of thee; so if the time thrust forth
A cause for thy repeal, we shall not send
O'er the vast world to seek a single man
And lose advantage, which doth ever cool
I' th' absence of the needer.

CORIOLANUS Fare you well.
Thou hast years upon thee, and thou art too full
Of the wars' surfeits to go rove with one
That's yet unbruised. Bring me but out at gate.—

58. **noble touch:** proven nobility

**4.2** Meeting the tribunes, Volumnia and Virgilia curse them.

---

9. **ancient:** former

Hercules holding the "mellow fruit" of the Hesperides. (4.6.126; see also 4.1.21)
From Vincenzo Cartari, *Le vere e noue imagini . . .* (1615).

Come, my sweet wife, my dearest mother, and
My friends of noble touch. When I am forth,
Bid me farewell, and smile. I pray you, come.
While I remain above the ground, you shall
Hear from me still, and never of me aught
But what is like me formerly.

MENENIUS That's worthily
As any ear can hear. Come, let's not weep.
If I could shake off but one seven years
From these old arms and legs, by the good gods,
I'd with thee every foot.

CORIOLANUS Give me thy hand.
Come.

*They exit.*

⌜Scene 2⌝

*Enter the two Tribunes, Sicinius, and Brutus, with the Aedile.*

SICINIUS
Bid them all home. He's gone, and we'll no further.
The nobility are vexed, whom we see have sided
In his behalf.

BRUTUS Now we have shown our power,
Let us seem humbler after it is done
Than when it was a-doing.

SICINIUS Bid them home.
Say their great enemy is gone, and they
Stand in their ancient strength.

BRUTUS Dismiss them home.

⌜*Aedile exits.*⌝

Here comes his mother.

*Enter Volumnia, Virgilia, and Menenius.*

SICINIUS Let's not meet her.

BRUTUS Why?

14. **mad:** (1) insane; (2) furious

16. **hoarded:** stored-up

17. **Requite:** repay

19. **could:** i.e., **could** speak

24. **mankind:** masculine, virago-like (Volumnia's response seems to be to another meaning, "human.")

26. **foxship:** cunning, craftiness

33. **Arabia:** i.e., the desert (where conventionally there is no law)

An Amazon. (2.2.107)
From Giovanni Battista Cavalleriis,
*Antiquarum statuarum* . . . (1585–94).

SICINIUS They say she's mad.

BRUTUS
They have ta'en note of us. Keep on your way.

VOLUMNIA
O, you're well met. The hoarded plague o' th' gods
Requite your love!

MENENIUS Peace, peace! Be not so loud.

VOLUMNIA, ⌜*to the Tribunes*⌝
If that I could for weeping, you should hear—
Nay, and you shall hear some. ⌜(*To Sicinius.*)⌝ Will
you be gone?

VIRGILIA, ⌜*to Brutus*⌝
You shall stay too. I would I had the power
To say so to my husband.

SICINIUS, ⌜*to Volumnia*⌝ Are you mankind?

VOLUMNIA
Ay, fool, is that a shame? Note but this, fool.
Was not a man my father? Hadst thou foxship
To banish him that struck more blows for Rome
Than thou hast spoken words?

SICINIUS O blessèd heavens!

VOLUMNIA
More noble blows than ever thou wise words,
And for Rome's good. I'll tell thee what—yet go.
Nay, but thou shalt stay too. I would my son
Were in Arabia and thy tribe before him,
His good sword in his hand.

SICINIUS What then?

VIRGILIA What then?
He'd make an end of thy posterity.

VOLUMNIA Bastards and all.
Good man, the wounds that he does bear for Rome!

MENENIUS Come, come, peace.

SICINIUS
I would he had continued to his country

46. **Cats:** term of contempt; **fitly:** properly
53. **meanest:** shabbiest, poorest
57–58. **baited / With:** i.e., tormented by
58. **wants:** lacks
61. **would:** wish
63. **unclog:** free (A *clog* is a **heavy** [line 64] piece of wood attached to the leg or neck of a person or animal to prevent its escape.)
65. **home:** i.e., bluntly, unsparingly
66. **sup:** have supper
68. **sup:** i.e., feed
71. **faint:** feeble; **puling:** whining, wailing
72. **Juno-like:** like Juno, queen of the Roman gods, implacable in her anger (See picture, below.)

The goddess Juno. (2.1.104; 4.2.72; 5.3.53)
From Johann Theodor de Bry,
*Proscenium vitae humanae . . .* (1627).

As he began, and not unknit himself
The noble knot he made.

BRUTUS I would he had.

VOLUMNIA
"I would he had"? 'Twas you incensed the rabble.
Cats, that can judge as fitly of his worth
As I can of those mysteries which heaven
Will not have earth to know.

BRUTUS, ⌜*to Sicinius*⌝ Pray, let's go.

VOLUMNIA Now, pray, sir, get you gone.
You have done a brave deed. Ere you go, hear this:
As far as doth the Capitol exceed
The meanest house in Rome, so far my son—
This lady's husband here, this, do you see?—
Whom you have banished, does exceed you all.

BRUTUS
Well, well, we'll leave you.

SICINIUS Why stay we to be baited
With one that wants her wits? *Tribunes exit.*

VOLUMNIA Take my prayers with
you.
I would the gods had nothing else to do
But to confirm my curses. Could I meet 'em
But once a day, it would unclog my heart
Of what lies heavy to 't.

MENENIUS You have told them home,
And, by my troth, you have cause. You'll sup with
me?

VOLUMNIA
Anger's my meat. I sup upon myself
And so shall starve with feeding.
⌜(*To Virgilia.*)⌝ Come, let's go.
Leave this faint puling, and lament as I do,
In anger, Juno-like. Come, come, come. *They exit.*

MENENIUS Fie, fie, fie!

*He exits.*

**4.3** A Roman informer tells a Volscian spy of Coriolanus's banishment.

---

5. **'em:** i.e., the Romans

9. **favor:** look; **approved:** established

10. **note:** i.e., written order

25. **This:** i.e., **this** conflict between nobles and people; **glowing:** i.e., like coals from a fire

31. **them:** i.e., the Volscians

Mars, the god of war. (1.4.14; 4.5.131, 212; 5.6.119)
From Vincenzo Cartari, *Le imagini de i dei de gli antichi* . . . (1587).

## ⌜Scene 3⌝

*Enter a Roman ⌜(Nicanor)⌝ and a Volsce ⌜(Adrian).⌝*

ROMAN I know you well, sir, and you know me. Your name I think is Adrian.

VOLSCE It is so, sir. Truly, I have forgot you.

ROMAN I am a Roman, and my services are, as you are, against 'em. Know you me yet?

VOLSCE Nicanor, no?

ROMAN The same, sir.

VOLSCE You had more beard when I last saw you, but your favor is well ⌜approved⌝ by your tongue. What's the news in Rome? I have a note from the Volscian state to find you out there. You have well saved me a day's journey.

ROMAN There hath been in Rome strange insurrections, the people against the senators, patricians, and nobles.

VOLSCE Hath been? Is it ended, then? Our state thinks not so. They are in a most warlike preparation and hope to come upon them in the heat of their division.

ROMAN The main blaze of it is past, but a small thing would make it flame again; for the nobles receive so to heart the banishment of that worthy Coriolanus that they are in a ripe aptness to take all power from the people and to pluck from them their tribunes forever. This lies glowing, I can tell you, and is almost mature for the violent breaking out.

VOLSCE Coriolanus banished?

ROMAN Banished, sir.

VOLSCE You will be welcome with this intelligence, Nicanor.

ROMAN The day serves well for them now. I have heard

32. **fittest:** most convenient

35–36. **in no request of:** i.e., unwanted by

37. **cannot choose: cannot** do otherwise

45. **charges:** i.e., those under their command (Originally each centurion commanded a hundred soldiers.) **distinctly:** individually; **billeted:** enrolled

45–46. **in th' entertainment:** taken into service, being paid

46. **on foot:** astir, in motion

48. **present:** immediate

51. **my part:** i.e., the words I should be saying

**4.4** Coriolanus comes to the Volscian city of Antium in search of Aufidius.

---

0 SD. **muffled:** his face covered

3. **'fore:** in the presence of; **wars:** assaults

it said the fittest time to corrupt a man's wife is when she's fall'n out with her husband. Your noble Tullus Aufidius ⌜will⌝ appear well in these wars, his great opposer Coriolanus being now in no request of his country.

VOLSCE He cannot choose. I am most fortunate thus accidentally to encounter you. You have ended my business, and I will merrily accompany you home.

ROMAN I shall between this and supper tell you most strange things from Rome, all tending to the good of their adversaries. Have you an army ready, say you?

VOLSCE A most royal one. The centurions and their charges, distinctly billeted, already in th' entertainment, and to be on foot at an hour's warning.

ROMAN I am joyful to hear of their readiness and am the man, I think, that shall set them in present action. So, sir, heartily well met, and most glad of your company.

VOLSCE You take my part from me, sir. I have the most cause to be glad of yours.

ROMAN Well, let us go together.

*They exit.*

## ⌜Scene 4⌝

*Enter Coriolanus in mean apparel, disguised, and muffled.*

CORIOLANUS
A goodly city is this Antium. City,
'Tis I that made thy widows. Many an heir
Of these fair edifices 'fore my wars
Have I heard groan and drop. Then, know me not,

5. **spits:** kitchen skewers

7. **Save you:** i.e., God **save you** (a conventional greeting in Shakespeare's time)

10. **lies:** dwells

17. **slippery:** fickle, faithless, deceitful; **turns:** changes; **fast:** firmly, earnestly

18. **double:** paired, coupled (but the word also means "deceitful")

20. **still:** always

21. **Unseparable:** i.e., inseparable; **within this:** i.e., in a single

22. **dissension of:** quarrel over; **doit:** a coin of trifling value (half a farthing, or one-eighth of a penny)

23. **fellest:** most savage

24. **plots:** schemes; **broke:** broken, disturbed

26. **take:** capture

27. **trick:** trifle

28. **interjoin their issues:** (1) arrange a marriage between their children; (2) join with one another in action

31. **give me way:** allow me liberty of action

Lest that thy wives with spits and boys with stones
In puny battle slay me.

*Enter a Citizen.*

Save you, sir.

CITIZEN
And you.

CORIOLANUS Direct me, if it be your will,
Where great Aufidius lies. Is he in Antium?

CITIZEN
He is, and feasts the nobles of the state
At his house this night.

CORIOLANUS Which is his house, beseech you?

CITIZEN
This here before you.

CORIOLANUS Thank you, sir. Farewell.

*Citizen exits.*

O world, thy slippery turns! Friends now fast sworn,
Whose double bosoms seems to wear one heart,
Whose hours, whose bed, whose meal and exercise
Are still together, who twin, as 'twere, in love
Unseparable, shall within this hour,
On a dissension of a doit, break out
To bitterest enmity; so fellest foes,
Whose passions and whose plots have broke their sleep
To take the one the other, by some chance,
Some trick not worth an egg, shall grow dear friends
And interjoin their issues. So with me:
My birthplace ⌜hate⌝ I, and my love's upon
This enemy town. I'll enter. If he slay me,
He does fair justice; if he give me way,
I'll do his country service.

*He exits.*

**4.5** Coriolanus offers to join Aufidius in making war on Rome.

---

2. **fellows:** fellow servants

6. **Appear not:** (1) do **not** look like; (2) do **not** arrive

8–9. **go to the door:** perhaps, get out; or, perhaps, go where the beggars sit by **the door**

10. **entertainment:** reception

14. **companions:** a term of contempt

19. **anon:** immediately

Apron-men (here, swordmakers). (4.6.122)
From Jan Luiken, *Spiegal . . .* (1704).

## ⌜Scene 5⌝

*Music plays. Enter a Servingman.*

FIRST SERVINGMAN Wine, wine, wine! What service is here? I think our fellows are asleep. ⌜*He exits.*⌝

*Enter another Servingman.*

SECOND SERVINGMAN Where's Cotus? My master calls for him. Cotus! *He exits.*

*Enter Coriolanus.*

CORIOLANUS
A goodly house. The feast smells well, but I
Appear not like a guest.

*Enter the First Servingman.*

FIRST SERVINGMAN What would you have, friend? Whence are you? Here's no place for you. Pray, go to the door. *He exits.*

CORIOLANUS
I have deserved no better entertainment
In being Coriolanus.

*Enter Second ⌜Servingman.⌝*

SECOND SERVINGMAN Whence are you, sir?—Has the porter his eyes in his head, that he gives entrance to such companions?—Pray, get you out.

CORIOLANUS Away!

SECOND SERVINGMAN Away? Get you away.

CORIOLANUS Now th' art troublesome.

SECOND SERVINGMAN Are you so brave? I'll have you talked with anon.

*Enter Third Servingman; the First, ⌜entering,⌝ meets him.*

THIRD SERVINGMAN What fellow's this?

25. **avoid:** leave

30. **marv'llous:** astonishingly

33. **station:** place to stand (with possible wordplay on "social status")

35. **Follow:** occupy yourself with; **function:** employment, calling (i.e., as a servant); **batten:** grow fat

36. **cold bits:** table scraps

45. **kites:** vultures

47. **daws:** jackdaws (equivalent to "fools" when applied to people) See picture, below.

49. **meddle with:** concern yourself with

51. **honester:** more honest (with wordplay on "more chaste"); **meddle:** have sexual intercourse

52. **Thou prat'st:** i.e., you chatter

53. **trencher:** wooden dish

Jackdaws. (4.5.47)
From Aesop, . . . *Fabulae* . . . (1587).

FIRST SERVINGMAN A strange one as ever I looked on. I cannot get him out o' th' house. Prithee, call my master to him. ⌜*He steps aside.*⌝

THIRD SERVINGMAN What have you to do here, fellow? Pray you, avoid the house.

CORIOLANUS Let me but stand. I will not hurt your hearth.

THIRD SERVINGMAN What are you?

CORIOLANUS A gentleman.

THIRD SERVINGMAN A marv'llous poor one.

CORIOLANUS True, so I am.

THIRD SERVINGMAN Pray you, poor gentleman, take up some other station. Here's no place for you. Pray you, avoid. Come.

CORIOLANUS Follow your function, go, and batten on cold bits. *Pushes him away from him.*

THIRD SERVINGMAN What, you will not?—Prithee, tell my master what a strange guest he has here.

SECOND SERVINGMAN And I shall.

*Second Servingman exits.*

THIRD SERVINGMAN Where dwell'st thou?

CORIOLANUS Under the canopy.

THIRD SERVINGMAN Under the canopy?

CORIOLANUS Ay.

THIRD SERVINGMAN Where's that?

CORIOLANUS I' th' city of kites and crows.

THIRD SERVINGMAN I' th' city of kites and crows? What an ass it is! Then thou dwell'st with daws too?

CORIOLANUS No, I serve not thy master.

THIRD SERVINGMAN How, sir? Do you meddle with my master?

CORIOLANUS Ay, 'tis an honester service than to meddle with thy mistress. Thou prat'st and prat'st. Serve with thy trencher. Hence! *Beats him away.*

⌜*Third Servingman exits.*⌝

69. **a command:** an authority; **tackle's:** ship's rigging is

70. **show'st:** appear to be

75. **mischief:** evil, injury

76. **painful:** laborious

79. **memory:** memorial

83. **envy:** malice

*Enter Aufidius with the ⌜Second⌝ Servingman.*

AUFIDIUS Where is this fellow?

SECOND SERVINGMAN Here, sir. I'd have beaten him like a dog, but for disturbing the lords within.

⌜*He steps aside.*⌝

AUFIDIUS Whence com'st thou? What wouldst thou? Thy name? Why speak'st not? Speak, man. What's thy name?

CORIOLANUS, ⌜*removing his muffler*⌝ If, Tullus,
Not yet thou know'st me, and seeing me, dost not
Think me for the man I am, necessity
Commands me name myself.

AUFIDIUS What is thy name?

CORIOLANUS
A name unmusical to the Volscians' ears
And harsh in sound to thine.

AUFIDIUS Say, what's thy name?
Thou hast a grim appearance, and thy face
Bears a command in 't. Though thy tackle's torn,
Thou show'st a noble vessel. What's thy name?

CORIOLANUS
Prepare thy brow to frown. Know'st thou me yet?

AUFIDIUS I know thee not. Thy name?

CORIOLANUS
My name is Caius Martius, who hath done
To thee particularly and to all the Volsces
Great hurt and mischief; thereto witness may
My surname Coriolanus. The painful service,
The extreme dangers, and the drops of blood
Shed for my thankless country are requited
But with that surname, a good memory
And witness of the malice and displeasure
Which thou shouldst bear me. Only that name remains.
The cruelty and envy of the people,

84. **dastard:** cowardly
86. **suffered:** allowed
87. **Whooped:** i.e., derisively shouted
91. **'voided:** avoided; **mere:** pure
92. **full:** fully; **quit of:** i.e., avenged on
94. **wreak:** vengeance
95–96. **maims / Of shame:** shameful injuries
96. **through:** throughout; **speed thee:** act with speed
97. **straight:** straightaway, immediately
101. **cankered:** corrupt, depraved; **spleen:** indignation
102. **under:** i.e., underworld
103. **prove:** try; **fortunes:** i.e., chances in war
106. **ancient:** long-standing
109. **tuns:** large barrels
115. **envy:** malice

Nettles. (2.1.204)
From John Gerard, *The herball* . . . (1597).

Permitted by our dastard nobles, who
Have all forsook me, hath devoured the rest,
And suffered me by th' voice of slaves to be
⌜Whooped⌝ out of Rome. Now this extremity
Hath brought me to thy hearth, not out of hope—
Mistake me not—to save my life; for if
I had feared death, of all the men i' th' world
I would have 'voided thee, but in mere spite,
To be full quit of those my banishers,
Stand I before thee here. Then if thou hast
A heart of wreak in thee, that wilt revenge
Thine own particular wrongs and stop those maims
Of shame seen through thy country, speed thee straight
And make my misery serve thy turn. So use it
That my revengeful services may prove
As benefits to thee, for I will fight
Against my cankered country with the spleen
Of all the under fiends. But if so be
Thou dar'st not this, and that to prove more fortunes
Thou'rt tired, then, in a word, I also am
Longer to live most weary, and present
My throat to thee and to thy ancient malice,
Which not to cut would show thee but a fool,
Since I have ever followed thee with hate,
Drawn tuns of blood out of thy country's breast,
And cannot live but to thy shame, unless
It be to do thee service.

AUFIDIUS O Martius, Martius,
Each word thou hast spoke hath weeded from my heart
A root of ancient envy. If Jupiter
Should from yond cloud speak divine things
And say 'tis true, I'd not believe them more
Than thee, all-noble Martius. Let me twine

119. **whereagainst:** against which
120. **grainèd ash:** (1) visibly grained ashen shaft of a spear; or (2) ashen-shafted spear with prongs
122. **clip:** embrace
128. **truer:** more faithful
129. **rapt:** ravished, enraptured
131. **Bestride:** step across; **Mars:** Roman god of war (See picture, page 190.)
132. **power:** army; **had purpose:** intended
133. **target:** shield; **brawn:** arm
134. **out:** outright, utterly
135. **several:** separate
137. **down:** i.e., on the ground
138. **helms:** helmets
144. **o'erbear 't:** overwhelm it
147. **prepared against:** i.e., ready to set out to attack
150. **absolute:** perfect, consummate

Hector. (1.3.44; 1.8.17)
From [Guillaume Rouillé,] . . . *Promptuarii iconum* . . . (1553).

Mine arms about that body, whereagainst
My grainèd ash an hundred times hath broke
And scarred the moon with splinters.
⌜*They embrace.*⌝
Here I clip
The anvil of my sword and do contest
As hotly and as nobly with thy love
As ever in ambitious strength I did
Contend against thy valor. Know thou first,
I loved the maid I married; never man
Sighed truer breath. But that I see thee here,
Thou noble thing, more dances my rapt heart
Than when I first my wedded mistress saw
Bestride my threshold. Why, thou Mars, I tell thee
We have a power on foot, and I had purpose
Once more to hew thy target from thy brawn
Or lose mine arm for 't. Thou hast beat me out
Twelve several times, and I have nightly since
Dreamt of encounters 'twixt thyself and me;
We have been down together in my sleep,
Unbuckling helms, fisting each other's throat,
And waked half dead with nothing. Worthy Martius,
Had we no other quarrel else to Rome but that
Thou art thence banished, we would muster all
From twelve to seventy and, pouring war
Into the bowels of ungrateful Rome,
Like a bold flood ⌜o'erbear 't.⌝ O, come, go in,
And take our friendly senators by th' hands,
Who now are here, taking their leaves of me,
Who am prepared against your territories,
Though not for Rome itself.

CORIOLANUS
You bless me, gods!

AUFIDIUS
Therefore, most absolute sir, if thou wilt have
The leading of thine own revenges, take

152. **commission:** authority (i.e., to make war); **set down:** resolve on, determine

157. **rudely:** violently; **visit them:** go to them with hostile intentions

159. **commend thee:** present you (as worthy of regard)

166. **strucken:** struck

167. **gave me:** i.e., suggested that

170. **set up: set** spinning

173. **methought:** it seemed to me

180. **he:** The reference for this third-person pronoun and a number that follow is unclear. "**He**" could refer equally well to Coriolanus or to Aufidius, as if the servants are afraid to admit to each other a preference for Coriolanus over their master. **wot:** know

183. **on him:** i.e., of him

Th' one half of my commission and set down—
As best thou art experienced, since thou know'st
Thy country's strength and weakness—thine own
ways,
Whether to knock against the gates of Rome,
Or rudely visit them in parts remote
To fright them ere destroy. But come in.
Let me commend thee first to those that shall
Say yea to thy desires. A thousand welcomes!
And more a friend than ere an enemy—
Yet, Martius, that was much. Your hand. Most
welcome! *⌜Coriolanus and Aufidius⌝ exit.*

*Two of the Servingmen ⌜come forward.⌝*

FIRST SERVINGMAN Here's a strange alteration!

SECOND SERVINGMAN By my hand, I had thought to have strucken him with a cudgel, and yet my mind gave me his clothes made a false report of him.

FIRST SERVINGMAN What an arm he has! He turned me about with his finger and his thumb as one would set up a top.

SECOND SERVINGMAN Nay, I knew by his face that there was something in him. He had, sir, a kind of face, methought—I cannot tell how to term it.

FIRST SERVINGMAN He had so, looking as it were—Would I were hanged but I thought there was more in him than I could think.

SECOND SERVINGMAN So did I, I'll be sworn. He is simply the rarest man i' th' world.

FIRST SERVINGMAN I think he is. But a greater soldier than he you wot one.

SECOND SERVINGMAN Who, my master?

FIRST SERVINGMAN Nay, it's no matter for that.

SECOND SERVINGMAN Worth six on him.

FIRST SERVINGMAN Nay, not so neither. But I take him to be the greater soldier.

190. **slaves:** rascals, fellows

194. **had as lief:** i.e., would **as** gladly

195. **Wherefore:** why

196. **wont:** accustomed

202. **fellows:** co-workers, associates

205. **directly:** entirely

206. **on 't:** i.e., of it; **before Corioles:** See 1.8, pages 57–59, above. **scotched:** scored, cut

207. **carbonado:** a piece of meat or fish, scored across for grilling or broiling

208. **An:** i.e., if; **given:** inclined, disposed

211. **so made on:** i.e., **made so** much of

212. **upper end:** i.e., place of greatest honor

214. **stand bald:** i.e., **stand** and remove their hats—two marks of respect

215. **makes a mistress of him:** allows him the upper hand

215–16. **sanctifies . . . hand:** i.e., represents the touch of his **hand** as if it were holy

216–17. **turns up . . . eye:** i.e., shows affected devotion

217. **bottom:** essence

218. **cut i' th' middle:** i.e., **cut** into two equal pieces (like a piece of meat)

SECOND SERVINGMAN Faith, look you, one cannot tell how to say that. For the defense of a town our general is excellent.

FIRST SERVINGMAN Ay, and for an assault too.

*Enter the Third Servingman.*

THIRD SERVINGMAN O slaves, I can tell you news, news, you rascals!

BOTH What, what, what? Let's partake!

THIRD SERVINGMAN I would not be a Roman, of all nations; I had as lief be a condemned man.

BOTH Wherefore? Wherefore?

THIRD SERVINGMAN Why, here's he that was wont to thwack our general, Caius Martius.

FIRST SERVINGMAN Why do you say "thwack our general"?

THIRD SERVINGMAN I do not say "thwack our general," but he was always good enough for him.

SECOND SERVINGMAN Come, we are fellows and friends. He was ever too hard for him; I have heard him say so himself.

FIRST SERVINGMAN He was too hard for him directly, to say the truth on 't, before Corioles; he scotched him and notched him like a carbonado.

SECOND SERVINGMAN An he had been cannibally given, he might have boiled and eaten him too.

FIRST SERVINGMAN But, more of thy news.

THIRD SERVINGMAN Why, he is so made on here within as if he were son and heir to Mars; set at upper end o' th' table; no question asked him by any of the senators but they stand bald before him. Our general himself makes a mistress of him, sanctifies himself with 's hand, and turns up the white o' th' eye to his discourse. But the bottom of the news is, our general is cut i' th' middle and but one half of

221. **sowl:** seize

223. **polled:** pillaged, plundered

226. **look you:** see

230. **directitude:** an important-sounding but meaningless word (The context demands a word that describes Coriolanus's current exiled and despised status.)

232. **they:** i.e., his **friends** (line 227), the Roman patricians or nobles

232–33. **his crest up:** i.e., him proud and self-confident

233. **in blood:** in full vigor, full of life

234. **coneys:** rabbits

237. **presently:** immediately

239. **parcel:** part

243. **increase tailors:** perhaps, profit **tailors** or increase the number of **tailors** (because idle men buy clothes)

245–46. **sprightly . . . vent:** language used to describe a hunting hound **audible:** able to be heard, i.e., barking **vent:** scent (of a hunted animal)

246. **apoplexy:** paralysis

247. **mulled:** stupefied; softened; **getter:** begetter, parent

251. **ravisher:** plunderer, rapist

what he was yesterday, for the other has half, by the entreaty and grant of the whole table. He'll go, he says, and sowl the porter of Rome gates by th' ears. He will mow all down before him and leave his passage polled.

SECOND SERVINGMAN And he's as like to do 't as any man I can imagine.

THIRD SERVINGMAN Do 't? He will do 't! For, look you, sir, he has as many friends as enemies, which friends, sir, as it were, durst not, look you, sir, show themselves, as we term it, his friends whilest he's in directitude.

FIRST SERVINGMAN Directitude? What's that?

THIRD SERVINGMAN But when they shall see, sir, his crest up again, and the man in blood, they will out of their burrows like coneys after rain, and revel all with him.

FIRST SERVINGMAN But when goes this forward?

THIRD SERVINGMAN Tomorrow, today, presently. You shall have the drum struck up this afternoon. 'Tis, as it were, a parcel of their feast, and to be executed ere they wipe their lips.

SECOND SERVINGMAN Why then, we shall have a stirring world again. This peace is nothing but to rust iron, increase tailors, and breed ballad-makers.

FIRST SERVINGMAN Let me have war, say I. It exceeds peace as far as day does night. It's sprightly walking, audible, and full of vent. Peace is a very apoplexy, lethargy; mulled, deaf, ⌜sleepy,⌝ insensible; a getter of more bastard children than war's a destroyer of men.

SECOND SERVINGMAN 'Tis so, and as wars in some sort may be said to be a ravisher, so it cannot be denied but peace is a great maker of cuckolds.

**4.6** The tribunes' delight in Coriolanus's banishment is interrupted by news that an army led by him and Aufidius has invaded Rome's territories.

---

2. **His remedies:** i.e., the **remedies** for Coriolanus (i.e., **remedies** for the disease or infection associated with Coriolanus's violence at 3.1.378 and 396); **tame:** i.e., what is **tame** (namely, **peace** and **quietness**). This line is opaque, and other readings are quite possible.

4. **hurry:** commotion, disturbance

7. **pest'ring:** overcrowding

9. **functions:** occupations

10. **stood to 't:** fought resolutely

16. **with:** by

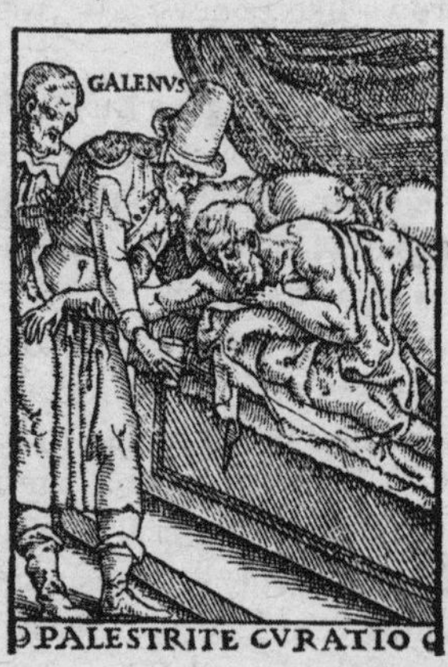


Galen tending the sick. (2.1.121)
From Galen, . . . *Omnia quae extant opera* . . . (1565).

FIRST SERVINGMAN Ay, and it makes men hate one another.

THIRD SERVINGMAN Reason: because they then less need one another. The wars for my money! I hope to see Romans as cheap as Volscians. ⌜(*Noise within.*)⌝ They are rising; they are rising.

⌜FIRST and SECOND SERVINGMEN⌝ In, in, in, in!

*They exit.*

## ⌜Scene 6⌝

*Enter the two Tribunes. Sicinius and Brutus.*

SICINIUS
We hear not of him, neither need we fear him.
His remedies are tame—the present peace,
And quietness of the people, which before
Were in wild hurry. Here do we make his friends
Blush that the world goes well, who rather had,
Though they themselves did suffer by 't, behold
Dissentious numbers pest'ring streets than see
Our tradesmen singing in their shops and going
About their functions friendly.

BRUTUS
We stood to 't in good time.

*Enter Menenius.*

Is this Menenius?

SICINIUS
'Tis he, 'tis he. O, he is grown most kind
Of late.—Hail, sir.

MENENIUS Hail to you both.

SICINIUS
Your Coriolanus is not much missed
But with his friends. The commonwealth doth stand,
And so would do were he more angry at it.

25. **Good e'en: good** evening

34. **comely:** agreeable

36. **confusion:** destruction

41. **affecting:** aiming at; **one sole:** a single; **assistance:** i.e., associates

44. **found:** i.e., have **found**

Pride. (2.1.19)
From Johann Theodor de Bry,
*Proscenium vitae humanae* . . . (1627).

MENENIUS
All's well, and might have been much better if
He could have temporized.

SICINIUS Where is he, hear you?

MENENIUS Nay, I hear nothing;
His mother and his wife hear nothing from him.

*Enter three or four Citizens.*

ALL ⌜CITIZENS, *to the Tribunes*⌝ The gods preserve
you both!

SICINIUS Good e'en, our neighbors.

BRUTUS
Good e'en to you all, good e'en to you all.

FIRST CITIZEN
Ourselves, our wives, and children, on our knees
Are bound to pray for you both.

SICINIUS Live, and thrive!

BRUTUS
Farewell, kind neighbors. We wished Coriolanus
Had loved you as we did.

ALL ⌜CITIZENS⌝ Now the gods keep you!

BOTH TRIBUNES Farewell, farewell. *Citizens exit.*

SICINIUS
This is a happier and more comely time
Than when these fellows ran about the streets
Crying confusion.

BRUTUS Caius Martius was
A worthy officer i' th' war, but insolent,
O'ercome with pride, ambitious, past all thinking
Self-loving.

SICINIUS
And affecting one sole throne, without assistance.

MENENIUS I think not so.

SICINIUS
We should by this, to all our lamentation,
If he had gone forth consul, found it so.

48. **slave:** used as a term of contempt

49. **Reports:** i.e., who **reports; several:** separate; **powers:** armies

51. **deepest:** most intense

55. **Thrusts . . . horns:** The image is of a snail putting its head out of its shell. (See picture, below.)

56. **inshelled:** withdrawn; **stood for:** defended

58. **what:** why

60. **break:** i.e., **break** their treaty (See 3.1.2–3.)

62. **record:** accented on the second syllable

64. **age:** lifetime; **reason:** talk

66. **information:** i.e., informant

A snail "thrust[ing] forth his horns." (4.6.55)
From George Wither, *A collection of emblemes* . . . (1635).

BRUTUS
The gods have well prevented it, and Rome
Sits safe and still without him.

*Enter an Aedile.*

AEDILE Worthy tribunes,
There is a slave, whom we have put in prison,
Reports the Volsces with two several powers
Are entered in the Roman territories,
And with the deepest malice of the war
Destroy what lies before 'em.

MENENIUS 'Tis Aufidius,
Who, hearing of our Martius' banishment,
Thrusts forth his horns again into the world,
Which were inshelled when Martius stood for Rome,
And durst not once peep out.

SICINIUS Come, what talk you of Martius?

BRUTUS
Go see this rumorer whipped. It cannot be
The Volsces dare break with us.

MENENIUS Cannot be?
We have record that very well it can,
And three examples of the like hath been
Within my age. But reason with the fellow
Before you punish him, where he heard this,
Lest you shall chance to whip your information
And beat the messenger who bids beware
Of what is to be dreaded.

SICINIUS Tell not me.
I know this cannot be.

BRUTUS Not possible.

*Enter a Messenger.*

MESSENGER
The nobles in great earnestness are going

73. **coming:** i.e., arriving in bits and pieces

74. **turns:** changes, alters

76. **raising:** instigation

79. **seconded:** supported

82. **spoke:** i.e., spoken

85–86. **as spacious as . . . thing:** i.e., **as** that space **between** (the two extremities) of youngest and **oldest**

88. **Raised:** originated, brought about, set going

90. **trick on 't:** clever expedient or device

92. **atone:** reconcile with each other

93. **violent'st contrariety:** the most opposed contraries

96. **rages:** rushes furiously

98. **O'erborne their way:** i.e., overwhelmed everything in **their** path; **took:** i.e., taken

All to the Senate House. Some news is coming
That turns their countenances.

SICINIUS 'Tis this slave—
Go whip him 'fore the people's eyes—his raising,
Nothing but his report.

MESSENGER Yes, worthy sir,
The slave's report is seconded, and more,
More fearful, is delivered.

SICINIUS What more fearful?

MESSENGER
It is spoke freely out of many mouths—
How probable I do not know—that Martius,
Joined with Aufidius, leads a power 'gainst Rome
And vows revenge as spacious as between
The young'st and oldest thing.

SICINIUS This is most likely!

BRUTUS
Raised only that the weaker sort may wish
Good Martius home again.

SICINIUS The very trick on 't.

MENENIUS This is unlikely;
He and Aufidius can no more atone
Than violent'st contrariety.

*Enter ⌜a Second⌝ Messenger.*

⌜SECOND⌝ MESSENGER You are sent for to the Senate.
A fearful army, led by Caius Martius
Associated with Aufidius, rages
Upon our territories, and have already
O'erborne their way, consumed with fire and took
What lay before them.

*Enter Cominius.*

COMINIUS, ⌜*to the Tribunes*⌝ O, you have made good work!

MENENIUS What news? What news?

103. **holp:** helped; **ravish:** rape

104. **leads:** roofs of lead; **pates:** heads

107. **in . . . cement:** i.e., into **their** mortar

108. **franchises:** freedoms, full rights of citizenship; **stood:** insisted

109. **auger's bore:** tiny hole made by an auger, a carpenter's drilling tool

122. **apron-men:** craftsmen who wear aprons (See picture, page 196.) **stood:** depended; insisted

123. **voice:** votes; **occupation:** tradesmen

124. **garlic eaters:** commoners (an allusion to garlic's strong smell, which would make it unappealing to the nobility)

126. **Hercules:** The eleventh labor of Hercules' twelve was to pick the apples from a tree in a garden guarded by a dragon. (See picture, page 184.)

131. **smilingly:** cheerfully; **who:** i.e., whoever

133. **constant:** resolute; loyal (i.e., to Rome)

COMINIUS, ⌜*to the Tribunes*⌝
You have holp to ravish your own daughters and
To melt the city leads upon your pates,
To see your wives dishonored to your noses—
MENENIUS What's the news? What's the news?
COMINIUS, ⌜*to the Tribunes*⌝
Your temples burnèd in their cement, and
Your franchises, whereon you stood, confined
Into an auger's bore.
MENENIUS Pray now, your news?—
You have made fair work, I fear me.—Pray, your news?
If Martius should be joined with Volscians—
COMINIUS If?
He is their god; he leads them like a thing
Made by some other deity than Nature,
That shapes man better; and they follow him
Against us brats with no less confidence
Than boys pursuing summer butterflies
Or butchers killing flies.
MENENIUS, ⌜*to the Tribunes*⌝ You have made good work,
You and your apron-men, you that stood so much
Upon the voice of occupation and
The breath of garlic eaters!
COMINIUS
He'll shake your Rome about your ears.
MENENIUS
As Hercules did shake down mellow fruit.
You have made fair work.
BRUTUS But is this true, sir?
COMINIUS Ay, and you'll look pale
Before you find it other. All the regions
Do smilingly revolt, and who resists
Are mocked for valiant ignorance
And perish constant fools. Who is 't can blame him?
Your enemies and his find something in him.

135. **undone:** destroyed

140. **For:** i.e., as **for**

141. **charged:** would exhort

144. **showed:** would show

146. **brand:** torch

147. **face:** impudence, effrontery

148–49. **You . . . hands:** Proverbial: "To make a **fair** hand of a thing," here used ironically to mean "You have made a mess."

150. **crafts:** i.e., handicraftsmen, tradesmen; **crafted:** (1) exercised your trade; (2) used crafty devices

154. **S' incapable:** i.e., so **incapable; help:** remedy (with wordplay on **help** as "cure" for the **trembling** of line 153)

157. **clusters:** crowds

160. **roar:** i.e., perhaps, in pain; or, perhaps, for mercy

161. **second name of men: second** most renowned man; **his points:** i.e., him in detail (A "**point** of war" is a signal sounded by a trumpet, drum, etc.)

162. **he were his officer:** i.e., Aufidius **were** Coriolanus's (well-trained, obedient) **officer**

MENENIUS We are all undone, unless
The noble man have mercy.
COMINIUS Who shall ask it?
The Tribunes cannot do 't for shame; the people
Deserve such pity of him as the wolf
Does of the shepherds. For his best friends, if they
Should say "Be good to Rome," they charged him
even
As those should do that had deserved his hate
And therein showed like enemies.
MENENIUS 'Tis true.
If he were putting to my house the brand
That should consume it, I have not the face
To say "Beseech you, cease."—You have made fair
hands,
You and your crafts! You have crafted fair!
COMINIUS You have
brought
A trembling upon Rome such as was never
S' incapable of help.
TRIBUNES Say not we brought it.
MENENIUS
How? Was 't we? We loved him, but like beasts
And cowardly nobles, gave way unto your clusters,
Who did hoot him out o' th' city.
COMINIUS But I fear
They'll roar him in again. Tullus Aufidius,
The second name of men, obeys his points
As if he were his officer. Desperation
Is all the policy, strength, and defense
That Rome can make against them.

*Enter a troop of Citizens.*

MENENIUS Here come the
clusters.—
And is Aufidius with him? You are they

172. **coxcombs:** fools' heads (literally, caps of professional fools) (See picture, below.)

175. **coal:** charred remnant, cinder

182. **That:** i.e., **that** which

183–84. **though . . . will:** This contradiction was apparently in use as a paradox. A sermon survives from 1609 on the topic "**willingly against** my **will.**"

186. **cry:** pack

187. **Shall 's:** i.e., **shall** we go

190. **side:** faction

A professional fool wearing a coxcomb. (4.6.172)
From George Wither, *A collection of emblemes* . . . (1635).

That made the air unwholesome when you cast
Your stinking, greasy caps in hooting at
Coriolanus' exile. Now he's coming,
And not a hair upon a soldier's head
Which will not prove a whip. As many coxcombs
As you threw caps up will he tumble down
And pay you for your voices. 'Tis no matter.
If he could burn us all into one coal,
We have deserved it.

ALL ⌜CITIZENS⌝ Faith, we hear fearful news.

FIRST CITIZEN For mine own part,
When I said banish him, I said 'twas pity.

SECOND CITIZEN And so did I.

THIRD CITIZEN And so did I. And, to say the truth, so did very many of us. That we did we did for the best; and though we willingly consented to his banishment, yet it was against our will.

COMINIUS You're goodly things, you voices!

MENENIUS
You have made good work, you and your cry!—
Shall 's to the Capitol?

COMINIUS O, ay, what else? *Both exit.*

SICINIUS
Go, masters, get you home. Be not dismayed.
These are a side that would be glad to have
This true which they so seem to fear. Go home,
And show no sign of fear.

FIRST CITIZEN The gods be good to us! Come, masters, let's home. I ever said we were i' th' wrong when we banished him.

SECOND CITIZEN So did we all. But, come, let's home.
*Citizens exit.*

BRUTUS I do not like this news.

SICINIUS Nor I.

199. **Would:** i.e., I wish

**4.7** Aufidius, offended by the Volscian soldiers' preference for Coriolanus, begins plotting against him.

---

3. **use him:** i.e., **use** his name; **grace:** short prayer; **meat:** food

5. **dark'ned:** eclipsed, deprived of renown (See picture of a **dark'ned** sun, page 230.) **action:** fight

6. **own:** i.e., **own** men

8. **means I lame:** i.e., such **means** that **I** would **lame**

9. **more proudlier:** i.e., **more** proudly

10. **to my person:** i.e., to me

12. **changeling:** (1) renegade; (2) fickle person

15. **for your particular:** i.e., as far as you are concerned

17. **of yourself:** i.e., by **yourself**

20. **his account:** answering for **his** conduct

21. **urge:** allege

23. **vulgar eye:** i.e., notice of the common people; **bears:** i.e., carries out

24. **husbandry for:** management of (i.e., for the profit of)

BRUTUS
Let's to the Capitol. Would half my wealth
Would buy this for a lie.

SICINIUS Pray, let's go.

*Tribunes exit.*

⌜Scene 7⌝

*Enter Aufidius with his Lieutenant.*

AUFIDIUS Do they still fly to th' Roman?

LIEUTENANT
I do not know what witchcraft's in him, but
Your soldiers use him as the grace 'fore meat,
Their talk at table, and their thanks at end;
And you are dark'ned in this action, sir,
Even by your own.

AUFIDIUS I cannot help it now,
Unless by using means I lame the foot
Of our design. He bears himself more proudlier,
Even to my person, than I thought he would
When first I did embrace him. Yet his nature
In that's no changeling, and I must excuse
What cannot be amended.

LIEUTENANT Yet I wish, sir—
I mean for your particular—you had not
Joined in commission with him, but either
Have borne the action of yourself or else
To him had left it solely.

AUFIDIUS
I understand thee well, and be thou sure,
When he shall come to his account, he knows not
What I can urge against him, although it seems,
And so he thinks and is no less apparent
To th' vulgar eye, that he bears all things fairly,
And shows good husbandry for the Volscian state,

25. **achieve:** succeed

29. **carry:** take by force

30. **sits down:** lays siege

32. **too:** Throughout the play the **Senators** and **Patricians** seem to be the **nobility of Rome** (line 31).

34. **the repeal:** i.e., **the repeal** of Coriolanus's banishment; **as hasty:** i.e., **as** they were **hasty**

36. **osprey:** sea eagle (which preys on **fish**)

39. **even:** even-temperedly

40. **out of:** as a consequence of; **daily fortune:** i.e., always being successful

41. **happy:** fortunate

42. **disposing:** management; **chances:** opportunities

45. **casque:** soldier's helmet (See picture, page 166.) **cushion:** i.e., of a state official

47. **austerity and garb:** austere style (hendiadys) **garb:** demeanor, style

48. **controlled:** commanded

49. **spices:** traces

50. **free:** absolve, acquit

51. **So:** therefore; **merit:** excellence

52. **it:** perhaps, any mention of a fault in him

53. **Lie in:** depend on

55. **chair:** rostrum for public orations (See longer note, page 289.)

57. **One . . . nail:** Both statements are proverbial.

Fights dragonlike, and does achieve as soon
As draw his sword; yet he hath left undone
That which shall break his neck or hazard mine
Whene'er we come to our account.

LIEUTENANT

Sir, I beseech you, think you he'll carry Rome?

AUFIDIUS

All places yields to him ere he sits down,
And the nobility of Rome are his;
The Senators and Patricians love him too.
The Tribunes are no soldiers, and their people
Will be as rash in the repeal as hasty
To expel him thence. I think he'll be to Rome
As is the osprey to the fish, who takes it
By sovereignty of nature. First, he was
A noble servant to them, but he could not
Carry his honors even. Whether ⌜'twas⌝ pride,
Which out of daily fortune ever taints
The happy man; whether ⌜defect⌝ of judgment,
To fail in the disposing of those chances
Which he was lord of; or whether nature,
Not to be other than one thing, not moving
From th' casque to th' cushion, but commanding
  peace
Even with the same austerity and garb
As he controlled the war; but one of these—
As he hath spices of them all—not all,
For I dare so far free him—made him feared,
So hated, and so banished. But he has a merit
To choke it in the utt'rance. So our ⌜virtues⌝
Lie in th' interpretation of the time,
And power, unto itself most commendable,
Hath not a tomb so evident as a chair
T' extol what it hath done.
One fire drives out one fire, one nail one nail;

58–59. **strengths . . . fail:** Proverbial: "The strong man meets a stronger."

The sun "dark'ned." (4.7.5)

From Richard Day, *A booke of Christian prayers* . . . (1590).

Rights by rights ⌜falter⌝; strengths by strengths do
fail.
Come, let's away. When, Caius, Rome is thine,
Thou art poor'st of all; then shortly art thou mine.
*They exit.*

# CORIOLANUS

ACT 5

**5.1** After Cominius fails to persuade Coriolanus not to destroy Rome, Menenius agrees to try.

---

1. **he:** i.e., Cominius
2. **Which:** who; **sometime:** formerly
3. **particular:** personal way
5. **knee:** i.e., walk on your knees (as if you were penitents approaching a shrine)
6. **coyed:** "condescended unwillingly, with reserve and coldness" (George Steevens, 1773)
8. **would not seem:** i.e., pretended **not**
15. **o' th' fire:** i.e., out of the **fire;** or, perhaps, in the **fire**
18. **wracked:** caused the ruin of
19. **coals:** charcoal (formed from the imperfect combustion of wood); **noble memory:** splendid memorial (ironic)

# ACT 5

## ⌜Scene 1⌝

*Enter Menenius, Cominius, Sicinius, Brutus (the two Tribunes), with others.*

MENENIUS
No, I'll not go. You hear what he hath said
Which was sometime his general, who loved him
In a most dear particular. He called me father,
But what o' that? Go you that banished him;
A mile before his tent, fall down, and knee
The way into his mercy. Nay, if he coyed
To hear Cominius speak, I'll keep at home.

COMINIUS
He would not seem to know me.

MENENIUS
Do you hear?

COMINIUS
Yet one time he did call me by my name.
I urged our old acquaintance, and the drops
That we have bled together. "Coriolanus"
He would not answer to, forbade all names.
He was a kind of nothing, titleless,
Till he had forged himself a name o' th' fire
Of burning Rome.

MENENIUS, ⌜*to the Tribunes*⌝
Why, so; you have made good work!
A pair of tribunes that have wracked Rome
To make coals cheap! A noble memory!

20. **minded:** reminded, admonished

21. **When . . . expected:** i.e., the less **it was expected**

22. **It:** i.e., Cominius's implied request for pardon; **bare:** paltry; worthless; **of:** from

26. **offered:** tried

28–31. **He could . . . offense:** See longer note, page 289. **stay to:** tarry or delay in order to **in a pile:** i.e., out of or from **a pile** (The image is of separating wheat from **chaff.**) **noisome:** ill-smelling, offensive **chaff:** husks **grain:** i.e., kernel of wheat **nose:** smell **th' offense:** i.e., the offensive **noisome musty chaff**

38. **this so-never-needed help:** i.e., on **this** occasion when your **help** is **needed** as **never** before

39. **sure:** surely

41. **the . . . make:** i.e., **the army we** could raise on the spur of the moment

45. **should I do:** i.e., would **I do** there

COMINIUS
I minded him how royal 'twas to pardon
When it was less expected. He replied
It was a bare petition of a state
To one whom they had punished.

MENENIUS Very well.
Could he say less?

COMINIUS
I offered to awaken his regard
For 's private friends. His answer to me was
He could not stay to pick them in a pile
Of noisome musty chaff. He said 'twas folly
For one poor grain or two to leave unburnt
And still to nose th' offense.

MENENIUS For one poor grain or two!
I am one of those! His mother, wife, his child,
And this brave fellow too, we are the grains;
You are the musty chaff, and you are smelt
Above the moon. We must be burnt for you.

SICINIUS
Nay, pray, be patient. If you refuse your aid
In this so-never-needed help, yet do not
Upbraid 's with our distress. But sure, if you
Would be your country's pleader, your good tongue,
More than the instant army we can make,
Might stop our countryman.

MENENIUS No, I'll not meddle.

SICINIUS Pray you, go to him.

MENENIUS What should I do?

BRUTUS
Only make trial what your love can do
For Rome, towards Martius.

MENENIUS Well, and say that
Martius
Return me, as Cominius is returned, unheard,

51. **But as:** i.e., what if Coriolanus return me **but as**

52. **Grief-shot:** i.e., grief-stricken

54–55. **after the . . . well:** i.e., to the full extent of the goodness of your intention

58. **hum:** i.e., make a sound of disapproval; **unhearts:** disheartens

59. **He was:** i.e., perhaps **he was;** or, undoubtedly **he was; taken well:** i.e., engaged at the right time

60. **The veins:** i.e., when **the veins** are

63. **conveyances:** i.e., channels

64. **suppler:** more compliant

66. **dieted to:** i.e., fed in preparation for

70. **prove:** try

71. **Speed how it will:** i.e., no matter what happens

72. **success:** outcome (good or bad)

75. **in gold:** i.e., **in** a chair of **gold,** on a throne

76. **his injury:** the wrongful treatment he suffered

79–82. **What . . . Conditions:** i.e., **he sent in writing after me** a list of **what he would do** and a list of **what he would not do,** having sworn **an oath** (perhaps to the Volscians) that we must **yield to his** listed **conditions**

83. **his noble . . . wife:** i.e., **his noble . . . wife** succeed (The sentence structure breaks down, but the sense is clear.)

What then? But as a discontented friend,
Grief-shot with his unkindness? Say 't be so?

SICINIUS Yet your good will
Must have that thanks from Rome after the measure
As you intended well.

MENENIUS I'll undertake 't.
I think he'll hear me. Yet to bite his lip
And hum at good Cominius much unhearts me.
He was not taken well; he had not dined.
The veins unfilled, our blood is cold, and then
We pout upon the morning, are unapt
To give or to forgive; but when we have stuffed
These pipes and these conveyances of our blood
With wine and feeding, we have suppler souls
Than in our priestlike fasts. Therefore I'll watch him
Till he be dieted to my request,
And then I'll set upon him.

BRUTUS
You know the very road into his kindness
And cannot lose your way.

MENENIUS Good faith, I'll prove him,
Speed how it will. I shall ere long have knowledge
Of my success. *He exits.*

COMINIUS He'll never hear him.

SICINIUS Not?

COMINIUS
I tell you, he does sit in gold, his eye
Red as 'twould burn Rome; and his injury
The jailor to his pity. I kneeled before him;
'Twas very faintly he said "Rise"; dismissed me
Thus with his speechless hand. What he would do
He sent in writing after me; what he
Would not, bound with an oath to yield to his
Conditions. So that all hope is vain
Unless his noble mother and his wife,
Who, as I hear, mean to solicit him

86. **fair:** kindly

**5.2** Menenius fails to shake Coriolanus's determination to destroy Rome.

---

1. **Whence:** from where
3. **by your leave:** an apology for taking a liberty
12. **Good my friends:** i.e., **my good friends**
14. **it is lots to blanks:** i.e., (1) "**it is** a thousand to one"; or, possibly, (2) "chances are"
16. **virtue:** power, influence
17. **passable:** sufficient
18. **fellow:** a term of contempt
19. **is my lover:** i.e., loves me, is my friend
22. **verified:** supported by testimony
23. **with all the size:** i.e., to the full extent
24. **suffer:** allow

For mercy to his country. Therefore let's hence
And with our fair entreaties haste them on.
*They exit.*

## ⌜Scene 2⌝

*Enter Menenius to the Watch, or Guard.*

FIRST WATCH Stay! Whence are you?
SECOND WATCH Stand, and go back.
MENENIUS
You guard like men; 'tis well. But by your leave,
I am an officer of state and come
To speak with Coriolanus.
FIRST WATCH From whence?
MENENIUS From Rome.
FIRST WATCH
You may not pass; you must return. Our general
Will no more hear from thence.
SECOND WATCH
You'll see your Rome embraced with fire before
You'll speak with Coriolanus.
MENENIUS Good my friends,
If you have heard your general talk of Rome
And of his friends there, it is lots to blanks
My name hath touched your ears. It is Menenius.
FIRST WATCH
Be it so; go back. The virtue of your name
Is not here passable.
MENENIUS I tell thee, fellow,
Thy general is my lover. I have been
The book of his good acts, whence men have read
His fame unparalleled happily amplified;
For I have ever verified my friends—
Of whom he's chief—with all the size that verity
Would without lapsing suffer. Nay, sometimes,

25. **bowl:** the ball in lawn bowling; **subtle:** tricky; **ground:** bowling green

26. **throw:** distance to be thrown

27. **stamped:** given the mark of approval to; **leasing:** lie, falsehood

32. **lie:** with possible wordplay on *fornicate*

34. **factionary on the party:** i.e., a member of the faction

36. **Howsoever:** however, notwithstanding that

44. **out your:** i.e., **out** of **your**

47. **front:** confront, face; **easy:** insignificant

49. **decayed:** impaired, physically wasted

50. **dotant:** dotard, one in his dotage

56. **Sirrah:** a term of address to a male social inferior

57. **use:** treat; **estimation:** esteem, respect

Alexander the Great. (5.4.23)
From Valentin Thilo, *Icones heroum* . . . (1589).

Like to a bowl upon a subtle ground,
I have tumbled past the throw, and in his praise
Have almost stamped the leasing. Therefore, fellow,
I must have leave to pass.

FIRST WATCH Faith, sir, if you had told as many lies in his behalf as you have uttered words in your own, you should not pass here, no, though it were as virtuous to lie as to live chastely. Therefore, go back.

MENENIUS Prithee, fellow, remember my name is Menenius, always factionary on the party of your general.

SECOND WATCH Howsoever you have been his liar, as you say you have, I am one that, telling true under him, must say you cannot pass. Therefore, go back.

MENENIUS Has he dined, can'st thou tell? For I would not speak with him till after dinner.

FIRST WATCH You are a Roman, are you?

MENENIUS I am, as thy general is.

FIRST WATCH Then you should hate Rome as he does. Can you, when you have pushed out your gates the very defender of them, and, in a violent popular ignorance given your enemy your shield, think to front his revenges with the easy groans of old women, the virginal palms of your daughters, or with the palsied intercession of such a decayed dotant as you seem to be? Can you think to blow out the intended fire your city is ready to flame in with such weak breath as this? No, you are deceived. Therefore, back to Rome and prepare for your execution. You are condemned. Our general has sworn you out of reprieve and pardon.

MENENIUS Sirrah, if thy captain knew I were here, he would use me with estimation.

FIRST WATCH Come, my captain knows you not.

MENENIUS I mean thy general.

61. **half pint of blood:** Age was thought to lessen or dry up the **blood.**

62. **of your having:** i.e., that you will get

65. **companion:** like *fellow,* a term of contempt

66. **say:** deliver; **errand:** message

67. **in estimation:** i.e., held in esteem

67–68. **Jack guardant:** knave of a guard **Jack:** knave **guardant:** a heraldic term referring to a beast that has its full face to the viewer

68. **office me:** drive me by virtue of his office

69. **entertainment with:** i.e., reception by

71. **spectatorship:** presentation to the eyes of spectators

72. **presently:** immediately

73–74. **The glorious gods sit:** i.e., may **the glorious gods sit**

74. **synod:** assembly

74–75. **particular:** personal

78. **hardly:** not easily; **moved:** persuaded

80–81. **your gates:** i.e., Rome's **gates**

81. **conjure:** appeal earnestly to

82. **petitionary:** petitioning

84. **varlet:** rascal; **block:** blockhead

88. **affairs:** pursuits

89. **servanted:** put in subjection; **owe:** own

90. **properly:** i.e., myself; **remission:** i.e., capacity to grant pardon

91–93. **That . . . much:** i.e., Rome's ungrateful **forgetfulness** will **poison** our former friendship, instead of **pity** taking note of **how** friendly we once were **familiar:** friendly

FIRST WATCH My general cares not for you. Back, I say, go, lest I let forth your half pint of blood. Back! That's the utmost of your having. Back!

MENENIUS Nay, but fellow, fellow—

*Enter Coriolanus with Aufidius.*

CORIOLANUS What's the matter?

MENENIUS ⌜*to First Watch*⌝ Now, you companion, I'll say an errand for you. You shall know now that I am in estimation; you shall perceive that a Jack guardant cannot office me from my son Coriolanus. Guess but ⌜by⌝ my entertainment with him if thou stand'st not i' th' state of hanging or of some death more long in spectatorship and crueler in suffering; behold now presently, and swoon for what's to come upon thee. ⌜(*To Coriolanus.*)⌝ The glorious gods sit in hourly synod about thy particular prosperity and love thee no worse than thy old father Menenius does! O my son, my son! ⌜(*He weeps.*)⌝ Thou art preparing fire for us; look thee, here's water to quench it. I was hardly moved to come to thee; but being assured none but myself could move thee, I have been blown out of your gates with sighs, and conjure thee to pardon Rome and thy petitionary countrymen. The good gods assuage thy wrath and turn the dregs of it upon this varlet here, this, who, like a block, hath denied my access to thee.

CORIOLANUS Away!

MENENIUS How? Away?

CORIOLANUS

Wife, mother, child, I know not. My affairs
Are servanted to others. Though I owe
My revenge properly, my remission lies
In Volscian breasts. That we have been familiar,
Ingrate forgetfulness shall poison rather

94. **suits:** petitions
95. **for:** because
99. **my beloved:** one loved by me
100. **temper:** temperament
104. **shent:** scolded
109. **For:** i.e., as **for**
110. **so slight:** of such little worth
111. **by himself:** i.e., by his own hand
112. **that:** i.e., **that** which
113. **long:** i.e., for a **long** time

**5.3** Volumnia, accompanied by Virgilia, Valeria, and young Martius, persuades Coriolanus to spare Rome.

---

2. **Set down:** encamp; **host:** army; **action:** i.e., campaign, military **action**

Than pity note how much. Therefore, begone.
Mine ears against your suits are stronger than
Your gates against my force. Yet, for I loved thee,
Take this along; I write it for thy sake,
⌜*He gives Menenius a paper.*⌝
And would have sent it. Another word, Menenius,
I will not hear thee speak.—This man, Aufidius,
Was my beloved in Rome; yet thou behold'st.

AUFIDIUS You keep a constant temper. *They exit.*
*The Guard and Menenius remain.*

FIRST WATCH Now, sir, is your name Menenius?

SECOND WATCH 'Tis a spell, you see, of much power. You know the way home again.

FIRST WATCH Do you hear how we are shent for keeping your Greatness back?

SECOND WATCH What cause do you think I have to swoon?

MENENIUS I neither care for th' world nor your general. For such things as you, I can scarce think there's any, you're so slight. He that hath a will to die by himself fears it not from another. Let your general do his worst. For you, be that you are, long; and your misery increase with your age! I say to you, as I was said to, away! *He exits.*

FIRST WATCH A noble fellow, I warrant him.

SECOND WATCH The worthy fellow is our general. He's the rock, the oak not to be wind-shaken.
*Watch exit.*

## ⌜Scene 3⌝

*Enter Coriolanus and Aufidius.*

CORIOLANUS
We will before the walls of Rome tomorrow
Set down our host. My partner in this action,

3. **plainly:** openly

5. **ends:** purposes

7. **general suit:** petition of the people

13. **godded me:** made me into a god; **latest:** last; **refuge:** means of obtaining safety

15. **showed:** appeared; **sourly:** as sullen, cross

16. **first conditions:** i.e., terms already offered Cominius

17. **to grace him only:** i.e., **only** for the purpose of conferring honor on **him**

18. **That:** who

20. **Nor:** i.e., neither

25. **mold:** matrix, model

26. **trunk:** body; **framed:** formed, fashioned

27. **out:** (1) i.e., begone, get **out;** or, (2) an expression of abhorrence

30. **doves' eyes:** See the Song of Solomon 1.14: "My love, behold thou art fair . . . : thine **eyes** are like the dove's."

32. **earth:** dust, clay (the supposed material of which the body is created) See Genesis 2.7.

34. **Olympus:** in classical mythology, the mountain that was the home of the gods

You must report to th' Volscian lords how plainly
I have borne this business.

AUFIDIUS Only their ends
You have respected, stopped your ears against
The general suit of Rome, never admitted
A private whisper, no, not with such friends
That thought them sure of you.

CORIOLANUS This last old man,
Whom with a cracked heart I have sent to Rome,
Loved me above the measure of a father,
Nay, godded me indeed. Their latest refuge
Was to send him, for whose old love I have—
Though I showed sourly to him—once more offered
The first conditions, which they did refuse
And cannot now accept, to grace him only
That thought he could do more. A very little
I have yielded to. Fresh embassies and suits,
Nor from the state nor private friends, hereafter
Will I lend ear to. *Shout within.*
Ha? What shout is this?
Shall I be tempted to infringe my vow
In the same time 'tis made? I will not.

*Enter Virgilia, Volumnia, Valeria, young Martius, with Attendants.*

My wife comes foremost, then the honored mold
Wherein this trunk was framed, and in her hand
The grandchild to her blood. But out, affection!
All bond and privilege of nature, break!
Let it be virtuous to be obstinate. ⌜*Virgilia curtsies.*⌝
What is that curtsy worth? Or those doves' eyes,
Which can make gods forsworn? I melt and am not
Of stronger earth than others. ⌜*Volumnia bows.*⌝
My mother bows,
As if Olympus to a molehill should
In supplication nod; and my young boy

36. **aspect:** facial expression; **intercession:** pleading

40. **author of:** the one who begets

44. **delivers:** presents (While Coriolanus's words in line 43 may imply that he or his eyes have changed, Virgilia states that what he sees, his family, has been changed by **sorrow.**)

47. **am out: am** at a loss from failure of memory and self-possession

49. **tyranny:** cruelty

50. **For that:** i.e., because I have asked your forgiveness

53. **jealous queen of heaven:** Juno, goddess of marriage and queen of the gods (See picture, page 188.)

54. **true:** faithful

55. **virgined it:** remained a virgin; **prate:** chatter

58. **deep:** profound; **more impression:** (1) stronger effect; (2) deeper mark in the earth

60. **blest:** i.e., with my maternal blessing

62–63. **unproperly . . . duty:** improperly **show** deference (By custom **the child** shows respect for the **parent** [line 64].)

66. **corrected:** chastised, rebuked

67. **hungry:** a word that usually modifies "sea," but that here is transferred to its **beach**

Hath an aspect of intercession which
Great Nature cries "Deny not!" Let the Volsces
Plow Rome and harrow Italy. I'll never
Be such a gosling to obey instinct, but stand
As if a man were author of himself,
And knew no other kin.

VIRGILIA
My lord and husband.

CORIOLANUS
These eyes are not the same I wore in Rome.

VIRGILIA
The sorrow that delivers us thus changed
Makes you think so.

CORIOLANUS
Like a dull actor now,
I have forgot my part, and I am out,
Even to a full disgrace. Best of my flesh,
Forgive my tyranny, but do not say
For that "Forgive our Romans." ⌜*They kiss.*⌝
O, a kiss
Long as my exile, sweet as my revenge!
Now, by the jealous queen of heaven, that kiss
I carried from thee, dear, and my true lip
Hath virgined it e'er since. You gods! I ⌜prate⌝
And the most noble mother of the world
Leave unsaluted. Sink, my knee, i' th' earth; *Kneels.*
Of thy deep duty more impression show
Than that of common sons.

VOLUMNIA
O, stand up blest,
⌜*He rises.*⌝
Whilst with no softer cushion than the flint
I kneel before thee and unproperly
Show duty, as mistaken all this while
Between the child and parent. ⌜*She kneels.*⌝

CORIOLANUS
What's this?
Your knees to me? To your corrected son?
⌜*He raises her up.*⌝
Then let the pebbles on the hungry beach

68. **Fillip:** strike against

70. **Murdering impossibility:** i.e., making anything possible

71. **slight:** trifling

73. **holp:** helped; **frame:** (1) form (see lines 25–26, above); (2) train, discipline

74. **Publicola:** an early Roman consul

75–77. **moon . . . temple: Valeria** is here described as being **as chaste as** Diana, **moon** goddess and goddess of chastity. **curdied:** congealed

78. **epitome:** condensed record, representation in miniature; abridgment

79. **interpretation:** explanation, commentary (and thus expansion)

80. **show like:** look **like**

81. **god of soldiers:** Mars

82. **inform:** imbue, inspire

84. **stick:** (1) stand fast; (2) stand out

85. **seamark:** conspicuous object, distinguishable at sea, that serves as a guide to sailors; **standing:** enduring; **flaw:** blast of wind

86. **eye thee:** keep you in view

87. **sirrah:** term of address to a male social inferior or, as here, to a boy

88. **brave:** a word expressing general admiration and praise ("good," "fine," "worthy," etc.)

90. **suitors:** petitioners

91. **peace:** silence

93. **forsworn:** sworn not

94. **held:** regarded; **denials:** as **denials** of what you ask

95. **capitulate:** negotiate

96. **mechanics:** craftsmen, working men

98. **allay:** assuage, alleviate

Fillip the stars! Then let the mutinous winds
Strike the proud cedars 'gainst the fiery sun,
Murdering impossibility to make
What cannot be slight work.

VOLUMNIA Thou art my warrior;
I ⌜holp⌝ to frame thee. Do you know this lady?

CORIOLANUS
The noble sister of Publicola,
The moon of Rome, chaste as the icicle
That's curdied by the frost from purest snow
And hangs on Dian's temple!—Dear Valeria.

VOLUMNIA, ⌜*presenting young Martius*⌝
This is a poor epitome of yours,
Which by th' interpretation of full time
May show like all yourself.

CORIOLANUS, ⌜*to young Martius*⌝ The god of soldiers,
With the consént of supreme Jove, inform
Thy thoughts with nobleness, that thou mayst prove
To shame unvulnerable, and stick i' th' wars
Like a great seamark standing every flaw
And saving those that eye thee.

VOLUMNIA, ⌜*to young Martius*⌝ Your knee, sirrah.
⌜*He kneels.*⌝

CORIOLANUS That's my brave boy!

VOLUMNIA
Even he, your wife, this lady, and myself
Are suitors to you. ⌜*Young Martius rises.*⌝

CORIOLANUS I beseech you, peace;
Or if you'd ask, remember this before:
The thing I have forsworn to grant may never
Be held by you denials. Do not bid me
Dismiss my soldiers or capitulate
Again with Rome's mechanics. Tell me not
Wherein I seem unnatural; desire not
T' allay my rages and revenges with
Your colder reasons.

101. **have said:** i.e., **have** thus **said**
104. **fail in:** i.e., **fail** to grant
106. **mark:** pay attention; **we'll:** i.e., I will
109. **raiment:** clothes
110. **state of bodies:** i.e., emaciated **state; bewray:** expose, reveal
111. **Think with thyself:** consider
121. **poor we:** i.e., **poor** us
122. **capital:** deadly
126. **Whereto we are bound:** to which (i.e., such prayer) **we are** obligated
127. **or we:** i.e., either **we**
130. **evident:** certain
131. **which:** i.e., whichever
132. **foreign recreant:** i.e., deserter to **a foreign** power

VOLUMNIA O, no more, no more!
You have said you will not grant us anything;
For we have nothing else to ask but that
Which you deny already. Yet we will ask,
That if you fail in our request, the blame
May hang upon your hardness. Therefore hear us.

CORIOLANUS
Aufidius, and you Volsces, mark, for we'll
Hear naught from Rome in private. ⌜*He sits.*⌝ Your request?

VOLUMNIA
Should we be silent and not speak, our raiment
And state of bodies would bewray what life
We have led since thy exile. Think with thyself
How more unfortunate than all living women
Are we come hither; since that thy sight, which should
Make our eyes flow with joy, hearts dance with comforts,
Constrains them weep and shake with fear and sorrow,
Making the mother, wife, and child to see
The son, the husband, and the father tearing
His country's bowels out. And to poor we
Thine enmity's most capital. Thou barr'st us
Our prayers to the gods, which is a comfort
That all but we enjoy. For how can we—
Alas, how can we—for our country pray,
Whereto we are bound, together with thy victory,
Whereto we are bound? Alack, or we must lose
The country, our dear nurse, or else thy person,
Our comfort in the country. We must find
An evident calamity, though we had
Our wish, which side should win, for either thou
Must as a foreign recreant be led
With manacles through our streets, or else

135. **bear the palm:** carry a branch of the palm tree as a sign of your victory

138. **determine:** end (and thereby **determine** one or the other outcome described in lines 131–36)

139. **grace:** mercy

150. **nor child:** i.e., neither **child**

158. **while:** at the same time that

161. **all-hail:** salutation of respect

163. **end:** result

167. **chronicle thus writ:** i.e., historical record will be written as follows

168. **it:** i.e., his nobility

Volumnia and other Roman ladies plead with Coriolanus. (5.3)
From Livy, *Decades* . . . [1511].

Triumphantly tread on thy country's ruin
And bear the palm for having bravely shed
Thy wife and children's blood. For myself, son,
I purpose not to wait on fortune till
These wars determine. If I cannot persuade thee
Rather to show a noble grace to both parts
Than seek the end of one, thou shalt no sooner
March to assault thy country than to tread—
Trust to 't, thou shalt not—on thy mother's womb
That brought thee to this world.

VIRGILIA Ay, and mine,
That brought you forth this boy to keep your name
Living to time.

YOUNG MARTIUS He shall not tread on me.
I'll run away till I am bigger, but then I'll fight.

CORIOLANUS
Not of a woman's tenderness to be
Requires nor child nor woman's face to see.—
I have sat too long. ⌜*He rises.*⌝

VOLUMNIA Nay, go not from us thus.
If it were so, that our request did tend
To save the Romans, thereby to destroy
The Volsces whom you serve, you might condemn
us
As poisonous of your honor. No, our suit
Is that you reconcile them, while the Volsces
May say "This mercy we have showed," the Romans
"This we received," and each in either side
Give the all-hail to thee and cry "Be blest
For making up this peace!" Thou know'st, great son,
The end of war's uncertain, but this certain,
That, if thou conquer Rome, the benefit
Which thou shalt thereby reap is such a name
Whose repetition will be dogged with curses,
Whose chronicle thus writ: "The man was noble,
But with his last attempt he wiped it out,

171. **affected:** assumed; aimed at; **fine strains:** niceties, refinements (Johnson 1765)

172. **graces of the gods:** described below in lines 173–75 as the terror inspired by Jupiter's thunderbolt, combined with the mercy of directing it only at **an oak** (See picture, page 146.)

173. **the wide . . . air:** In maps of this period, the winds are pictured as issuing from puffed-out cheeks associated with Aeolus, god of the winds.

174. **charge:** arm, load; **sulfur:** lightning and thunder; **bolt:** thunderbolt

177. **Still:** always

179. **move:** persuade

181. **prate:** chatter

182. **Like one . . . stocks:** i.e., to no effect (The **stocks** were an instrument of punishment and public shaming that imprisoned the ankles in a wooden frame.)

184. **fond of:** eager for; **second brood:** further offspring

186. **Loaden:** loaded

187. **spurn:** thrust

189. **thou restrain'st:** you withhold; **duty:** respect

192. **'longs:** belongs

195. **behold 's:** i.e., **behold** us

196. **tell:** say; **would:** wishes to

197. **for fellowship:** i.e., because the rest of us do

198. **reason:** support by argument

200. **to his:** i.e., for **his**

Destroyed his country, and his name remains
To th' ensuing age abhorred." Speak to me, son.
Thou hast affected the ⌜fine⌝ strains of honor
To imitate the graces of the gods,
To tear with thunder the wide cheeks o' th' air
And yet to ⌜charge⌝ thy sulfur with a bolt
That should but rive an oak. Why dost not speak?
Think'st thou it honorable for a noble man
Still to remember wrongs?—Daughter, speak you.
He cares not for your weeping.—Speak thou, boy.
Perhaps thy childishness will move him more
Than can our reasons.—There's no man in the world
More bound to 's mother, yet here he lets me prate
Like one i' th' stocks. Thou hast never in thy life
Showed thy dear mother any courtesy
When she, poor hen, fond of no second brood,
Has ⌜clucked⌝ thee to the wars and safely home,
Loaden with honor. Say my request's unjust
And spurn me back; but if it be not so,
Thou art not honest, and the gods will plague thee
That thou restrain'st from me the duty which
To a mother's part belongs.—He turns away.—
Down, ladies! Let us shame him with our knees.
To his surname Coriolanus 'longs more pride
Than pity to our prayers. Down! An end.
⌜*They kneel.*⌝
This is the last. So, we will home to Rome
And die among our neighbors.—Nay, behold 's.
This boy that cannot tell what he would have,
But kneels and holds up hands for fellowship,
Does reason our petition with more strength
Than thou hast to deny 't.—Come, let us go.
⌜*They rise.*⌝
This fellow had a Volscian to his mother,
His wife is in Corioles, and his child

202. **dispatch:** dismissal

203. **hushed:** silenced

207. **unnatural scene:** i.e., family tableau that is **unnatural** in that the mother, who had knelt to her son, is now, in effect, sacrificing him for her own and the city's good

209. **happy:** fortunate

212. **mortal:** i.e., mortally, fatally

213. **true wars:** i.e., **wars** according to my promise

214. **convenient:** suitable, proper

217. **withal:** i.e., with it, by it

220. **sweat compassion:** i.e., weep

223. **Stand to:** support

225. **At difference:** in disagreement; **in thee:** i.e., within yourself; **work:** shape, form

226. **Myself:** i.e., for **myself; a former fortune:** i.e., a prosperous condition such as I had before

227. **by and by:** soon

228. **drink together:** i.e., according to custom when a peace is concluded (See, for example, Shakespeare's *Henry IV, Part 2* 4.1.311–24.)

228–29. **bear . . . words:** i.e., take **back** a written treaty

230. **like conditions:** i.e., the same **conditions** as already expressed in **words** (line 229); **countersealed:** sealed with an additional seal by way of sanctioning them

Like him by chance.—Yet give us our dispatch.
I am hushed until our city be afire,
And then I'll speak a little.
*⌜He⌝ holds her by the hand, silent.*

CORIOLANUS O mother, mother!
What have you done? Behold, the heavens do ope,
The gods look down, and this unnatural scene
They laugh at. O, my mother, mother, O!
You have won a happy victory to Rome,
But, for your son—believe it, O, believe it!—
Most dangerously you have with him prevailed,
If not most mortal to him. But let it come.—
Aufidius, though I cannot make true wars,
I'll frame convenient peace. Now, good Aufidius,
Were you in my stead, would you have heard
A mother less? Or granted less, Aufidius?

AUFIDIUS
I was moved withal.

CORIOLANUS I dare be sworn you were.
And, sir, it is no little thing to make
Mine eyes to sweat compassion. But, good sir,
What peace you'll make advise me. For my part,
I'll not to Rome. I'll back with you; and pray you,
Stand to me in this cause.—O mother!—Wife!
*⌜He speaks with them aside.⌝*

AUFIDIUS, *⌜aside⌝*
I am glad thou hast set thy mercy and thy honor
At difference in thee. Out of that I'll work
Myself a former fortune.

CORIOLANUS, *⌜to the Women⌝* Ay, by and by;
But we will drink together, and you shall bear
A better witness back than words, which we,
On like conditions, will have countersealed.
Come, enter with us. Ladies, you deserve
To have a temple built you. All the swords

233. **her confederate arms:** i.e., Italy's united **arms** (weapons and armor)

**5.4** News arrives in Rome of Volumnia's success.

---

1. **yond:** yonder

1–2. **coign, cornerstone:** names for the large stones used in forming the corners of buildings

8. **stay upon:** wait for

10. **condition:** character, moral nature

11. **differency:** difference; **grub:** larva

12. **your butterfly:** i.e., this **butterfly**

17. **an . . . horse:** i.e., **an . . . horse** remembers its dam, or mother

18. **tartness of:** i.e., severe expression on

19. **engine:** machine used in war (a battering ram, catapult, etc.)

21. **corslet:** body armor; **knell:** the ringing of a bell to announce a death; **hum:** murmur; or, sound of disapproval

22. **battery:** artillery bombardment (an anachronism); **state:** raised chair of state, throne

22–23. **thing . . . Alexander:** statue **made** to resemble **Alexander** the Great, who conquered Greece and Asia in the fourth century B.C.E. (See picture, page 242.)

24–25. **He wants . . . throne in:** In Isaiah, God is described as inhabiting **eternity** and as saying "the **heaven** is my **throne**" (58.15; 66.1). **wants:** lacks

27. **in the character:** i.e., according to what his looks indicate; **Mark:** observe

In Italy, and her confederate arms,
Could not have made this peace.

*They exit.*

## ⌜Scene 4⌝

*Enter Menenius and Sicinius.*

MENENIUS See you yond coign o' th' Capitol, yond cornerstone?

SICINIUS Why, what of that?

MENENIUS If it be possible for you to displace it with your little finger, there is some hope the ladies of Rome, especially his mother, may prevail with him. But I say there is no hope in 't. Our throats are sentenced and stay upon execution.

SICINIUS Is 't possible that so short a time can alter the condition of a man?

MENENIUS There is differency between a grub and a butterfly, yet your butterfly was a grub. This Martius is grown from man to dragon. He has wings; he's more than a creeping thing.

SICINIUS He loved his mother dearly.

MENENIUS So did he me; and he no more remembers his mother now than an eight-year-old horse. The tartness of his face sours ripe grapes. When he walks, he moves like an engine, and the ground shrinks before his treading. He is able to pierce a corslet with his eye, talks like a knell, and his hum is a battery. He sits in his state as a thing made for Alexander. What he bids be done is finished with his bidding. He wants nothing of a god but eternity and a heaven to throne in.

SICINIUS Yes, mercy, if you report him truly.

MENENIUS I paint him in the character. Mark what mercy his mother shall bring from him. There is

31. **long of:** because of

37. **fly:** flee

39. **hale:** drag

41. **death by inches:** i.e., a slow **death**

44. **are dislodged:** have left their place of encampment

46. **expulsion of the Tarquins:** i.e., **expulsion of** Rome's last kings and the beginning of the Roman Republic

50. **lurked:** hidden, lived in retirement

51. **arch:** i.e., of a bridge; **blown:** wind-blown; swollen

52. **the recomforted:** those who have experienced relief

52 SD. **hautboys:** wooden double-reed wind instruments (See picture, page 268.)

53. **sackbuts:** bass trumpets with slides like trombones; **psalteries:** stringed instruments somewhat like harps

54. **Tabors:** small drums

no more mercy in him than there is milk in a male tiger. That shall our poor city find, and all this is long of you.

SICINIUS The gods be good unto us.

MENENIUS No, in such a case the gods will not be good unto us. When we banished him, we respected not them; and he returning to break our necks, they respect not us.

*Enter a Messenger.*

MESSENGER, ⌜*to Sicinius*⌝
Sir, if you'd save your life, fly to your house.
The plebeians have got your fellow tribune
And hale him up and down, all swearing if
The Roman ladies bring not comfort home,
They'll give him death by inches.

*Enter another Messenger.*

SICINIUS What's the news?

⌜SECOND⌝ MESSENGER
Good news, good news! The ladies have prevailed.
The Volscians are dislodged and Martius gone.
A merrier day did never yet greet Rome,
No, not th' expulsion of the Tarquins.

SICINIUS Friend,
Art thou certain this is true? Is 't most certain?

⌜SECOND⌝ MESSENGER
As certain as I know the sun is fire.
Where have you lurked that you make doubt of it?
Ne'er through an arch so hurried the blown tide
As the recomforted through th' gates. Why, hark you!

*Trumpets, hautboys, drums beat, all together.*

The trumpets, sackbuts, psalteries, and fifes,
Tabors and cymbals, and the shouting Romans
Make the sun dance. Hark you! *A shout within.*

62. **doit:** Dutch copper coin of small value

62 SD. **Sound still with:** i.e., continue the sound of

67. **at point:** about

**5.5** The Romans honor Volumnia as she returns.

---

3. **fires:** bonfires (an English, not a Roman, mode of celebration)

6. **Repeal him:** recall him from exile

"Hark, the trumpets!" (2.1.161–62)
From Guillaume Du Choul, *Los discursos de la religion* . . . (1579).

MENENIUS This is good news.
I will go meet the ladies. This Volumnia
Is worth of consuls, senators, patricians
A city full; of tribunes such as you
A sea and land full. You have prayed well today.
This morning for ten thousand of your throats
I'd not have given a doit. Hark, how they joy!
*Sound still with the shouts.*

SICINIUS, ⌜*to Second Messenger*⌝ First, the gods bless you for your tidings; next, accept my thankfulness.

⌜SECOND⌝ MESSENGER
Sir, we have all great cause to give great thanks.

SICINIUS They are near the city?

⌜SECOND⌝ MESSENGER Almost at point to enter.

SICINIUS We'll meet them, and help the joy.
*They exit.*

## ⌜Scene 5⌝

*Enter two Senators, with Ladies* ⌜*(Volumnia, Virgilia, Valeria)*⌝ *passing over the stage, with other Lords.*

SENATOR
Behold our patroness, the life of Rome!
Call all your tribes together, praise the gods,
And make triumphant fires. Strew flowers before
them,
Unshout the noise that banished Martius,
Repeal him with the welcome of his mother.
Cry "Welcome, ladies, welcome!"

ALL Welcome, ladies, welcome!
*A flourish with drums and trumpets.*
⌜*They exit.*⌝

**5.6** Aufidius and his fellow conspirators, on their return to Corioles, publicly assassinate Coriolanus.

---

6. **Him:** i.e., he whom

7. **ports:** gates

9. **purge himself:** establish his innocence; **Dispatch:** complete this business

13. **alms:** good works

14. **with his:** i.e., by **his**

17. **parties:** partners, accessories

18. **Of your:** i.e., from **your**

22. **difference:** disagreement

25–26. **admits . . . construction:** i.e., can be interpreted favorably

26. **raised:** promoted, elevated; **pawned:** pledged

27. **truth:** loyalty; **heightened:** exalted

An hautboy. (5.4.52 SD)
From Balthasar Küchler,
*Repraesentatio der fürstlichen Auffzug* . . . [1611].

⌜Scene 6⌝

*Enter Tullus Aufidius, with Attendants.*

AUFIDIUS
Go tell the lords o' th' city I am here.
Deliver them this paper. ⌜*(He gives them a paper.)*⌝
Having read it,
Bid them repair to th' marketplace, where I,
Even in theirs and in the commons' ears,
Will vouch the truth of it. Him I accuse
The city ports by this hath entered and
Intends t' appear before the people, hoping
To purge himself with words. Dispatch.
⌜*The Attendants exit.*⌝

*Enter three or four Conspirators of Aufidius's faction.*

Most welcome!

FIRST CONSPIRATOR
How is it with our general?

AUFIDIUS
Even so
As with a man by his own alms empoisoned
And with his charity slain.

SECOND CONSPIRATOR
Most noble sir,
If you do hold the same intent wherein
You wished us parties, we'll deliver you
Of your great danger.

AUFIDIUS
Sir, I cannot tell.
We must proceed as we do find the people.

THIRD CONSPIRATOR
The people will remain uncertain whilst
'Twixt you there's difference, but the fall of either
Makes the survivor heir of all.

AUFIDIUS
I know it,
And my pretext to strike at him admits
A good construction. I raised him, and I pawned
Mine honor for his truth, who, being so heightened,

28. **his new plants:** i.e., the Volscians

31. **free:** unrestrained

32. **stoutness:** stubbornness, arrogance

35. **spoke of:** i.e., if you had not interrupted me

38. **Made . . . me:** united with him on equal terms in the service of the state; **gave him way:** i.e., **gave way** to **him**

40. **files:** rows of troops

41. **designments:** designs, undertakings

42. **holp:** helped

43. **end:** gather as, store as

46. **waged:** paid, rewarded; **countenance:** demeanor; look

47. **mercenary:** a hired soldier

49. **in the last:** at **last**

50. **carried:** won; **that we:** i.e., we

52. **There:** i.e., that

53. **sinews:** strength; nerves; **upon:** against

54. **rheum:** i.e., tears

56. **action:** i.e., campaign

57. **me:** myself

58. **native town:** See longer note, page 289. **post:** messenger

He watered his new plants with dews of flattery,
Seducing so my friends; and to this end,
He bowed his nature, never known before
But to be rough, unswayable, and free.

THIRD CONSPIRATOR Sir, his stoutness
When he did stand for consul, which he lost
By lack of stooping—

AUFIDIUS That I would have spoke of.
Being banished for 't, he came unto my hearth,
Presented to my knife his throat. I took him,
Made him joint servant with me, gave him way
In all his own desires; nay, let him choose
Out of my files, his projects to accomplish,
My best and freshest men; served his designments
In mine own person; holp to reap the fame
Which he did end all his; and took some pride
To do myself this wrong; till at the last
I seemed his follower, not partner; and
He waged me with his countenance as if
I had been mercenary.

FIRST CONSPIRATOR So he did, my lord.
The army marvelled at it, and, in the last,
When he had carried Rome and that we looked
For no less spoil than glory—

AUFIDIUS There was it
For which my sinews shall be stretched upon him.
At a few drops of women's rheum, which are
As cheap as lies, he sold the blood and labor
Of our great action. Therefore shall he die,
And I'll renew me in his fall. But hark!

*Drums and trumpets sounds, with great shouts of the people.*

FIRST CONSPIRATOR
Your native town you entered like a post

61. **patient:** long-suffering

64. **at your vantage:** i.e., while you have the opportunity

65. **move:** persuade

67. **along:** stretched out (i.e., dead)

68. **After . . . pronounced:** i.e., **his** story told as you would have it told (i.e., **after your way**)

69. **reasons:** justifications

74. **heed:** careful attention

79. **found:** suffered; **easy:** small, slight; **fines:** penalties

81. **benefit of our levies:** advantage gained by the armies we had mustered

81–82. **answering . . . charge:** recompensing **us with our own** expenses; defending himself to us by invoking the authority we granted him

83. **yielding:** surrender

86. **infected with:** i.e., affected by, influenced by

And had no welcomes home, but he returns
Splitting the air with noise.

SECOND CONSPIRATOR And patient fools,
Whose children he hath slain, their base throats tear
With giving him glory.

THIRD CONSPIRATOR Therefore at your vantage,
Ere he express himself or move the people
With what he would say, let him feel your sword,
Which we will second. When he lies along,
After your way his tale pronounced shall bury
His reasons with his body.

AUFIDIUS Say no more.

*Enter the Lords of the city.*

Here come the lords.

ALL LORDS
You are most welcome home.

AUFIDIUS I have not deserved it.
But, worthy lords, have you with heed perused
What I have written to you?

ALL ⌜LORDS⌝ We have.

FIRST LORD And grieve to hear 't.
What faults he made before the last, I think
Might have found easy fines, but there to end
Where he was to begin and give away
The benefit of our levies, answering us
With our own charge, making a treaty where
There was a yielding—this admits no excuse.

*Enter Coriolanus marching with Drum and Colors, the Commoners being with him.*

AUFIDIUS He approaches. You shall hear him.

CORIOLANUS
Hail, lords! I am returned your soldier,
No more infected with my country's love

87. **hence:** from here; **subsisting:** remaining

89. **prosperously:** successfully; **attempted:** made an effort

93. **counterpoise . . . part:** more than compensate for fully one-third of (or, perhaps, compensate by more than fully one-third)

94. **charges:** expenses

97. **Subscribed:** signed

99. **compounded:** agreed

101. **tell . . . degree:** perhaps, **tell** this worst of traitors; or, perhaps, **tell** to the fullest extent this **traitor**

103. **How now:** i.e., what did you say?

107. **grace:** honor

111. **drops of salt:** i.e., tears

113. **his oath and resolution:** i.e., sworn purpose (hendiadys)

114. **twist:** thread, cord; **admitting:** acknowledging

115. **Counsel o' th' war:** i.e., military advice

117. **That pages:** i.e., so **that** boys serving knights (an anachronism); **heart:** courage

118. **wond'ring each at other:** i.e., **at each other** in astonishment

Than when I parted hence, but still subsisting
Under your great command. You are to know
That prosperously I have attempted, and
With bloody passage led your wars even to
The gates of Rome. Our spoils we have brought
home
Doth more than counterpoise a full third part
The charges of the action. We have made peace
With no less honor to the Antiates
Than shame to th' Romans, and we here deliver,
Subscribed by' th' Consuls and patricians,
Together with the seal o' th' Senate, what
We have compounded on.

⌜*He offers the lords a paper.*⌝

AUFIDIUS Read it not, noble lords,
But tell the traitor in the highest degree
He hath abused your powers.

CORIOLANUS "Traitor"? How now?

AUFIDIUS Ay, traitor, Martius.

CORIOLANUS Martius?

AUFIDIUS
Ay, Martius, Caius Martius. Dost thou think
I'll grace thee with that robbery, thy stol'n name
Coriolanus, in Corioles?
You lords and heads o' th' state, perfidiously
He has betrayed your business and given up
For certain drops of salt your city Rome—
I say your city—to his wife and mother,
Breaking his oath and resolution like
A twist of rotten silk, never admitting
Counsel o' th' war, but at his nurse's tears
He whined and roared away your victory,
That pages blushed at him and men of heart
Looked wond'ring each at ⌜other.⌝

CORIOLANUS Hear'st thou, Mars?

122. **No more:** perhaps, **no more** talk; or, perhaps, **no more** than the "**boy**" I called you

123. **Measureless:** infinite

126. **scold:** use violent language in public rebuke

128. **give . . . the lie:** accuse this dog to his face of lying; **notion:** understanding

129. **stripes:** strokes, blows; **that:** who (i.e., Aufidius)

130–31. **join . . . him:** i.e., take part in forcing back **the lie** against **him**

134. **Stain:** (1) color with my blood; (2) defile; **edges:** swords

135. **true:** i.e., truly; **there:** in **your annals**

136. **dovecote:** building that shelters doves

137. **Fluttered:** threw into confusion

140. **blind fortune:** pure luck

144. **presently:** immediately

148. **folds in:** embraces, wraps

149. **This orb o' th' earth:** i.e., the world, the **earth; last:** latest

150. **judicious:** (1) judicial; (2) unbiased; **Stand:** stop

AUFIDIUS Name not the god, thou boy of tears.

CORIOLANUS Ha?

AUFIDIUS No more.

CORIOLANUS
Measureless liar, thou hast made my heart
Too great for what contains it. "Boy"? O slave!—
Pardon me, lords, 'tis the first time that ever
I was forced to scold. Your judgments, my grave
lords,
Must give this cur the lie; and his own notion—
Who wears my stripes impressed upon him, that
Must bear my beating to his grave—shall join
To thrust the lie unto him.

FIRST LORD Peace, both, and hear me speak.

CORIOLANUS
Cut me to pieces, Volsces. Men and lads,
Stain all your edges on me. "Boy"? False hound!
If you have writ your annals true, 'tis there
That like an eagle in a dovecote, I
⌜Fluttered⌝ your Volscians in Corioles,
Alone I did it. "Boy"!

AUFIDIUS Why, noble lords,
Will you be put in mind of his blind fortune,
Which was your shame, by this unholy braggart,
'Fore your own eyes and ears?

ALL CONSPIRATORS Let him die for 't.

ALL PEOPLE Tear him to pieces! Do it presently! He killed my son! My daughter! He killed my cousin Marcus! He killed my father!

SECOND LORD Peace, ho! No outrage! Peace!
The man is noble, and his fame folds in
This orb o' th' earth. His last offenses to us
Shall have judicious hearing. Stand, Aufidius,
And trouble not the peace.

152. **that:** i.e., I wish **that**

153. **his tribe: his** race, i.e., everyone related to him

154. **lawful sword:** i.e., **sword** of **lawful** war

156 SD. **kills:** i.e., they kill

157. **Hold:** stop

160. **whereat:** at which

161. **Masters:** sirs, gentlemen

165. **owe:** bear

166. **Please it:** i.e., if **it please**

167. **deliver:** report, express in words; also, perhaps, present

169. **censure:** judicial sentence

172. **corse:** corpse

172–73. **herald . . . urn:** The funeral procession described here and in lines 180–81 is like that given to such fallen heroes as Sir Philip Sidney in Shakespeare's England, where heralds accompanied the coffin, where drummers beat **a dead march** (line 185 SD, below), and where soldiers trailed their **pikes** (line 181) as a sign of mourning. **urn:** grave, tomb

174. **His:** i.e., Coriolanus's; **impatience:** irascibility

179. **be one:** i.e., **be** the fourth bearer

180. **speak:** sound

CORIOLANUS, ⌜*drawing his sword*⌝ O, that I had him,
With six Aufidiuses, or more, his tribe,
To use my lawful sword.

AUFIDIUS Insolent villain!

ALL CONSPIRATORS Kill, kill, kill, kill, kill him!

*Draw the Conspirators, and kills Martius, who falls.*
*Aufidius stands on him.*

LORDS Hold, hold, hold, hold!

AUFIDIUS
My noble masters, hear me speak.

FIRST LORD O Tullus!

SECOND LORD
Thou hast done a deed whereat valor will weep.

THIRD LORD
Tread not upon him.—Masters, all be quiet.—
Put up your swords.

AUFIDIUS
My lords, when you shall know—as in this rage,
Provoked by him, you cannot—the great danger
Which this man's life did owe you, you'll rejoice
That he is thus cut off. Please it your Honors
To call me to your senate, I'll deliver
Myself your loyal servant or endure
Your heaviest censure.

FIRST LORD Bear from hence his body,
And mourn you for him. Let him be regarded
As the most noble corse that ever herald
Did follow to his urn.

SECOND LORD His own impatience
Takes from Aufidius a great part of blame.
Let's make the best of it.

AUFIDIUS My rage is gone,
And I am struck with sorrow.—Take him up.
Help, three o' th' chiefest soldiers; I'll be one.—
Beat thou the drum that it speak mournfully.—

181. **Trail . . . pikes:** i.e., drag along the ground behind you the pointed ends of your **pikes** **pikes:** long wooden shafts with pointed heads of **steel** or iron (See picture, below.)

182. **unchilded:** killed the child of

184. **memory:** memorial

185 SD. **dead march:** piece of solemn music played at a funeral procession

Mourners trailing "steel pikes." (5.6.181)
From Thomas Lant,
*Sequitur celebritas & pompa funeris* . . . (1587).

Trail your steel pikes. Though in this city he
Hath widowed and unchilded many a one,
Which to this hour bewail the injury,
Yet he shall have a noble memory.
Assist.

*They exit bearing the body of Martius.*
*A dead march sounded.*

# Longer Notes

1.1.58 SP. SECOND CITIZEN: Since the eighteenth century, editors have changed the Folio's designation of the citizen who converses with Menenius. From 1.1.58 on, the speeches assigned by the Folio to the Second Citizen are given by these editors to the First Citizen. The ground for this editorial change has been the conviction that the First Citizen, who seems so aggressive and assertive up to this point in the scene, would not stand silent during the debate with Menenius, which begins here. A further ground is these editors' characterization of the Second Citizen, in the early part of the scene, as more sympathetic to the patricians. A few recent editors have departed from this tradition and have followed the Folio's speech assignments. These editors point out that it is impossible to dismiss the Folio assignments as error, given the frequency with which they occur; a scribe or compositor would have had to misread copy repeatedly in order to persist in such error. We agree with this assessment. Further, we would argue that the earlier editorial tradition, which characterizes the citizens as a mob misled by a single leader, has profound ideological implications. If the people have more than one spokesman, as in the Folio, then the citizens appear not as a mob but as a group of individuals who share a sense of oppression by the patricians—a sense that a number of them can articulate equally well. We would also argue that the traditional view of the Second Citizen, in the early part of the scene, is inaccurate, in that he in no way disputes the shared purpose of those assembled; he differs from the First Citizen only in how much of the blame for patrician abuse of the people he ascribes to Martius.

1.1.286. **puts well forth:** In the Folio, the citizens exit after Martius's sarcastic remark; if one chooses this option, stage action needs to be introduced to occasion this comment. In our edition, the remark is addressed to the citizens' backs as they steal away.

1.3.85–87. **You . . . moths: Penelope** told the suitors pressing her to remarry that she must first weave her father-in-law's shroud. Each day **she spun yarn** and wove the shroud, and each night she unraveled all she had woven that day.

1.5.17. **course of fight:** This is one of the play's several associations of feasting and fighting. Another comes at 1.9.11–12, when Cominius describes Martius's late arrival at the battlefield after having conquered Corioles: "Yet cam'st thou to a morsel of this feast [the battle], / Having fully dined before [at Corioles]." The association appears again at 4.5.239–40, where the Third Servingman describes a coming battle between Volsces and Romans as "a parcel of their feast, and to be executed ere they wipe their lips."

1.9.22. **overta'en:** When Martius declares that "He that has but effected his good will / Hath overta'en mine act," he implies that he himself was not able to effect "his" own "good will," or accomplish his purpose. There is perhaps a further implication—that he thinks himself capable of realizing an ambition to do yet more on another occasion. He does not explain either of these hints.

1.9.52. **ovator:** This word is one solution to a much-debated verbal problem raised by the First Folio, which here reads "Ouerture." Some editors have kept the Folio word and emended its context to read "let *hymns* be made / An overture for th' wars." Another solution is to change the Folio's "Ouerture" to "coverture" (a covering, clothing), referring to **the parasite's silk.** The word **ovator** was first proposed as a solution by Hilda M. Hulme in *Explorations in Shakespeare's Language* (1962), pp. 155–56, and given further support by David George in *Notes & Queries* 242 (1997): 508–12. "When steel grows / Soft as the parasite's silk, let him be made / An ovator for th' wars," as the lines are printed in this edition, carries on Martius's objection to what he regards as the misuse of the drums and trumpets, properly employed to give signals during battle, to give praise to him. He presents **steel,** or armor and weapons, as suffering the same degradation as the **drums and trumpets:** it **grows soft as** the clothing worn by the despicable flatterer, who therefore ought to be the one who is greeted with shouts of acclamation for achievements on the battlefield that are, obviously, not his to claim.

1.10.33. **south the city mills:** This topographical detail seems to locate the scene in Shakespeare's London, rather than in the classical world that is properly the play's setting. There were four flour mills on the south bank of the Thames, in the neighborhood of the Globe playhouse.

2.1.154–55. **repulse of Tarquin:** The last king of Rome, **Tarquin** Superbus (i.e., **Tarquin** the Proud), after having been driven from Rome, made several attempts to return. At the battle where **Tarquin** was finally defeated, Coriolanus, though yet a boy, gained great fame for valor. Plutarch (as translated by North) describes the action as follows:

> The first time he went to the wars, being but a stripling, was when *Tarquin* surnamed the proud (that had been king of Rome, and was driven out for his pride,

> after many attempts made by sundry battles to come in again, wherein he was ever overcome) did come to Rome with all the aid of the Latins, and many other people of Italy: even as it were to set up his whole rest upon a battle by them, who with a great and mighty army had undertaken to put him into his kingdom again. . . . In this battle, wherein were many hot and sharp encounters of either party, Martius valiantly fought in the sight of the Dictator; and a Roman soldier being thrown to the ground . . . Martius straight bestrid him, and slew the enemy with his own hands that had before overthrown the Roman. Hereupon, after the battle was won, the Dictator did not forget so noble an act, and therefore first of all he crowned Martius with a garland of oaken boughs. For whosoever saveth the life of a Roman, it is a manner among them to honor him with such a garland. (Spelling modernized.)

The two marginal notes that accompany this passage in North's translation read "*Coriolanus first going to the wars*" and "*Coriolanus crowned with a garland of oaken boughs.*"

2.1.166 SD. **Titus Lartius:** Lartius's silent appearance in this scene in the Folio stands in contradiction to other parts of the *Coriolanus* text. The only acknowledgment of him in the scene (aside from this entrance direction) seems to be Menenius's mention of "You . . . three" (199), presumably referring to Cominius, Coriolanus, and Lartius. Near the end of Act 1 Lartius was delegated the responsibility of dealing with the Volscians by Cominius after their victory outside Corioles: "You, Titus Lartius, / Must to Corioles back" (1.9.82–83). Lartius is still in Corioles at 2.2.38. When he appears at the beginning of Act 3, he is represented as having just arrived back in Rome from his duties in Corioles. Evidently his appearance in 2.1, which thus sets up a contradiction within the play's action, was either not noticed or not thought in need of correction in the manuscript from which the Folio text was printed in 1623.

2.1.203. **grafted . . . relish: Crab trees** were **grafted** with apple **trees,** usually so as to produce a better tree and sweeter fruit. In *Henry VI, Part 2* (3.2.221–23), however, the image is used to insult Warwick's birth: "noble stock / Was graft with **crab-tree** slip, whose fruit thou art."

2.1.232. **variable complexions:** In the physiology and natural philosophy of Shakespeare's time, *complexion* referred to (1) the proportion of supposed qualities (*cold* or *hot,* and *moist* or *dry*) that determined the nature of a body, plant, etc.; and (2) the proportion of the four "humors" of the body (*blood, phlegm, black bile,* and *yellow bile*) or the bodily habit attributed to such a combination, i.e., "temperament."

2.1.260. **napless vesture:** Roman custom called for the candidate standing for election as consul to present himself to the people dressed only in a toga—a long piece of fine white wool that, draped around the body, was the formal attire of the male Roman citizen. Ordinarily, a tunic (i.e., shirt or gown) was worn under the toga; by wearing only the toga, the candidate could display his scars to the people as evidence of his having warred on Rome's behalf. Shakespeare's immediate source for the play, Thomas North's English translation of a French translation of Plutarch's biography of Coriolanus, mistranslated the description of the toga without the tunic as a "poor gowne" and "meane apparell," and thereby led Shakespeare to misrepresent the toga as a **napless vesture,** or threadbare garment.

2.3.266–72. **Ancus . . . ancestor:** Coriolanus's ancestors, as here recounted, are an odd mixture. Three are legendary or semilegendary kings, who are usually said to have succeeded each other in the following order: **Numa** Pompilius (Rome's second king), Tullus **Hostilius, Ancus Martius.** No one has identified **Publius,** but **Quintus** apparently is **Quintus** Martius Rex, from the second century B.C.E.—long after Coriolanus, who dates from the sixth and fifth centuries. Another anachronism is the inclusion of Caius Martius Rutilius, **surnamed Censorinus,** who lived in the third century B.C.E.

These errors originate not with Shakespeare but with his source, Plutarch's *The Lives of the Noble Grecians and Romanes*. It is Shakespeare's close reliance on this source that allows editors speculatively to supply a line—in our text, line 270—which dropped out of the play during its transcription or printing. The corresponding passage in Plutarch, as translated into English by Thomas North in 1579, reads "Censorinus also came of that familie, that was so surnamed, bicause the people had chosen him Censor twise" (1595 edition, the one Shakespeare probably used).

3.1.92. **cockle:** In Matthew 13.24–30, it is the enemy who sows **cockle** (called *tares* in the Geneva Bible) in the field of a farmer who has sowed good seed; discovering what the enemy has done to his wheat field, the farmer chooses to let both wheat and cockle grow together, then gather the cockle first and burn it.

3.1.370. **one danger:** Some editors interpret the **danger** as the alienation of the patricians or at least of Coriolanus's friends. Others understand **one danger** as "**one** kind of **danger,**" to be distinguished from the other **danger**—that is, **death.** In some editions **one danger** is emended to "our **danger,**" which neatly balances **our certain death** in line 371.

4.7.55. **chair:** The statement "power, unto itself most commendable, / Hath not a tomb so evident as a chair / T' extol what it hath done" seems deliberately obscure. It may mean, in the paraphrase of Samuel Johnson in his edition of 1765, "the virtue which delights to commend itself will find the surest *tomb* in the *chair* wherein it holds forth its own commendation."

5.1.28–31. **He could . . . offense:** See Matthew 3.12: "Whose fan is in his hand, and he will thoroughly purge his floor, and gather his wheat up into the garner, but he will burn up the **chaff** with unquenchable fire." See also Genesis 18.24–33, where we read that too few righteous people are to be found in Sodom to spare it from divine wrath.

5.6.58. **native town:** As established at 1.6.68–69, Aufidius is an Antiate, a man from Antium, which would thus be his **native town.** Line 5.6.58 seems, then, to set scene 5.6 in Antium. (See also the lords' "welcome home" to Aufidius at line 72 and the reference to Antiates in line 95, below.) However, by lines 106–8, the setting of this scene is clearly Corioles, a shift that Shakespeare no doubt made to take advantage of Coriolanus's association with that Volscian city.

# Textual Notes

The reading of the present text appears to the left of the square bracket. Unless otherwise noted, the reading to the left of the bracket is from **F,** the First Folio text (upon which this edition is based). The earliest sources of readings not in F are indicated as follows: **F2** is the Second Folio of 1632; **F3** is the Third Folio of 1663–64; **F4** is the Fourth Folio of 1685; **Ed.** is an earlier editor of Shakespeare, beginning with Rowe in 1709. No sources are given for emendations of punctuation or for corrections of obvious typographical errors, like turned letters that produce no known word. **SD** means stage direction; **SP** means speech prefix; ***uncorr***. means the first or uncorrected state of the First Folio; ***corr***. means the second or corrected state of the First Folio; **~** stands in place of a word already quoted before the square bracket; **∧** indicates the omission of a punctuation mark.

**1.1** 15. on] F (one); 34. SP SECOND CITIZEN] Ed.; *All*. F; 47. o'] F (a'); 49. SD *Enter Menenius Agrippa.*] *1 line later in* F; 60. which] F ($^{c}_{w}$); 68. you. . . . wants,] ~ . . . ~. F; 94. stale] Ed.; scale F; 101, 126, 160, 234. o'] F (a); 106. appetite∧] ~; F; 109. you.] ~∧ F; 112. tauntingly] F4; taintingly F; 117. what?] ~∧ F; 118. crownèd] F (crown'd); 159. cares,] ~; F; 183. geese. . . . are∧] ~∧ . . . ~: F; 224. eat,] ~∧ F; 235. Shouting] F (Shooting); 240. unroofed] Ed.; vnroo'st F; 250. SD *Junius*] *Annius* F; *Brutus*,] ~∧ F; *Cominius*] *Cominisn* F; 268. Lartius] Ed.; *Lucius* F; 271 *and hereafter in this scene*. SP LARTIUS] Ed.; *Tit*. F; 284. SD *Citizens steal away*.] *2 lines later in* F; 286. SD *Sicinius*] F (*Sicin.*)

**1.2** 0. SD *Corioles*] F (*Coriolus*); 5. on] F (one); 18. *Whither*] F (Whether); 33. Corioles.] ~^ F

**1.3** 39. that's] F2; that F; 46. sword,] ~. F; contemning] Ed.; *Contenning* F; 47. SD *Gentlewoman*] F (*Gent.*); 60, 61. O'] F (A); 61, 112. o'] F (a); 62. H'as] F (ha's); 84. SP VIRGILIA] F (*Vlug.*); 87. Ithaca] *Athica* F; 100. whom] F (whõ); 102. Corioles] *Carioles* F; 108. lady. . . . now,] ~, . . . ~: F

**1.4** 0, 17. SD *Corioles*] F (*Corialus*); 23. up.] ~^ F; 42. Boils] F (Byles); 54. trenches. Follow 's] F (Trenches followes); 54. SD *Another . . . them.*] Ed.; *Another Alarum, and Martius followes them to gates, and is shut in.* F; 58. SD *Martius . . . in.*] Ed.; *Enter the Gati.* F (*See also note to* 54 SD.); 63. SP LARTIUS] Ed.; *Tit.* F; 75. Cato's] Ed.; *Calues* F

**1.5** 3. SD *Enter . . . Trumpet.*] Ed.; *exeunt.* | *Alarum continues still a- farre off.* | *Enter Martius, and Titus with a Trumpet.* F; 5. drachma] Drachme F; 7. them,] ~. F; 8. up.] ~, F; 9. him!] ~^ F; 31. o'] F (a')

**1.6** 33. from] F (frõ); 40. heart^] ~; F; 60. o'] F (a'); 64. which] F ($\binom{c}{w}$); 68. Antiates] Ed.; Antients F; 89. Lesser] F3; Lessen F; 103. I] Ed.; foure F

**1.7** 0. SD *Corioles*] *Carioles* F

**1.8** 16. Wert] F (Wer't); 19. SD *Aufidius*] F (*Auffi.*); 22. SD *Martius fights . . . breathless.*] *2 lines earlier in* F

**1.9** 0. SD *Alarum . . . Flourish.*] Ed.; *Flourish. Alarum . . . sounded.* F; 13. SP LARTIUS] Ed.; *Titus Lartius* F; 37. store—of all^] ~^ . . . ~, F; 47. May] Ed.; *Mar.* May F; 52. ovator] Ed.; Ouerture F; 55. shout] F (shoot); 71, 73. Martius] F (*Marcus*); 74 *and hereafter in this scene.* SP CORIOLANUS] Ed.; *Martius.* F; 106. SD *A flourish . . . exit.*] Ed.; *Exeunt.* F (*See next note.*)

**1.10** 0. SD *Enter . . . Soldiers*] Ed.; *A flourish. Cornets. Enter . . . Souldiers* F; 32. cypress] F (Cyprus)

**2.1** 1. augurer] Agurer F; 22. o'] F (a'); 57–58. cannot] Ed.; can F; 65. bisson] F (beesome); 73.

faucet] F (Forset); 88. are. . . . purpose,] ~, . . . ~. F; 96. Good e'en] F (Godden); 99. SD *Brutus and Sicinius stand aside.*] F (*Bru. and Scic. Aside.*); 111. SP VALERIA, VIRGILIA] Ed.; 2. *Ladies.* F; 127. pocket,] ~? F; 135. Corioles] Carioles F; 166. SD *A sennet. Enter . . . Lartius . . . Herald. Trumpets sound.*] Ed.; *A Sennet. Trumpets sound. Enter . . . Latius . . . Herauld.* F; 170. Coriolanus] Ed.; *Martius Caius Coriolanus* F 171. SD *Sound*‸] ~. F; 188. Corioles] Carioles F; wear] F (were); 192. SP CORIOLANUS] Ed.; *Com.* F; 199. You] F2; Yon F; 223. SD *Brutus . . . come forward.*] Ed.; *Enter Brutus and Scicinius.* F; 240. human] F (humane); 274. authority's‸] Authorities, F; 279. human] F (humane); 286. touch] Ed.; teach F

**2.2** 54. o'] F (a'); 97. one on 's] F (on ones); 107. chin] F (Shinne); 124. took; . . . foot‸] ~‸ . . . ~: F; 127. o'] F (of); 130. Corioles] Carioles F; 183. SP SENATORS] Ed.; *Senat.* F; 189. here.] ~‸ F

**2.3** 21. colored] Coulord F; 24, 81. o'] F (a'); 28–29. block-head] F *corr.* (blocke-head); blocke head F *uncorr.*; 39–40. it. I say,] ~, ~~. F; 55. tongue] tougne F; 56. country's] F (Countries); 69. SD *Enter three of the Citizens.*] *2 lines earlier in* F; 75. not] Ed.; *omit* F; 93. SD *These citizens exit.*] Ed.; *Exeunt.* F; 97, 100, 116. SP FOURTH CITIZEN] Ed.; I. F; 114. SP FIFTH CITIZEN] Ed.; 2. F; 124. hire] F2; higher F; 125. toge] Ed.; tongue F; 143. SP SIXTH CITIZEN] Ed.; I. F; 145. SP SEVENTH CITIZEN] Ed.; 2. F; 166. SD *Coriolanus and Menenius*] F (*Coriol. and Mene.*); 189. you.] ~‸ F; 266. Numa's] *Numaes* F; 270. And . . . surnamed] Ed.; *not in* F; 274. besides] F (beside)

**3.1** 2 *and hereafter in this scene.* SP LARTIUS] Ed.; *Latius.* F; 58. suppliants‸] ~: F; 95. honored] hoaor'd F; 106, 147, 176. o'] F (a'); 123. good] Ed.; God F; 181. human] F (Humane); 183. Where one] Ed.; Whereon F; 204. 'Has] F (Has); 205. 'Has] F

(Ha's); 210. bench? . . . rebellion,] ~, . . . ~: F; 217. SD *Enter an Aedile.*] *1 line earlier in* F; 225. Agèd] F (Ag'd); 256, 292. SP CORIOLANUS] Ed.; *Com.* F; 270. SP ALL PLEBEIANS] F (*All Ple.*); 280. SD *Coriolanus*] F (*Corio.*); 288. SD *In . . . in.*] Ed.; *Exeunt.* | *In . . . in.* F; 289. your] Ed.; our F; 300. SP COMINIUS] F2; *Corio.* F; 301. SP CORIOLANUS] Ed.; *Mene.* F; 391. SP SICINIUS] Ed.; *Menen.* F; 412. bring him] Ed.; bring him in peace F

**3.2** 14. SD *Enter Volumnia.*] *8 lines earlier in* F; 25. thwartings] Ed.; things F; 41. herd] Ed.; heart F; 42. o'] F (a'); 125. bear? Well,] ~∧ ~? F.

**3.3** 19, 23. o'] F (a'); 42. for th'] F2; fourth F; 47. Throng] Ed.; Through F; the] F ($\overset{e}{\text{y}}$); 73. accents] Ed.; Actions F; 89. hell∧] ~. F; 92. clutched∧ . . . millions,] ~: . . . ~∧ F; 93. numbers,] ~. F; 126. it,] ~. F; 126, 151. o'] F (a'); 138. for] Ed.; from F; 142. wife's] F (Wiues); 164. city,] ~. F; 165. SD *with others*] F (*Cumalijs*); 167. SD *They . . . caps.*] *2 lines earlier in* F

**4.1** 5. chances∧] ~. F; 29. thee] F (the); 41. Whither] F (Whether); wilt] Ed.; will F; 43. exposure] exposture F; 45. SP VIRGILIA] Ed.; *Corio.* F

**4.2** 16. The] F (Th'); o'] F (a'); 30. thou] F ($\overset{u}{\text{y}}$); words,] ~. F

**4.3** 9. approved] Ed.; appear'd F; 34. will] F2; well F

**4.4** 29. hate] Ed.; haue F

**4.5** 3. master] F (M.); 11. SD *Servingman*] Ed.; *Seruant* F; 57, 71. thou] F ($\overset{u}{\text{y}}$); 87. Whooped] Ed.; Hoop'd F; 144. o'erbear 't] Ed.; o're-beate F; 163. SD. *Coriolanus and Aufidius exit.*] Ed.; *Exeunt.* F; *Two of the Servingmen come forward.*] Ed.; *Enter two of the Seruingmen.* F; 194. lief] F (liue); 247. sleepy] F3; sleepe F; 259. SP FIRST and SECOND SERVINGMEN] F (*Both.*)

**4.6** 43. lamentation] Lamention F; 94. SP SECOND

MESSENGER] Ed.; *Mes.* F; 175. one] oue F; 196. SD *Citizens exit.*] F (*Exit Cit.*)

**4.7** 39. even] eeuen F; 'twas] F3; 'was F; 41. defect] F2; detect F; 52. virtues] F2; Vertue F; 58. falter] Ed.; fouler F (David George, "*Cum Notis Variorum*: The Proverb in Shakespeare," *Shakespeare Newsletter* [Fall 1998]: 65.)

**5.1** 15. o'] F (a'); 18. wracked] This ed.; wrack'd for F; 86. haste] F (hast)

**5.2** 69. by] Ed.; *not in* F; 93. pity‸] ~: F

**5.3** 19. embassies] F (*E*mbasses); 55. prate] Ed.; pray F; 73. holp] Ed.; hope F; 147. SP YOUNG MARTIUS] Ed.; *Boy*. F; 171. fine] Ed.; fiue F; 172. gods,] ~. F; 173. o'] F (a'); 174. charge] Ed.; change F; 185. clucked] F2; clock'd F; 191. him with] F2; him with him with F

**5.4** 1. coign] F (Coin); o'] F (a'); 52. SD *all together*] F (*altogether*)

**5.6** 1. o'] F (a'); 67–68. second. . . . way‸] ~, . . . ~. F; 70. SD *Enter . . . city.*] *1 line later in* F; 83. SD *Enter . . . him.*] *1 line later in* F; 98, 109, 115, 179. o'] F (a'); 118. other] Ed.; others F; 133. Volsces.] ~‸ F; 137. Fluttered] F3; Flatter'd F; 138. it.] ~, F; 156. SD *Draw the Conspirators*] Ed.; *Draw both the Conspirators* F

# *Coriolanus:* A Modern Perspective

Heather James

Shakespeare's Coriolanus labors to establish his reputation as Rome's most valiant son, but his relentless verbal attacks on his fellow Romans and strenuous defenses of himself cause him to lose respect almost as quickly as he earns it. Though no one doubts his valor, many question the virtue from which his valiant deeds must spring if they are to be entirely admirable. Even before he first appears in the play, one of Rome's common citizens casts plausible suspicion on him: Coriolanus performs heroics on the battlefield, he says, "to please his mother and to be partly proud" (1.1.38–39). Two acts later, his own mother, exasperated by his reluctance to show his battle wounds to the commons (as political custom dictates), snaps at her son, "Thy valiantness was mine; thou suck'st it from me, / But owe [i.e., own] thy pride thyself" (3.2.157–58). According to Shakespeare's main historical source, Plutarch's "Life of Caius Martius Coriolanus," Coriolanus's enemies and intimates alike seem to doubt that the warrior possesses the "inner armor" necessary for full respect: "outward he esteemed armour to no purpose, unless one were naturally armed within."[1]

The warrior does not fare much better with some literary critics, who feel that any character displaying so much self-righteousness forfeits the benefit of the doubt owed to the flawed protagonists of Shakespeare's tragedies. For these critics, Coriolanus's failure to draw sympathy even throws doubt on his status as a tragic hero: some view him as an antihero, set in opposition to Rome and his fellow citizens, while others see him as a grotesquely comic figure, who passes through the tragic machinery of suffering, enlightenment, and loss without any of it touching his mind. For many, Coriolanus is the least self-reflective of Shakespeare's tragic protagonists. It does not help that the play presents him mainly in external views, without employing soliloquies and revealing dialogue. It is true that something happens within the warrior when he goes into exile as a muffled traveler and emerges as a virtual god of war. And something yet more profound takes place within him when he yields to his mother's appeals and grants mercy to Rome. In both cases, Coriolanus *chooses* his metamorphoses, first into "a lonely dragon" (4.1.35) breathing wrath on Rome and then, less explicably, into a figure as vulnerable as the butterfly (classically, an image of the mutable soul) that his small son chases and rips to shreds (1.3.63–68). But we do not know why he makes these choices: we are led to the threshold of insight but not taken into his confidence.

The most damaging argument is the one against interiority, which dispels the fascination or charisma associated with the tragic hero. There is no getting to the heart of his mystery if Coriolanus ignores his interior life to pursue martial performances that make even his friends see him, ambivalently, as "a thing of blood" (2.2.125) and "an engine" (5.4.19) of war mowing down all in sight. Indeed, it seems that if we opened up Coriolanus to look inside, we might find yet more armor, his breastplate covering up defensive machinery, not the "inner armor" of Stoic fortitude that protects the self against the insults of worldly experience. But this view presumes too much about the models of selfhood available to Shakespeare and of dramatic interest to him.

In fact, Coriolanus is intensely preoccupied with the analysis and evaluation of his deeds. As Lee Bliss points out, he "never asks 'Who am I?' or 'What have I become?'"[2] He seems more likely to ask, "Have I done anything today for which I am ashamed?" Coriolanus frustrates the model of selfhood associated with Hamlet, who defines the tragic hero of Shakespeare's mature plays for modern critics and audiences. Hamlet focuses his entire attention on a single momentous act—the murder of the king—and subordinates every consideration and character to it: Rosencrantz and Guildenstern, Polonius, and Ophelia are victims and casualties of the tragic plot focused on kings. Whereas the Danish prince takes just one deed with him to the bar of conscience, Coriolanus subjects each daily act, no matter how inconsequential in the eyes of others, to minute scrutiny. Behind his awkward expressions of modesty lies a noisy conscience: "Did I once relax my vigor in battle? Did I slack in my duty to lambaste the cowardly and embolden the good? Was it my fault, or his, that Aufidius and I were separated in combat? Was it wrong to let my praises be read to the populace in 'acclamations hyperbolical' (1.9.56)? Will I lose my dignity in pursuit of public office?"

Let us consider the most famous act that Coriolanus submits to the business of self-auditing: his effort to serve convention and show his wounds to the Roman commons. Although he tries to do as he is told, the implications of exchanging a view of his wounds for their voices paralyze him. If he shows his wounds, he must identify his labor and dignity with theirs (a thing he cannot do) and bind his duties as consul to their rights and liberties (a thing he wants to avoid). The people long to show their "noble acceptance" of his "noble deeds" (2.3.8–9) and affirm their voice in Roman politics. While the Roman nobles routinely and insincerely make these connections in their political rhetoric, Coriolanus does not—and for good reason: unlike the other nobles, he would feel obliged to represent the people in his office of consul if he said or implied he was going to do so. The "chief enemy to the people" (1.1.7–8) would have to be their friend and advocate.

When so much rides on his every gesture, it is no wonder that Coriolanus worries about his social performances. In psychoanalytic readings of his anxiety, the warrior comes up short, since the terms of analysis—paranoia and narcissism—allow no room for his deliberative agency. He fares better if his restless self-audits are referred to moral philosophy, particularly the Stoic self-scrutiny that Shakespeare's contemporaries knew best from Seneca (a philosopher and the counselor of the emperor Nero) and that the philosopher Michel Foucault has revived in modern criticism.[3] In Shakespeare's play, Coriolanus constantly battles temptations to conform to social norms and values.[4] To embrace Stoic values and resist the outer world order—a witch's brew of fiction, coercion, and ideology—Coriolanus must retreat to an inner world, in which his battles are moral, his weapon is his reason, and his goal is the defense of the fortress of himself.

Before exile forces his full retreat into himself, Coriolanus looks to one person for guidance in his constant testing of convention and reality: his mother, whom he reveres for her indomitable will and fortitude of mind. In his eyes, Volumnia is a mirror in which he may confidently view ideals of conduct and review his own shortcomings. As she is the first to say, she took risks with her only son at a tender age, when no mother would wish to "sell him an hour from her beholding": putting his honor before her desire, she "let him seek danger where he was like to find fame," sending him to a "cruel war . . . from whence he returned, his brows bound with oak" (1.3.9–16), the honor bestowed on soldiers who save the life of a citizen in battle. These admissions are meant not to inspire admiration in the tenderhearted (like Virgilia) but to explain a way of life based on the defiance of custom, no matter how great the personal risk. This is mother's milk to Coriolanus, for whom the battlefield is a proving ground of moral as well as martial virtue.

Yet nothing, not even Volumnia, can force Coriolanus to reexamine the act for which history will judge him: he flatly refuses to see his campaign against Rome as treason. In an effort to awaken the conscience of its wrathful son, Rome sends three embassies to Coriolanus, who sits in the Volscian camp like an avenging deity, poised to wreak devastation on the ungrateful city. Coriolanus easily discerns the long arm of the state reaching out to touch him in the persons of his intimate friends, Cominius and Menenius, and he sends both on their way with cold words. He is not, in the end, able to dismiss the third embassy, led by Volumnia. But no change of heart is brought about by anything his mother says in the way of logic: his invasion of Rome divides the loyalties of his household between family and state; his reputation in the historical record hangs in jeopardy; and mercy might be regarded as a worthy alternative to victory. In her lucid and powerful arguments he hears the same unwelcome challenge to his autonomy represented by the first two embassies. Rather than capitulate to Rome, he chooses to test and face down the massive weight of the cultural traditions that claim to shape his identity.

Rome's embassies to Coriolanus are on a collision course with what we might call the warrior's experiments in divinity, his effort to shake off the controls of civilization and forge an autonomous self or "I" able to defy the claims of the world. He begins this massive effort when he desperately reverses the terms of his exile: "I banish you!" (3.3.153), he thunders at the Romans who condemn him. His exile further kindles his desire to forge his identity in the fire of Stoic denial. As Paul Veyne puts it, the Stoics of the late Roman Empire aimed to create the impression that

> the *I* is all-powerful, that only it matters, and that it can be sufficient unto itself. In order for unhappiness and death not to matter, it is enough to consider them as nothing; if the world is hostile, it is enough to ignore it. . . . In the face of death, the *I*, with its capacity for denial, is the only weapon remaining to us.[5]

Shakespeare's Coriolanus nearly realizes the Stoic fantasy, according to Cominius's account of the wrathful warrior:

> "Coriolanus"
> He would not answer to, forbade all names.
> He was a kind of nothing, titleless,
> Till he had forged himself a name o' th' fire
> Of burning Rome.
> (5.1.12–16)

In Coriolanus's wishful phrase, he would be "author of himself, / And know no other kin" (5.3.40–41).

Tellingly, Coriolanus utters this wish at the first moment he glimpses its impossibility, when Rome's third embassy arrives in camp: "My wife comes foremost, then the honored mold / Wherein this trunk was framed" (5.3.25–26). For him, the third embassy is something like the last temptation of Christ. He must first deny the protocols of war (Cominius), and then the more endearing face of Roman public life (his surrogate father, Menenius). The ties of blood represent Rome's last effort. To the claims of family, Coriolanus yields and kneels. The question posed to Shakespeare's audiences has long vexed and inspired the interpreters of history: why?

Two main explanations circulated in Shakespeare's day. One account emphasizes the obedience of child to parent and views Coriolanus's performance of his duties as doubly ennobling: the son redeems himself through his obedience to his parent, while the mother illustrates the moral excellence of women. Volumnia's story appears, for example, in Cornelius Agrippa's book *Treatise of the nobilitie and excellencye of vvoman kynde,* as David Clapham rendered the title in his English translation of 1542. Shakespeare takes a marked interest in Volumnia's ability to control her son's acts and compel his obedience. In the confrontation of mother and son, he locates her victory over Coriolanus at the precise moment when she abandons argumentation and turns to coercion. Her success wins her a triumph in Rome. Yet her moment of glory seems, in Shakespeare's play, to diminish rather than confirm her moral stature.

The second version focuses on Coriolanus, who recognizes his fault, repents, and dies of grief. In the first account, Volumnia proves the capacity of women to rise above historical and social constraints and to achieve moral dignity. In the second, she disappears from the story, leaving her son to discover the meaning of treason on his own. An early English printed commonplace book lists his story under two headings, "Of Grief" ("Coriolanus, finding his offence / For warring gainst his country, dyde with griefe") and "Of Tears" ("Braue Coriolanus being banisht Rome, / Toucht with his fault, went forth, and dide in teares").[6] From this story, Shakespeare takes Coriolanus's tears, which he relocates in time, transferring them from the moment of the warrior's death to the act that precipitates it: his choice to yield to his mother's demands without believing in her arguments. The tears that Coriolanus sheds express not contrition (the work of grace) but compassion (the labor of moral philosophy): "[I]t is no little thing to make / Mine eyes to sweat compassion" (5.3.219–20), says Rome's fierce warrior, who has hitherto only "sweat with wrath" (1.4.37).

What leads Shakespeare's Coriolanus to give up his wrath for mercy and, simultaneously, to enter into a bad-faith relationship with Rome and the social institutions whose lies and limitations he deplores? Why does he submit to demands that he fully believes to be violations of natural and divine law? To date, the most influential reading of his submission is the psychoanalytic one advanced by Janet Adelman just thirty years ago: for all of his violent performances of masculinity on the battlefield, Coriolanus remains, in his eyes and his mother's, her "warrior," whom she "holp to frame" (5.3.72–73) and without whom he has no more moral or martial agency than an infant. He cannot be "author of himself" and know "no other kin," but must be his mother's "corrected son" (66), with his shame, dependency, and mortality on display for all to see.[7] This is Volumnia's perspective and story.

There is another story to be told about Coriolanus's encounter with human fragility, however, in which he learns something more terrible, and more common, than his dependency on his mother. That story reveals the growing dependency of Volumnia, once so invulnerable in his eyes, on her adult son and, worse, her incapacity to accept any change in their positions. She brings this lesson home to her son, however inadvertently, when she gives up on persuasion and produces a savagely ironic performance of her weakness. Seeing him turn away, she rallies Virgilia and Valeria to participate in a mock display of feminine submission: "Down, ladies! Let us shame him with our knees" (5.3.191), she cries, and the women fall to their knees in petition. Volumnia intends to shame her son with a charade of their dependence, when she seems to believe that the reverse is true: "There's no man in the world / More bound to 's mother, yet here he lets me prate / Like one i' th' stocks" (180–82). What brings Coriolanus to his knees in this reading is his slow recognition of her frailty and its consequence to him: he must assume the humbling responsibilities he owes to the members of his household, including his once formidable mother, who depend on him.

Coriolanus knows, as she does not, that she really has mistaken the relationship of parent to child all this while, as she said without meaning it. In the end, he assumes the position of her "corrected son," in full recognition of the tragic ironies. In what seems to be a private aside, because it is impossible to imagine she is listening, he evokes the gods, who look down at the tragic spectacle, in which both mother and son violate the laws of nature and the gods:

O mother, mother!
What have you done? Behold, the heavens do ope,
The gods look down, and this unnatural scene
They laugh at. O, my mother, mother, O!
You have won a happy victory to Rome,
But, for your son—believe it, O, believe it!—
Most dangerously you have with him prevailed,
If not most mortal to him. But let it come.
(5.3.205–12)

The speech is remarkable for the compassion it shows to his mother, who can see no ill in her actions and cannot take his word on faith. Abandoning the principle of strict justice by which he has striven to live, Coriolanus acts to protect his mother from the knowledge of her dependency on him and, more horrifyingly, on the outer world of determinism and fate that he believes she sent him out to combat. Rather than force on her the unbearable knowledge of her vulnerability and illusions, he gives her what he denied to the people: the right to think well of herself. In doing so, he relaxes his moral labors against the fates: "But let it come."

As the scene unfolds, it pushes the play's tragic plot in two directions at once: toward the grand space occupied by moral philosophy and the humble space of domestic life. Coriolanus's discoveries are in some ways comparable to those made by many citizens of the modern (especially Western) world, who spend the first part of their adult lives observing the biblical injunction to leave their parents' house and establish financial and domestic autonomy only to discover that the second portion of their adulthood will be spent seeking the means to provide care for aging and failing parents, whose greatest horror is at their own dependency. Without entirely collapsing the differences between the modern world and Shakespeare's, it seems pertinent to ask if Shakespeare's Coriolanus shares some of the dilemmas faced by another adult child of a willful parent, *King Lear*'s Cordelia.

It is cruel of Aufidius to tell Coriolanus, who can brave an armed and hostile city with the rigor of his violence, that he is a "boy of tears" (5.6.120), unworthy of the name of the god of war (the name *Martius* derives from Mars). By throwing Coriolanus's tears back in his face, Aufidius denies their status as signs of the moral labor that went into his most heroic act. Left to his own devices, Coriolanus would spend a lifetime sweating with wrath on the battlefield and auditing his performance for minute lapses. What brings him to man's estate and the threshold of tragedy is his consent to identifying with the members of society who are forced to depend on others. Had he learned these lessons earlier, perhaps he would have revealed his wounds to the people of Rome.

---

1. *The liues of the noble Grecians and Romanes*, translated by Thomas North (1579), p. 238.

2. Lee Bliss, ed., *Coriolanus* (Cambridge: Cambridge University Press, 2000), p. 40.

3. Of Seneca's moral essays, "On Anger," "On Mercy," and "On the Tranquility of Mind" were among the most important in Shakespeare's day. Foucault discusses "the care of the self" in volume 3 of *The History of Sexuality,* translated by Robert Hurley (New York: Pantheon, 1986), and, of more direct interest to the concerns of Shakespeare's play, in his remarks on truth-telling, *Fearless Speech,* edited by Joseph Pearson (Los Angeles: Semiotext(e), 2001).

4. For an account of Seneca's distinction between the outer world, which is subject to fate, and the inner world, which allows human beings to escape such determinism, see William J. Bouwsma, "The Two Faces of Humanism: Stoicism and Augustinianism in Renaissance Thought," in *A Usable Past: Essays in European Cultural History* (Berkeley: University of California Press, 1990), pp. 19–73.

5. Paul Veyne, *Seneca: The Life of a Stoic* (London: Routledge, 2002), p. ix.

6. John Bodenham, *Bel-vedére, or the Garden of the Muses* (1600), pp. 144, 190.

7. Janet Adelman, "'Anger's My Meat': Feeding, Dependency, and Aggression in *Coriolanus*," in *Representing Shakespeare: New Psychoanalytic Essays*, edited by Murray M. Schwartz and Coppélia Kahn (Baltimore: Johns Hopkins University Press, 1980), pp. 129–49.

# Further Reading

## *Coriolanus*

Abbreviations: *Ant.* = *Antony and Cleopatra; Cym.* = *Cymbeline; JC* = *Julius Caesar; Lear* = *King Lear; Luc.* = *Lucrece; Mac.* = *Macbeth;* RSC = Royal Shakespeare Company; *Titus* = *Titus Andronicus*

Adelman, Janet. "'Anger's My Meat': Feeding, Dependency, and Aggression in *Coriolanus.*" In *Shakespeare, Pattern of Excelling Nature*, edited by David Bevington and Jay L. Halio, pp. 108–24. Cranbury, N.J.: Associated University Presses; Newark: University of Delaware Press, 1978. [Reprinted in *Representing Shakespeare: New Psychoanalytic Essays*, edited by Murray M. Schwartz and Coppélia Kahn, pp. 129–49 (Baltimore: Johns Hopkins University Press, 1980); and in *Shakespeare: An Anthology of Criticism and Theory, 1945–2000*, edited by Russ McDonald, pp. 323–37 (Oxford: Blackwell, 2004). Revised and incorporated in Janet Adelman, *Suffocating Mothers: Fantasies of Maternal Origin in Shakespeare's Plays, "Hamlet" to "The Tempest,"* chapter 6 (pp. 130–64, esp. 146–64) (New York: Routledge, 1991).]

In this frequently cited feminist/psychoanalytic reading, Adelman argues that the image of phallic Oedipal aggression suggested by the uprising of the hungry crowd in 1.1 operates in "not only the political but also the intrapsychic world" of *Coriolanus*—especially in the titular figure, a man whose life is a "kind of phallic exhibitionism," committed to disproving any suggestion of human vulnerability and to fulfilling a desire to be the "author of himself" (5.3.40). Just as Mother Rome has failed to nurture her children, so Volumnia, who equates the need for food with weakness, has failed to nourish her son. Her contempt for feeding and dependence is reflected in Coriolanus's self-sufficiency, in his view of food as poisonous (1.1.189–90; 3.1.198–99), and in his belief that "the only thing he can imagine nourishing is rebellion" (see 3.1.91–92, 151). For both mother and son, masculine identity "depends on [the] transformation of . . . vulnerability [the oral neediness of the infant's feeding mouth] into an instrument of attack [the phallic aggression of the honorable warrior's bleeding wound]," a transformation graphically imaged in Volumnia's disturbing linkage of Hecuba's lactating breasts and Hector's forehead spitting blood (1.3.43–46). In turning his back on Rome, Coriolanus turns against his mother to seek in the camp of Aufidius a safe male world where hunger can be openly felt and satisfied with needed food. The supplication scene (5.3), however, places the hero in the presence of his mother and his own child, with the result that he becomes a child again, admitting his own neediness. The play's conclusion leaves us feeling uneasy because of the divided response prompted by the final confrontation between mother and son. On one hand, we want Coriolanus to acquiesce and save Rome; on the other, we desire him not to submit to Volumnia, thus allowing us to maintain our own fantasies of "omnipotence and independence." Neither solution is satisfactory. Whereas dependency registers the fullness of our humanity in *Lear* and *Ant.*, it "brings only the total collapse of the self" in *Coriolanus*, whose central image is of a woman who has not fed her son enough.

In the revised book chapter titled "Escaping the Matrix: The Construction of Masculinity in *Macbeth* and *Coriolanus*," Adelman discerns a "heroic masculinity" in both titular figures that "turns on leaving the mother behind. . . . [B]oth plays enact the paradox through which the son is never more the mother's creature than when he attempts to escape her." In *Coriolanus*, "maternal malevolence" is less "horrific" than in *Mac.* because it is "localize[d] and domesticate[d] . . . in the literal relation of mother and son." Nevertheless, Volumnia's "equation of starvation and masculinity" emerges as the "psychic equivalent" of the more melodramatic "disruptions of the feeding situation" associated with the witches and Lady Macbeth.

Barton, Anne. "Livy, Machiavelli, and Shakespeare's *Coriolanus*." *Shakespeare Survey* 38 (1985): 115–29.

While Thomas North's 1579 translation of *Plutarch's Lives* provided the basic narrative of Shakespeare's play, Livy's *The Romane Historie* (translated by Philemon Holland in 1600) shaped its overall attitude, one skeptical toward Coriolanus's virtue as a warrior and more receptive to the need for political compromise and diplomacy. Unlike the biographer Plutarch, the historian Livy focused on the city of Rome and its development as a republic; consequently, Coriolanus's life became important not for underscoring valor as the chief virtue (Plutarch's take on the story) but rather for showing how Rome, through the efforts of her women, escaped destruction and how the struggle between patricians and plebeians, with right on both sides, reached a new stage. Livy's communal emphasis is seen in Shakespeare's treatment of the Roman people, who, in contrast to the mob in *JC*, come across as individuals capable of intelligent opinion: "In fact, [*Coriolanus*] is unique in the canon for the tolerance and respect it accords an urban citizenry." Menenius, Cominius, Volumnia, and the senators eventually recognize that governmental change is inevitable and that the city belongs to patricians and plebeians alike. Only Coriolanus refuses to accept this change. For Livy, men like Coriolanus, "[h]owever useful in time of war, . . . are a threat to the balance of the state, to an evolving republic which must try to take them with it but, if it cannot, has no option but to discard them by the way." Barton connects Livy's view of Coriolanus with that of the sixteenth-century political theorist Niccolò Machiavelli, whose *Discorsi*, a commentary on the first ten books of Livy, was available to Shakespeare and his contemporaries in Italian and in translated manuscript versions. For Machiavelli, who distinguished between dissension and factionalism, the tension between plebeian and patrician was a positive development, and the expulsion of the rigid Roman aristocrat, whom he treats more harshly than Livy and more dismissively than Shakespeare, was "fit and useful." Barton devotes the final pages of the essay to Coriolanus's life in exile, where the hero finds "a world elsewhere" (3.3.165) in the martial habitat of the Volscians. There, Coriolanus "becomes genuinely popular," but no fundamental change in his character occurs. Although he recognizes his common humanity and the importance of family bonds in the supplication scene (5.3), the communal rapport suggested in the stage direction at 5.6.83 abruptly disappears and the old antiplebeian Coriolanus resurfaces at Aufidius's inflammatory accusation of "traitor." The play is a tragedy in that the truths Coriolanus learns about his changing world come too late for him to make use of them; when read in light of Livy's history and Machiavelli's commentary, however, *Coriolanus* becomes "predominantly a history—indeed, Shakespeare's most political play, the only one specifically about the *polis*."

Cavell, Stanley. "*Coriolanus* and Interpretations of Politics (Who Does the Wolf Love?)." In *Themes out of School,* pp. 60–96. San Francisco: North Point Press, 1984. [Reprinted under the title "'Who Does the Wolf Love?': *Coriolanus* and Interpretations of Politics," in *Shakespeare and the Question of Theory,* edited by Patricia Parker and Geoffrey Hartman, pp. 245–72 (New York: Methuen, 1985); and in Stanley Cavell, *Disowning Knowledge in Six Plays of Shakespeare,* pp. 143–77 (Cambridge: Cambridge University Press, 1987).]

Distinguishing between the political and politics per se, Cavell explores the play's iterative food and cannibal imagery to argue that *Coriolanus* is essentially about the formation of the political. In its depiction of a protagonist who refuses to acknowledge "his participation in finite human existence," the play illustrates "skepticism as a form of [incestuous] narcissism." Volumnia and Coriolanus are portrayed as starvers and hungerers caught in the "paradox [and reciprocity] of hungering not to hunger, of wanting not to want, of asking not to ask." Their starving suggests the "infiniteness of desire" not as the cause of "human insatiability" but as its effect, a fact that underscores "their sense of being cannibalized." This cannibalistic motif pervades the dramatic action from the opening sequence with the people imaged as lambs for patrician wolves to the closing scenes in which Rome is imaged as devouring itself. Detecting parallels between Coriolanus (as a kind of sacrificial lamb butchered for the salvation of the city) and Christ, the author emphasizes the play's concern with sacrificial feasts, particularly the Christian ritual of Communion. In the end, however, because he is sacrificed by his mother instead of his father—a mother, moreover, who does not believe that he is a god—Coriolanus's sacrifice is not redemptive: "He can provide spiritual food but he cannot make himself into food[;] . . . hence one may say his tragedy is that he cannot achieve tragedy." Cavell concludes that the play imagines the "creation of the political as the overcoming of narcissism, incestuousness, and cannibalism"—i.e., as a "beneficial, mutual consumption." In contrast to the essay's focus on the play's "orality," a postscript included in the two reprints addresses its "anality."

Doran, Madeleine. "'All's in anger': The Language of Contention in *Coriolanus*." In *Shakespeare's Dramatic Language*, pp. 182–217. Madison: University of Wisconsin Press, 1976.

Doran explores how Shakespeare uses "the language of contention to give life to his contentious plot." Whereas hyperbole, "the language of largesse," is the appropriate figurative device for the "magnificence, sensuousness, and openness" of *Ant.*, the dominant "figures of opposition or contrariety" (e.g., antithesis, synoeciosis, paradox, and dilemma) are perfectly suited to the "closeness, hardness, and harshness" of *Coriolanus*, a play built upon a "scheme of conflicts" and designed to assault the ear with the noise of trumpets, battles, and shouting voices. Doran praises Shakespeare's flexible and fluid use of figures of opposition, claiming that "while the whole tissue of *Coriolanus* is antithetical, [the] contraries are managed with such variety and freedom that they never grow stale"; she attributes this stylistic felicity to the playwright's refusal to allow antithetical pairs to settle into the "stultifying formality" of rigid and steady patterns of repetition, perfectly balanced members, and parallel syntax. In Coriolanus's speech urging the senators to abolish the office of the tribunes (3.1.129–36), for example, the antithetical pairs are kept from perfectly matching by the uneven members, by a shift of metaphor, and by the change from "unmetaphoric comparison" to "metaphoric action."

In the scenes following Martius's victory at Corioles, Shakespeare combines a narrowly focused hyperbole (the praise heaped on the hero) with "its opposite figure of extenuation" (the meiosis of the hero's own self-belittling) to create an "adjunct to the dominant figures of opposition." Finally, turning to Coriolanus's "two points of stress"—the obligation imposed on him to sue for the consulship and the maternal appeal to spare Rome—the author discusses how in both instances choices are presented "in the form of dilemmas of action": i.e., as the paradox of "a right choice [being] a wrong choice." With joyous shouts and the sounds of drums quickly changing to discord and accusations of treason, Coriolanus's entry into the Volscian city in 5.6 provides an antithetic and ironic parallel to his earlier triumphant entry into Rome. In his final lines, the hero repeats the antithetical images of hardness and fracture that run throughout the play, and "we sense below the rational, reflective level, the ruin of Coriolanus as a jolting fracture." Contending that "Mars alone, not entangled with Venus, requires harsher music," Doran finds the language of Coriolanus no "less masterly" than the hyperbolic and sensuous style of *Ant.* The realm of experience dramatized may be less sympathetic but Shakespeare "penetrates [it] no less profoundly."

George, David, ed. *Coriolanus, Shakespeare: The Critical Tradition.* London: Thoemmes Continuum, 2004.

The volume excerpts important and representative criticism, mostly in English, selected from the years 1682 to 1940. Performance-related studies are generally excluded. Among the seventy-nine entries are passages from the following critics: Samuel Johnson (on "the petty cavils of petty minds"), Thomas Davies (on "the good sense and shrewd wit of Menenius"), Francis Gentleman (on the play's savage kind of heroism), William Hazlitt (on "pretensions, arrogance, and absurdity"), Samuel Taylor Coleridge (on the "wonderfully philosophic impartiality" of Shakespeare's politics), Charles Knight (on "the stuff of a great general"), H. N. Hudson (on Coriolanus's "great virtues as well as great faults"), John Ruskin (on Virgilia as the "perfect type of wife and mother"), F. J. Furnivall (on Volumnia as "the grandest woman" in Shakespeare), Kenneth Deighton (on Coriolanus's Titanic pride), Frederick Boas (on "war as a gigantic duel"), Edmund K. Chambers (on "the subtle sin of egoism"), George Bernard Shaw (on the play as the "greatest" of Shakespeare's comedies), A. C. Bradley (on Coriolanus as "a noble, even a lovable, being"), John Middleton Murry (on the "golden silence of Virgilia"), Agnes Mure Mackenzie (on Volumnia's "false idea of greatness"), D. A. Traversi (on Coriolanus's "rather absurd and ironic death"), and Peter Alexander (on "heroic fidelity to an ideal"). An introductory overview of the play's scholarship from 1682 to 1940 is treated under seven headings: "Adaptation and Neoclassicism" (1682–1775), "Revolution and Romanticism" (1784–1824), "Conservative Morality" (1833–73), "Academic Criticism" (1873–98), "Scholars and Socialists" (1896–1918), "Cynicism and Specialization" (1918–30), and "New Beginnings, Old Reprises" (1931–40). Along with headnotes to excerpted passages, the editor provides a select bibliography and an index.

Kahn, Coppélia. "Mother of Battles: Volumnia and Her Son in *Coriolanus*." Chapter 6 in *Roman Shakespeare: Warriors, Wounds, and Women,* pp. 144–59. Feminist Readings of Shakespeare. London: Routledge, 1997. [The chapter incorporates the similarly titled article that first appeared in *Differences: A Journal of Feminist Cultural Studies* 4 (1992): 154–70.]

Kahn "interrogates the gender ideologies that uphold 'Roman virtue'" by examining "the wound as a fetish of Roman masculinity" in *Luc., Titus, JC, Ant., Coriolanus*, and *Cym.* In the chapter on *Coriolanus,* she explores the relationship between the hero and his mother to argue that the play "offers a troubling, richly problematic treatment of the cultural nexus between bearing children and bearing arms." By moving the feminine from the margins of *JC* to center stage in *Coriolanus*'s Volumnia, Shakespeare makes "mother" a term that cannot be placed securely on either side of a "male/female, public/private, war-making/mothering binarism." While Cicero differentiates the physical nurturing provided by the mother from the ideological indoctrination performed by her, Shakespeare conflates these duties in Volumnia, whose authority issues "equally from her social identity as a mother and from her identification with the masculinist, militarist ideology of Rome." The linked imagery of Hecuba's maternal breasts and Hector's bleeding forehead (1.3.43–46) provides a "striking paradigm for the social and psychological structures that bind [Volumnia's] performance as a mother to [her son's] performance as Rome's champion fighter." Significantly, the instrument of aggression in the passage is "not a sword but a wound . . . that behaves like a sword," spewing forth blood against an armed opponent. When Coriolanus moves from the battlefield to the forum, he is required to use words to dissemble his feelings and to reveal his wounds to the people. "Both words and wounds are linked problematically to gender difference": the wounds sought by the man of martial prowess "assert . . . the impregnability of the male body," whereas the woman's "wound [with which she is born] . . . implies pregnability—her capacity to bear sons." Volumnia's identification of her son's planned invasion of Rome with treading on her womb (5.3.140–43) underscores the value of women to Rome as the way the state reproduces itself. Ironically, it is her maternal power that "lock[s Coriolanus] into the fatal contradiction of his manhood and turn[s] him into an enemy of the state." The absence of a closing pietà image makes clear that Coriolanus's death changes nothing: "As long as Roman mothers 'frame' their sons, 'the Roman state . . . will on / The way it takes, cracking ten thousand curbs'" (1.1.71–72).

King, Bruce. *Coriolanus.* Critics Debate. Atlantic Highlands, N.J.: Humanities Press International, 1989.

The volume, divided into two parts, provides a summary and evaluation of critical studies of *Coriolanus.* Part 1 surveys critical approaches under the headings "Contextual," "Textual and Formal," "Religious, Sociological and Anthropological," "Interdisciplinary," and "Theatrical." Part 2 offers an appraisal of interpretive issues relating to such matters as staging, treatment of the crowd, the character of Coriolanus, warfare, sexuality, power, and notions of the heroic. A select bibliography and index round out the volume. Finding that no single interpretation is adequate, the author draws on both the conventions of Jacobean theater and studies concerned with imagery, psychoanalysis, and the epic genre in order to place *Coriolanus* in its Jacobean political and social context. King argues that in its use of alienation and distancing techniques, *Coriolanus* is Shakespeare's "most modern play."

Luckyj, Christina. "Volumnia's Silence." *Studies in English Literature* 31 (1991): 327–42.

Drawing on both the critical and performance histories of *Coriolanus,* Luckyj examines Volumnia's silent "passing over the stage" (5.5.0 SD) to argue for a reevaluation of the character and her relationship to her son and to the play as a whole. While literary critics and some directors (e.g., Terry Hands, RSC, 1978 and 1989–90) see a Volumnia who basks in the welcoming praise heaped on her as "our patroness, the life of Rome" (5.5.1)—i.e., a triumphant, delighted woman who shows no recognition of being the cause of her son's imminent death—a theatrical conception has developed since the 1950s that portrays a mother acutely aware of and visibly distressed at the prospect of the human cost of her political success (5.3.210–12). As evidence, Luckyj cites Irene Worth's widely praised 1984 interpretation at the National Theatre in which the character's silence was "rendered . . . as mute devastation"; included in this "venerable modern tradition" are productions at the Old Vic (1951), the RSC (1972), and Stratford, Ontario (1961 and 1981). Luckyj takes issue with the emphasis of recent feminist criticism on the character's military method of mothering (see Adelman and Kahn, above); instead, she focuses on the "vulnerability underlying [her] maternal self-denial," for in Volumnia, as in Lear and Coriolanus, Shakespeare presents us with a character "both enormous in will and profoundly self-ignorant." Arguing for a figure of psychological depth who, like her son, changes, the author charts an evolution from the "formidable virago" of Act 1 through the "near-comic bourgeois matriarch" of Act 2, the "dissembler" of Act 3, and "the angry, devastated mother" of Act 4 to the "powerful advocate" of Act 5. To view her as capable of change allows for ways of reading and performing Volumnia's silences (both immediately after her successful supplication [5.3] and moments later in her celebrated return to Rome [5.5]) that depart from the common conception of her as the "mother-destroyer" of her son. "That Shakespeare knew and exploited the ambiguities of feminine silence should make critics wary of too hastily judging Volumnia's."

Marshall, Cynthia. "*Coriolanus* and the Politics of Theatrical Pleasure." In *Companion to Shakespeare's Works,* edited by Richard Dutton and Jean E. Howard, 4 vols., 1:452–72. Malden, Mass.: Blackwell, 2003.

In her examination of the critical and modern theatrical afterlife of *Coriolanus,* Marshall contends that Shakespeare's "act of turning a violent political history to the uses of theatrical pleasure . . . help[ed] to inaugurate a modern culture of entertainment in which political questions of social discord and harmony are subordinated to individual questions of autonomy and pleasure." As evidenced by the 1933 Comédie Française production that provoked supporters of both left and right ideologies to riot in the streets, *Coriolanus* does not attempt to indoctrinate viewers into a particular political perspective or nationalistic cause. Instead, by establishing "the gap between subjective identity and shaping ideological codes . . . as a site of pleasure," *Coriolanus* "works the rift opened by the *performance* of politics" and "anticipates modern debates about the theatrical dimension of political life and about the political valency of entertainment." As an early example of dramatizing politics for theatrical delight, the play heralds a process that would come to include the work of Sade and Masoch. Marshall relates Kenneth Burke's interest in the "cathartic pleasure of painful emotion" ("*Coriolanus*—and the Delights of Faction," in *Language as Symbolic Action* [1966]) to her argument that *Coriolanus* "accords with an aesthetic of masochism," not as self-punishment but as "a way of elaborating and interpreting the pleasurable tensions of violence, toward which viewers are inevitably drawn." Choosing to "foreground . . . the performative aspects of the [titular] role as a theatrical event," Laurence Olivier (RSC, 1959) made clear the play's movement in the direction of sadomasochism. As an example, the author cites Olivier's death leap: hurling himself backward from a high rock only to be caught at the last second by his ankles, "the actor br[ought] his audience to heel, and then submitt[ed] the character's integration and his own physical safety to a cruelly punishing ordeal, enact[ing] a profoundly sadomasochistic rhythm." Olivier had intuited what the play encourages: namely, the spectator's response to character and spectacle rather than to ideology. In *Coriolanus,* Shakespeare showed that he clearly understood "the pleasure audiences would derive from the theatrical dissolution of established norms and identities."

Parker, R. B. "Coriolanus and 'th'interpretation of the time.'" In *Mirror up to Shakespeare: Essays in Honour of G. R. Hibbard*, edited by J. C. Gray, pp. 261–76. Toronto: University of Toronto Press, 1984.

Parker begins his study of the play with "one of Shakespeare's bleakest comments on human history": the "pragmatic cynicism" of Aufidius's lines on the impermanence of human values and the transitory nature of political power (4.7.52–59). In order to grasp what Shakespeare poses as an alternative to the historical relativism of the Volscian leader (a view that Coriolanus also articulates at 4.4.17–23), Parker examines the play's two main political issues—the class conflict between patricians and plebeians and the "more basic question of patriotism"—in light of Shakespeare's developing political thought, his departures from Plutarch (the main source), and the drama's topical reflection of sensitive matters in the early 1600s (e.g., bad harvests, escalating food prices, outbreaks of rioting in northern and midland counties, and the growing "arrogance of the gentry," two of whom, the second earl of Essex and Sir Walter Raleigh, "stand out" as possible models for Shakespeare's titular character).

By the time Shakespeare wrote *Coriolanus,* his understanding of the "political" had widened from the narrower meaning of the early plays—i.e., the struggle for power and the determination of the best institutions for authority—to the broader, anthropological sense of culture: i.e., a "triple interaction" involving the individual, institutions (including the basic institution of the family), and society at large. Parker claims that Shakespeare tests two clichés in the play: that of the "body politic ideal" and that of the mother country as a nurturing force. By assigning the parable of the belly to the "voluptuary" Menenius and by making clear that in this version there is no head, only members and the "sovereign belly," Shakespeare exposes the reality behind the "body politic" as static, inflexible, and "dehumanizing" (1.1.68–74). With Rome (like Shakespeare's England) in transition from an "apparently benign political state" to a society caught up in factional strife, Coriolanus pledges his loyalty not to mother Rome but to his own mother. Parker locates "both the psychological and the political heart" of the play in the term "boy" (5.6.120), because "clearly Coriolanus is Volumnia's creation as Volumnia is Rome's." The play achieves "genuine tragedy . . . because though . . . it will not last, and nothing can be built upon it," Coriolanus's selfless decision in 5.3, "made not as a Roman but a son," affirms the familial bond "on which a healthy society has to be built and which Shakespeare had come to see as the truly *political* core of human society set against the constant flux of history."

Paster, Gail Kern. "To Starve with Feeding: The City in *Coriolanus*." *Shakespeare Studies* 11 (1978): 123–44.

In *Coriolanus,* Shakespeare italicizes the idea of the "city" as "the symbol of human community" by opening and closing the action with two angry groups of citizens: the first from Rome wishes for the hero's death; the second from a Volscian city carries out that wish. This framing technique suggests "that the tragic outcome of what happens to [Coriolanus] in the forum has as much to do with the nature of the forum as with the nature of [the protagonist himself]." Paster notes the iteration of "Rome" and "Capitol" (each word occurs more frequently than in *JC* and *Ant.*), the class division between plebeians and patricians (which results in contrasting views of the city), the importance of ceremony, and the absence of private moments and settings (even the ostensibly domestic sewing episode in 1.3 is charged with public, civic meaning). In a play which leaves no room for a "private realm," our understanding of Coriolanus's tragedy is entwined with the value we place on the city that survives him, a value "compounded of paradox": "Rome . . . is at once the source of life and the instrument of death, the agent of immortality and the exactor of a sacrifice which diminishes the city's existence in preserving it. . . . Indeed the city in *Coriolanus* . . . represents collectively held ideals of individual aspirations and creates possibilities for achieving them even as it moves with a compulsive, predatory savagery to destroy the heroic man who manifests the very qualities it holds up to emulation." Volumnia, who views motherhood as a civic duty, embodies this paradox of Rome as both nurturer and destroyer. Through her, the vocabulary of kinship and the predatory imagery of body parts, animals, and food fuse in "a final image of the city which . . . shapes our response to the death of Coriolanus." For Volumnia and Rome, the play ends on a comic note in that the community survives (5.5). For both the audience and the titular figure, however, the penultimate scene acquires a "heavily ironic cast," because the play is not over and the audience recognizes that "tragedy will follow comedy": "Coriolanus's decision to spare Rome and die—in a way, to starve with feeding—reveals the community to be in truth the mother who eats her own children."

Patterson, Annabel. *Fables of Power: Aesopian Writing and Political History.* Durham: Duke University Press, 1991.

Chapter 4 of Patterson's book is titled "Body Fables" and includes a section on *Coriolanus* (pp. 118–26), a play that Shakespeare saw "as a medium for the discussion of contemporary sociopolitical and socioeconomic issues." The author focuses on the fable of "The Belly and the Members" and compares Shakespeare's telling (1.1.91–169) to the account found in Edward Forset's *Comparative Discourse of the Bodies Naturall and Politique* (1606), the "official version of the Belly fable for the early Jacobean state." Whereas Forset used the digestive metaphor abstractly in order to address economic questions and achieve "political consensus as to how and by whom the *financial* resources of the state should be controlled," Shakespeare shifted the fable "back toward its literal, bodily content." As evidence of this shift, Patterson cites the oft-noted topical importance of the Midlands Rising (1607) to the play and Shakespeare's condensing into one scene of popular unrest two distinct insurrections found in Plutarch (one occasioned by usury and the other by famine). Choosing to make famine the pretext for Menenius's telling of the belly fable, Shakespeare (as Philip Brockbank noted in the 1976 Arden edition) "made visible the essential flaw in its argument": namely, that food in the Rome of *Coriolanus* is not being distributed to the people. Unlike most critics, who view the play as antidemocratic, the citizens as rabble, and the belly fable as illustrating the fatal consequences of allowing the populace their will, Patterson contends that Shakespeare used the fable to showcase economic injustice and to portray the people as skeptical and articulate. The citizens understand why the food that could relieve the famine is instead being wasted on the patricians: the patricians "*need* the dearth as a physical demonstration of their own wealth" (i.e., their hierarchical authority) (1.1.19–21). The belly fable, which the citizens discredit before Menenius's delivery of it (1.1.81–88), not only fails to pacify the plebeians but is also shown to be irrelevant, since, while it is being told, their "petition" for formal representation is being approved by the Senate (1.1.227–38). In Patterson's reading, the opening scenes of *Coriolanus* serve as "a damning indictment of socioeconomic inequality, focused as they are on the primal issue of hunger": in his treatment of the fable, Shakespeare "transformed a metaphorical rebellion *against* the Belly (the original plot of The Belly and the Members) into a literal rebellion *of* the Belly—the hungry plebeians," who "appeal to a 'moral economy.'"

Phillips, James E., ed. *Twentieth Century Interpretations of "Coriolanus."* Englewood Cliffs, N.J.: Prentice-Hall, 1970.

This collection of important earlier twentieth-century criticism reprints abridged versions of the following commentaries: G. Wilson Knight, "The Royal Occupation: An Essay on *Coriolanus*" (from *The Imperial Theme: Further Interpretations of Shakespeare's Tragedies Including the Roman Plays* [1931]); Oscar James Campbell, "*Coriolanus*" (from *Shakespeare's Satire* [1943]); Harley Granville-Barker, "*Coriolanus*" (from *Prefaces to Shakespeare,* vol. 2 [1947]); Donald A. Stauffer, "Roads to Freedom: *Coriolanus*" (from *Shakespeare's World of Images: The Development of His Moral*

*Ideas* [1949]); Willard Farnham, "*Coriolanus*" (from *Shakespeare's Tragic Frontier: The World of His Final Tragedies* [1950]); A. P. Rossiter, "*Coriolanus*" (from *Angel with Horns,* edited by Graham Storey [1961]); Maurice Charney, "The Dramatic Use of Imagery in Shakespeare's *Coriolanus*" (*ELH* 23 [1956]: 183–93); and Charles K. Hofling, M.D., "An Interpretation of Shakespeare's *Coriolanus*" (*American Imago* 14 [1957]: 407–35). Also represented are excerpted viewpoints relating to theme and structure (Kenneth Burke, "*Coriolanus*—and the Delights of Faction" [*Hudson Review* 19 (1966): 185–202]) and to specific characters: Coriolanus (T. S. Eliot, *Coriolan II: Difficulties of a Statesman* [1932], and Paul A. Jorgensen: "Shakespeare's Coriolanus: Elizabethan Soldier" [*PMLA* 64 (1949): 221–35]); Volumnia (Rufus Putney, "Coriolanus and His Mother" [*Psychoanalytic Quarterly* 31 (1962): 364–81]); the Citizens (A. A. Smirnov, *Shakespeare: A Marxist Interpretation* [1936], and Brents Stirling, *The Populace in Shakespeare* [1949]); Menenius (Derek Traversi, "Coriolanus" [*Scrutiny* 6 (1937): 43–58]); the Tribunes (John Palmer, *Political Characters of Shakespeare* [1945]); Virgilia (John Middleton Murry, "A Neglected Heroine of Shakespeare," in *Countries of the Mind: Essays in Literary Criticism* [1922]); and Aufidius (Eugene M. Waith, *The Herculean Hero in Marlowe, Chapman, Shakespeare and Dryden* [1962]). In the introductory essay, Phillips situates *Coriolanus* in relation to Shakespeare's personal and professional life in 1608 (the year often assigned to the play's composition); comments on its critical and theatrical afterlife, observing that it wasn't until shortly before World War II that Shakespeare's "last tragedy" and "last dramatization of Roman history" began to enjoy success both in the study and on the stage; addresses the character of Coriolanus; and discusses the significance of the belly fable (1.1.91–169) for the "imagery of a diseased body that dominates the play as all parties violate the natural order." Phillips credits T. S. Eliot with recognizing in his *Coriolan* poems the play's relevance to the twentieth century in terms of both the psychological dilemma posed by a domineering mother and the political dilemma of a "brilliant military leader . . . forced, against his own nature and temperament, into a position of governmental leadership for which he is hopelessly unqualified."

Ripley, John. *"Coriolanus" on Stage in England and America, 1609–1994.* Madison, N.J.: Fairleigh Dickinson University Press; London: Associated University Presses, 1998.

Following an introductory overview of the play's critical afterlife from Restoration commentators to modern critics, Ripley provides an extensive and detailed performance history of *Coriolanus* under the following headings: "The Jacobean and Caroline Era," "From Tate to Thomson: The Age of Propaganda (1681–1749)," "From Sheridan to Kemble: The Making of a Production Tradition (1752–1817)," "The Kemble Tradition Challenged: Elliston-Kean (1820)," "The Kemble Tradition in England (1819–1915)," "The Kemble Tradition in America (1796–1885)," "Modernism and Elizabethan Methodism (1920–1938)," "From Olivier to Olivier: A Romantic Interlude (1938–1959)," and "Psychoanalysis, Politics, and Postmodernity (1961–1994)." The volume includes a chronological list of performances in London; Stratford-upon-Avon; New York; Stratford, Ontario; and Stratford, Connecticut, spanning the years 1609 to 1994. The play's stage history is "driven by the theater's conviction that [*Coriolanus*] is the product not of aesthetic strategy but defective craft." While the theater's assessment may be right,

Ripley nevertheless asks what an experiment based on "a calculated aesthetic, however unconventional," and undertaken by a major acting company, might yield. His afterword attempts to answer that question. For Ripley, the "aesthetics of the play privilege uncertainty." He urges resistance to the modern impulse to impose a "tight-knit" unity on the script and calls on directors to balance the mother-son theme (the dominant focus of most of the play's stage history) against the "crucial resonance of battlefield and Forum," without which the "tortured attachment" of Coriolanus and Volumnia "is at best the stuff of Tennessee Williams melodrama or at worst Freudian analysis."

Ripley, John. "*Coriolanus*'s Stage Imagery on Stage, 1754–1901." *Shakespeare Quarterly* 38 (1987): 338–50. (Reprinted in Wheeler, below.)

Operating on the assumption that the working dynamics of Shakespeare's presentational images are best demonstrated in performance, Ripley examines how eighteenth- and nineteenth-century productions staged three scenes in *Coriolanus*: the titular figure's triumphal return from Corioles (2.1), the opening of the pleading scene (5.3), and Coriolanus's assassination (5.6). What emerges from this examination of entrances, groupings, gestures, sounds, and costumes is "largely a recital of mutilations and distortions" of Shakespeare's economical and precise visual eloquence; Ripley attributes this wide-scale mutilation to "audience tastes, managerial ambitions, and financial exigency." Using the stage directions found in the First Folio and verbal clues embedded in the dialogue, he notes how Shakespeare sets up Coriolanus's entrance in 2.1 on a barish stage with the protagonist flanked by his generals; later, when he sees his mother downstage, Coriolanus crosses and kneels to her. In contrast to this simplicity and blurring the clarity of Coriolanus's movement from a military group to a domestic one in the Folio text, Thomas Sheridan (1754), John Philip Kemble (1811), Charles Macready (1838), and Henry Irving (1901) had Volumnia exit before her son entered; she, along with her companions, later returned as part of a massive downstage procession, which, in the case of Macready, included 300 people. A similar bias toward spectacle and sheer numbers is found in the pleading scene, where—unlike the Folio, which indicates only a few people onstage—Kemble showed Coriolanus and Aufidius on thrones, with 240 people onstage, a choice that deprived the episode of its poignant intimacy. Finally, in contrast to Shakespeare's use of only a few soldiers to assist Aufidius in killing Coriolanus, Edwin Forrest (1855) had a large group surround him, hiding the murder from the squeamish and robbing the audience of "the transcendent instant when the lonely dragon passes from titanic rage to dispassionate death." Although such flagrant departures from Shakespeare's "minimalist design" occur less frequently today, "visual philistinism" still remains a problem in staging *Coriolanus*. The reason, Ripley contends, is the failure of theater artists to recognize an indisputable fact: "Where Shakespeare's stagecraft is concerned, less is often more."

Shrank, Cathy. "Civility and the City in *Coriolanus*." *Shakespeare Quarterly* 54 (2003): 406–23.

Shrank examines the interplay of language and politics, the two recurrent concerns of criticism on *Coriolanus,* within the context of Elizabethan monarchical government and the "ideology—with its rhetoric of civility and iconography of the city—that informed local civil government life" in early modern England. Analysis of the play's politics demands consideration of more localized contexts in order to reconcile its political nature and republican setting with the monarchical society surrounding its production. While awareness of "monarchical republicanism" remained alive among those close to the workings of power in seventeenth-century England, a form of republican thought and a belief in active political participation were particularly strong in the "civic politics" of the 204 English towns and cities that had been incorporated by 1610, and that, because of their "limited self-government," were compared by visiting dignitaries to "republics." The centrality of this civic culture to the English political system was "underpinned" by the humanist curriculum promoted in English grammar schools, where schoolboys were taught not only to "emulate and admire Roman ideals of civic duty" but also to master the Ciceronian argument that language is both a sign of civility and the means by which it is achieved. Emphasizing the "link between *civil* and *civic,"* Shrank places politics at the center of the play to argue that the protagonist's "uncivil language is a natural extension of his antipathy to the civic community": through Coriolanus's "indecorous speech," which derives from both his being a professional soldier (one meaning of "civil" at the time was "nonmilitary") and his having been deprived of the kind of education that early modern conceptions of civility and civil language encompassed, Shakespeare "signals his protagonist's inability to live within the urban community and, beyond that, his ultimately detrimental effect on civic society." Fittingly, Shakespeare builds the play's two crises—the titular figure's failure to participate decorously in the election rituals and his threat to invade the city with an enemy force—around Coriolanus's strong aversion to the civic body. Shrank concludes that an understanding of the linkage between *civil* and *civic* in early modern England can help to "unravel some of the problems of interpretation that have dogged the play with its complex—yet confusing—politics and uncompromising, alienating protagonist."

Walker, Jarrett. "Voiceless Bodies and Bodiless Voices: The Drama of Human Perception in *Coriolanus.*" *Shakespeare Quarterly* 43 (1992): 170–85.

Concerned with the "ontological differences between speech and the body" as manifested in the theater, Walker observes that in moments of violence, such as the mutilation of Lavinia in *Titus,* the body, when divorced from speech, attests not to the linear time insisted on by the latter but to "time bifurcated into before and after by a single violent moment." Similarly, dead bodies onstage at the end of many tragedies "testify to a time that has stopped," notwithstanding the voices that go on speaking, "unconvincingly marking time toward a peaceful, linear future." In *Coriolanus,* the Shakespearean tragedy "most obsessed" with the "body/voice polarity," Walker argues that the titular figure's disdain for the spoken word reveals "a contempt for linear time and a desire to live in a single transcendent moment such as the moment of violence." Even the names Caius Martius and Coriolanus signify the tension between "the realm of the voice" (where the linear time of birth and death prevails) and "the realm of the body" (where one act of violence—i.e., the conquest of Corioles—"can overwhelm time and record itself in eternity"). The linear realm of the play's strong narrators—Cominius, Menenius, and Volumnia—for whom the conversion of bodily action into spoken narrative implies that the body exists for the purpose of the voice contrasts with the hero's "alternate universe in which there are *only* bodies, active or still, violent or sexual, but never needing words." For Walker, the interplay of temporal speech and atemporal presence informs the crisis at the gates of Rome (5.3). After Volumnia begs her son not to attack the city of his birth and Coriolanus recognizes that all further speech and action are denied him, the Folio has the only stage direction in Shakespeare that "specifically demands a total stop to both speech and action": "Holds her by the hand, silent" (5.3.204 SD). The question that follows—"What have you done?"—indicates a change in the mind of the protagonist. What precipitates the change, Walker argues, is not the temporality of Volumnia's narrative but the "atemporal level" of Coriolanus's "ongoing perceptions" of the bodies of his "two erotic objects," Aufidius and Virgilia. The complete silence at the moment of choice "contains nothing but presence, but it is created out of speech, by the speaker's decision to fall silent." The conflict between the body and the voice that pervades *Coriolanus* "evokes a world where there are only . . . bodies seen and voices heard—all struggling in vain to become persons."

Wheeler, David, ed. *Coriolanus: Critical Essays.* New York: Garland, 1995.

Designed to collect the "most influential historical criticism, the most significant contemporary interpretations, and reviews of the most influential productions," this anthology devoted to *Coriolanus* reprints twenty-two critical extracts and essays spanning the years 1682–1994, and eighteen reviews of eight productions between 1901 and 1988. Extracts are taken from Tyrone Guthrie, *In Various Directions: A View of the Theatre* (1955); Lawrence Danson, *Tragic Alphabet: Shakespeare's Drama of Language* (1974); and Kristina Bedford, *Coriolanus at the National* (1992). Reprinted essays include the following: A. C. Bradley, "*Coriolanus*" (1912); Paul A. Jorgensen, "Shakespeare's Coriolanus:

Elizabethan Soldier" (1949); James L. Calderwood, "*Coriolanus:* Wordless Meanings and Meaningless Words" (1966); Emmett Wilson, "Coriolanus: The Anxious Bridegroom" (1968); J. L. Simmons, "*Antony and Cleopatra* and *Coriolanus,* Shakespeare's Heroic Tragedies: A Jacobean Adjustment" (1973); Patricia K. Meszaros, "'There is a world elsewhere': Tragedy and History in *Coriolanus*" (1976); Felicia Hardison Londre, "Coriolanus and Stavisky: The Interpenetration of Art and Politics" (1986); Madelon Sprengnether, "Annihilating Intimacy in *Coriolanus*" (1986); John Ripley, "*Coriolanus's* Stage Imagery on Stage, 1754–1901" (1987); Zvi Jagendorf, "*Coriolanus:* Body Politic and Private Parts" (1990); and Martin Scofield, "Drama, Politics and the Hero: *Coriolanus,* Brecht, and Grass" (1990). The collection also provides two new essays: Karen Aubry, "Shifting Masks, Roles, and Satiric Personae: Suggestions for Exploring the Edge of Genre in *Coriolanus,*" and David Wheeler, "To Their Own Purpose: The Treatment of *Coriolanus* in the Restoration and Eighteenth Century." Theatrical reviews are reprinted for productions in London (Sir Henry Irving, 1901, and Peter Hall, 1985), Paris (La Comédie-Française, 1933), Stratford-upon-Avon (Peter Hall, 1959), and New York (John Houseman, 1954, and the New York Shakespeare Festival, 1965, 1979, and 1988). Wheeler focuses his introductory essay on the "conflict between the intellectual engagement the play offers those who study it, and the absence of emotional engagement for the general audiences who view it."

## Shakespeare's Life

Baldwin, T. W. *William Shakspere's Petty School.* Urbana: University of Illinois Press, 1943.

Baldwin here investigates the theory and practice of the petty school, the first level of education in Elizabethan England. He focuses on that educational system primarily as it is reflected in Shakespeare's art.

Baldwin, T. W. *William Shakspere's Small Latine and Lesse Greeke*. 2 vols. Urbana: University of Illinois Press, 1944.

Baldwin attacks the view that Shakespeare was an uneducated genius—a view that had been dominant among Shakespeareans since the eighteenth century. Instead, Baldwin shows, the educational system of Shakespeare's time would have given the playwright a strong background in the classics, and there is much in the plays that shows how Shakespeare benefited from such an education.

Beier, A. L., and Roger Finlay, eds. *London 1500–1700: The Making of the Metropolis*. New York: Longman, 1986.

Focusing on the economic and social history of early modern London, these collected essays probe aspects of metropolitan life, including "Population and Disease," "Commerce and Manufacture," and "Society and Change."

Bentley, G. E. *Shakespeare's Life: A Biographical Handbook*. New Haven: Yale University Press, 1961.

This "just-the-facts" account presents the surviving documents of Shakespeare's life against an Elizabethan background.

Chambers, E. K. *William Shakespeare: A Study of Facts and Problems*. 2 vols. Oxford: Clarendon Press, 1930.

Analyzing in great detail the scant historical data, Chambers's complex, scholarly study considers the nature of the texts in which Shakespeare's work is preserved.

Cressy, David. *Education in Tudor and Stuart England.* London: Edward Arnold, 1975.

This volume collects sixteenth-, seventeenth-, and early eighteenth-century documents detailing aspects of formal education in England, such as the curriculum, the control and organization of education, and the education of women.

Dutton, Richard. *William Shakespeare: A Literary Life.* New York: St. Martin's Press, 1989.

Not a biography in the traditional sense, Dutton's very readable work nevertheless "follows the contours of Shakespeare's life" as Dutton examines Shakespeare's career as playwright and poet, with consideration of his patrons, theatrical associations, and audience.

Honan, Park. *Shakespeare: A Life.* New York: Oxford University Press, 1998.

Honan's accessible biography focuses on the various contexts of Shakespeare's life—physical, social, political, and cultural—to place the dramatist within a lucidly described world. The biography includes detailed examinations of, for example, Stratford schooling, theatrical politics of 1590s London, and the careers of Shakespeare's associates. The author draws on a wealth of established knowledge and on interesting new research into local records and documents; he also engages in speculation about, for example, the possibilities that Shakespeare was a tutor in a Catholic household in the north of England in the 1580s and that he played particular roles in his own plays, areas that reflect new, but unproven and debatable, data—though Honan is usually careful to note where a particular narrative "has not been capable of proof or disproof."

Schoenbaum, S. *William Shakespeare: A Compact Documentary Life*. New York: Oxford University Press, 1977.

This standard biography economically presents the essential documents from Shakespeare's time in an accessible narrative account of the playwright's life.

## Shakespeare's Theater

Bentley, G. E. *The Profession of Player in Shakespeare's Time, 1590–1642*. Princeton: Princeton University Press, 1984.

Bentley readably sets forth a wealth of evidence about performance in Shakespeare's time, with special attention to the relations between player and company, and the business of casting, managing, and touring.

Berry, Herbert. *Shakespeare's Playhouses*. New York: AMS Press, 1987.

Berry's six essays collected here discuss (with illustrations) varying aspects of the four playhouses in which Shakespeare had a financial stake: the Theatre in Shoreditch, the Blackfriars, and the first and second Globe.

Berry, Herbert, William Ingram, and Glynne Wickham, eds. *English Professional Theatre, 1530–1660*. Cambridge: Cambridge University Press, 2000.

Wickham presents the government documents designed to control professional players, their plays, and playing places. Ingram handles the professional actors, giving as representative a life of the actor Augustine Phillips, and discussing, among other topics, patrons, acting companies, costumes, props, playbooks, provincial playing, and child actors. Berry treats the twenty-three different London playhouses from 1560 to 1660 for which there are records, including four inns.

Cook, Ann Jennalie. *The Privileged Playgoers of Shakespeare's London*. Princeton: Princeton University Press, 1981.

Cook's work argues, on the basis of sociological, economic, and documentary evidence, that Shakespeare's audience—and the audience for English Renaissance drama generally—consisted mainly of the "privileged."

Greg, W. W. *Dramatic Documents from the Elizabethan Playhouses*. 2 vols. Oxford: Clarendon Press, 1931.

Greg itemizes and briefly describes many of the play manuscripts that survive from the period 1590 to around 1660, including, among other things, players' parts. His second volume offers facsimiles of selected manuscripts.

Gurr, Andrew. *Playgoing in Shakespeare's London*. 2nd ed. Cambridge: Cambridge University Press, 1996.

Gurr charts how the theatrical enterprise developed from its modest beginnings in the late 1560s to become a thriving institution in the 1600s. He argues that there were important changes over the period 1567–1644 in the playhouses, the audience, and the plays.

Harbage, Alfred. *Shakespeare's Audience*. New York: Columbia University Press, 1941.

Harbage investigates the fragmentary surviving evidence to interpret the size, composition, and behavior of Shakespeare's audience.

Hattaway, Michael. *Elizabethan Popular Theatre: Plays in Performance*. London: Routledge and Kegan Paul, 1982.

Beginning with a study of the popular drama of the late Elizabethan age—a description of the stages, performance conditions, and acting of the period—this volume concludes with an analysis of five well-known plays of the 1590s, one of them (*Titus Andronicus*) by Shakespeare.

Shapiro, Michael. *Children of the Revels: The Boy Companies of Shakespeare's Time and Their Plays*. New York: Columbia University Press, 1977.

Shapiro chronicles the history of the amateur and quasi-professional child companies that flourished in London at the end of Elizabeth's reign and the beginning of James's.

## The Publication of Shakespeare's Plays

Blayney, Peter W. M. *The First Folio of Shakespeare*. Hanover, Md.: Folger, 1991.

Blayney's accessible account of the printing and later life of the First Folio—an amply illustrated catalog to a 1991 Folger Shakespeare Library exhibition—analyzes the mechanical production of the First Folio, describing how the Folio was made, by whom and for whom, how much it cost, and its ups and downs (or, rather, downs and ups) since its printing in 1623.

Hinman, Charlton. *The Norton Facsimile: The First Folio of Shakespeare*. 2nd ed. New York: W. W. Norton, 1996.

This facsimile presents a photographic reproduction of an "ideal" copy of the First Folio of Shakespeare; Hinman attempts to represent each page in its most fully corrected state. The second edition includes an important new introduction by Peter W. M. Blayney.

Hinman, Charlton. *The Printing and Proof-Reading of the First Folio of Shakespeare*. 2 vols. Oxford: Clarendon Press, 1963.

In the most arduous study of a single book ever undertaken, Hinman attempts to reconstruct how the Shakespeare First Folio of 1623 was set into type and run off the press, sheet by sheet. He also provides almost all the known variations in readings from copy to copy.

# Key to Famous Lines and Phrases

[T]he gods sent not
Corn for the rich men only.

[*Coriolanus*—1.1.225–27]

[T]hey threw their caps
As they would hang them on the horns o' th' moon,
Shouting their emulation.

[*Coriolanus*—1.1.232–35]

[A]ll the yarn she spun in Ulysses' absence did but fill Ithaca full of moths.

[*Valeria*—1.3.86–87]

Nature teaches beasts to know their friends.

[*Sicinius*—2.1.6]

[A] cup of hot wine with not a drop of allaying Tiber in 't[.]

[*Menenius*—2.1.48–49]

My gracious silence, hail.

[*Coriolanus*—2.1.184]

[H]e himself stuck not to call us the many-headed multitude.

[*First Citizen*—2.3.16–17]

Bid them wash their faces
And keep their teeth clean.

[*Coriolanus*—2.3.68–69]

Hear you this Triton of the minnows? Mark you
His absolute "shall"?

[*Coriolanus*—3.1.119–20]

What is the city but the people?

[*Sicinius*—3.1.249]

His nature is too noble for the world.
He would not flatter Neptune for his trident
Or Jove for 's power to thunder. His heart's his
mouth;
What his breast forges, that his tongue must vent[.]

[*Menenius*—3.1.326–30]

The beast
With many heads butts me away.

[*Coriolanus*—4.1.1–2]

He wants nothing of a god but eternity and a heaven to throne in.

[*Menenius*—5.4.24–25]

They'll give him death by inches.

[*Messenger*—5.4.41]

Thou hast done a deed whereat valor will weep.

[*Second Lord*—5.6.160]

[H]e shall have a noble memory.

[*Aufidius*—5.6.184]

SIMON & SCHUSTER
PAPERBACKS
A CBS COMPANY